Strategic Human Resource Development

Jim Grieves

SAGE Publications
London • Thousand Oaks • New Delhi

First published 2003

 SAGE Publications Ltd
6 Bonhill Street
London EC2A 4PU

SAGE Publications Inc
2455 Teller Road
Thousand Oaks, California 91320

SAGE Publications India Pvt Ltd
B-42, Panchsheel Enclave
Post Box 4109
New Delhi - 100 017

British Library Cataloguing in Publication Data

A catalogue record for this book is available from the British
Library

ISBN 0 7619 4934 7
ISBN 0 7619 4944 5 (pbk)

Library of Congress Control Number available

Typeset by Photoprint, Torquay, Devon
Printed and in Great Britain by The Cromwell Press Ltd,
Trowbridge, Wiltshire

Contents

Acknowledgements

I would like to acknowledge the various critical debates with managers and students for their practical focus in relation to affairs of the imagination.

Three people deserve special mention for the insights provided. Both Trudi Fellows and Joanne Flood each provided excellent examples of change agent practice and these are illustrated in Chapter 6. Bob Hamlin offered some very practical advice on the manuscript prior to publication and I am therefore grateful for his critical insight regarding the relationship between organizational change and Strategic Human Resource Development.

Finally, special mention goes to Kiren Shoman of Sage to whom I am grateful for help and advice in guiding the manuscript to its final conclusion.

Introduction

The subject of *Strategic Human Resource Development* has emerged as the logical development of the Organizational Development (OD) tradition. *Strategic Human Resource Development* combines three things: (a) an awareness of the complexities of change management; (b) a desire to rescue the concept of Human Resource Development from a mundane existence in the depths of training programmes; and, finally, (c) a new perspective which provides direction for the twenty-first century. *Strategic Human Resource Development* promotes a more enlightened, ethical and skills-focused change management that puts human resources back where they belong – at the forefront of the change agenda.

This book represents the fusion of three disciplines – Human Resource Development (HRD), Organizational Development (OD), and Strategic Management. Two things might be said about this. First, the demarcation between disciplines is often arbitrary and constructed for convenience. In reality, however, the management of organizations requires a more eclectic approach driven by the pragmatic needs of managers and the organization's members.

Second, there has been fusion of these three areas in recent years as middle managers have become increasingly involved in managing change. This, in fact, represents the more recent thinking about pro-active change in contrast to the older planned change approaches.

One major problem with the various debates on Human Resource Development, Organizational Development and Strategic Management is the reactive nature of these disciplines to change. This book seeks to draw the boundaries for a new discipline that views change management as a strategic process-driven approach that emerges from within the organization rather than due to the pressures of external forces. It is in this sense that it should be regarded as pro-active since the purpose is continual transformation of the organization's products and services.

The book is informed by the transformation of Organizational Development, with its origins in twentieth-century management, to a new terrain in which learning is placed at the forefront. This is, in part, a challenge to the reactive formulations of change management we have seen in the past 20 years. However, it also represents a determined effort to challenge the complacency of managers in the twenty-first century who may think that manipulative programmes were a product of the past. Change often seems like a reshuffled pack of cards in which the contents of each hand change but the form of the game remains the same. Not wishing to be too cynical, it is nevertheless clear that people still become alienated, stressed and exploited, by new organizational forms: by employers who use Information Communications Technologies as mechanisms to control and manipulate or by companies, such as Marconi or Enron, who fail their own workforce as well as other stakeholders – shareholders, local communities and even the nation–state.

THE STRUCTURE OF THE BOOK

Chapter 1, 'The Roots of Strategic Human Resource Development', sets the scene by looking at the roots of the subject in Organizational Development and organizational theory that goes back to the beginning of the twentieth century. This history is important in order to remind ourselves of the dangers of the reductionist thinking in the various value-free 'scientific' discourses that are still available today. It is important, therefore, to promote humanistic values and adopt a critique that seeks to deconstruct reality prior to offering an interpretation.

Chapter 2, 'Planned Strategies for Change: The Evolution of Strategic Human Resource Development', focuses on six strategies that were central to the development of organizational efficiency in the twentieth century. These are: organizational design, innovation and enterprise, empowerment, strategic downsizing, programmed approaches such as Total Quality Management and Business Process Reengineering, and, finally, teamwork. These strategies have all influenced our understanding of the management of change. The strategies mirror the chronological development of late capitalism from early twentieth-century monopoly capitalism to twenty-first-century global capitalism. Furthermore, while these strategies are today driven by globalization, each contains its own ideology for managing change. A review of these strategies enables an enlightened move forward into the twenty-first century.

Chapter 3, 'Analysing Culture', argues that if all change strategies contain contradictions, then the wise change agent will recognize the importance of organizational culture to the objectives of the organization. The problem, however, is that most populist writing has adopted a functional analysis which requires the integration of activities and the identification of dysfunctions. The difficulty with this is the temporary nature of the integration – if it can be achieved at all – and the fact that the organization's values are viewed differently from various positions within the organization. By contrast, the interpretive approach focuses on the drama and discourse of organizational life. The interpretive approach therefore provides more sophisticated insights into organizational behaviour. But, these insights also have a practical value and are developed further in Chapters 5 and 6.

Chapter 4, 'The Emergence of Strategic Human Resource Development', argues that, by the end of the twentieth century, Organizational Development had developed a mature perspective for managing change. This perspective had become more flexible than the planned change programmes of the 1970s. It remained experimental and forward-looking but, above all, influenced by interpretive analyses, it had become much more aware of the behavioural dynamics that influenced change. There is a problem, however. As organizations changed by flattening hierarchies, downsized and delayered, the responsibility for change management was passed on, down the line, to middle managers, supervisors and team leaders armed with pre-packaged programmes for managing change at a variety of levels throughout their organizations. Prescriptive programmes based on half-baked theories, lacking analytical awareness, organizational diagnosis, and methodological rigour were driven by the myopic vision of a garden pruned and maintained by managers looking for a quick technical fix. It is in this sense that the case for Strategic Human Resource Development has now emerged in order to progress a more enlightened, methodological, and ethical change management that puts human resources back where they belong – at the top of the change agenda.

Chapter 5, 'Consultants, Clients and Change Agents', addresses the 'craft knowledge' of the change agent. Change agents must focus on the historical, processual and contextual issues that inform change and develop an ability to analyse situations, mobilize commitment, and establish mechanisms for change. If change is to become a successful learning process, then it requires internal change agents who are able to develop expertise. In order to facilitate organizational learning they require a methodology focused on (a) the role of the change agent within the Strategic Human Resource Development framework outlined in Chapter 4; and (b) the acquisition of appropriate knowledge and skills in relation to organizational analysis and diagnosis. In addition, the various types of Strategic Human Resource Development interventions require an ability to manage the relationship between the client and consultant through process consultation. Not only is it critically important to understand the complexity of dealing with internal clients but the depth of the intervention also needs to be identified. This 'craft knowledge' also requires knowledge of and an ability to apply four metaphors – *machine*, *organism*, *drama* and *discourse*.

Chapter 6, 'Strategic Human Resource Development Interventions', explores examples of change interventions through five case studies. The case studies demonstrate practical examples of change agents operating within organizations. The examples are related to the issues developed in Chapter 5. The case studies reflect (a) the complexities of contracting with the client;

(b) the difficulties faced in becoming an internal consultant; (c) the use of the organism metaphor to improve processes by examining functional inter-relationships; (d) the use of the drama metaphor to understand the underlying dynamics of organizational life; and (e) the use of discourse as a vehicle for learning conversations.

Finally, the book provides the basis for a new organizational development in which managers become more sensitive to the dynamics of change. Although the book is a practical guide for managers it should also be read as a cautionary warning about quick fix solutions to management problems. The scandal of Enron illustrates this. The unscrupulous management of change at Enron plunged the company's stock rating, worth $60 billion, into bankruptcy virtually overnight. The dramatic bankruptcy registration, on 2 December 2001, saw the company move from seventh on the Fortune list of US companies into the biggest corporate loss in US history. But, the real warning here is with the ideas that lay behind the reengineering of Enron by McKinsey, whose process of 'atomizing' was based on the ideas of management gurus and certain seminal texts including 'In Search of Excellence'. The company's human resource strategies (the annual hire and fire of MBA graduates), together with its decision-making and ethical practices (the so called 'stock-lock' which meant that whereas executives with inside information could sell shares before the price collapsed, other employees were legally restricted from selling their share options) failed to focus on personal and organizational development. Consequently, the quick fix was overtaken by the doomsday scenario. Without recourse to a process of proactive change enabled by Strategic Human Resource Development, the simple McKinsey 'loose-tight' management model, or the 'think outside the box' formula for success, was not enough to sustain competitive advantage.

The roots of strategic human resource development

INTRODUCTION: THE ARGUMENT FOR STRATEGIC HUMAN RESOURCE DEVELOPMENT

Fritz Lang's film *Metropolis* was a masterpiece of early twentieth-century film-making. The film's main theme was workers revolting against exploitation by management. The sub-themes were domination and control by technology and the construction of what has become referred to today as the hierarchical stratification of employees represented by senior managers at the top and an underclass of workers, who have only marginal rights, at the bottom. As images go, this is one of the most remarkable of the twentieth century since it was produced in 1927, long before the structural problems and unintended consequences of Taylorism and Fordism appeared. Indeed, *Metropolis* was such a powerful image of soulless machines and new technology that it was celebrated by the public and reviewers as a warning about the future. But critics claimed that it contained an anti-Fordist interpretation of new organizational design and life. They criticized the film for its implicit rejection of the production line mentality.

This image of the future is still as potent today despite the passage of time because we are still dealing with the deliberate or unintended consequences of organizational systems, power structures, decisions that affect the lives of millions of people, not only in the advanced capitalist economies, but also in the industrializing world of sweatshops and child labour. Organizations such as Marconi and Enron, the champions of the brave new world of global capitalism, have made bad decisions that affect the lives of too many people – shareholders, local communities and employees – to suggest that we have learned from the mistakes of the past.

This book begins from such a position but it seeks to reposition human resources centre-stage by making them strategic assets rather than costs. This is not a new argument but, in reviewing the last ten years of the twentieth century, it is worrying that the trends appear ominous.

This chapter takes its lead from the discipline of Organizational Development (OD), partly because it has been incorporated into various other discipline areas of the management agenda but also because change management is now the main subject of academic inquiry within these disciplines. There is, therefore, a very real danger of misapplying the tacit frameworks and debates in relation to change. Strategic Human Resource Development (SHRD) has its roots in OD although it is clear that Human Resource Management and Performance Management have extended the discourse in relation to improving organizational performance.

The learning objectives for this chapter are:

1   *Twentieth-century management* – Functionalism and early industrial sociology, Behaviourism and the emergence of industrial psychology, Scientific Management, Fordism and the elimination of uncertainty.
2   *The problem of control and compliance* – Modernity and the study of alienation and anomie. The application of technology and the origins of Organizational Behaviour.
3   *Organizational analysis as critique* – Strategic Human Resource Development as critical theory. Critical theory and the deconstruction of reality.

ORGANIZATIONAL DEVELOPMENT (OD)

Most OD texts identify the birth of the discipline in the late 1950s with its flowering in the 1960s (Albrecht, 1983). A thumbnail sketch of the history of OD would reveal that the 1960s was not only the decade of the T-group (Argyris, 1962; Harrison, 1963, 1966; Schein and Bennis, 1965) but saw the introduction of OD 'technology' beginning with Lewin's Force Field Analysis and the emergence of organizational theory in the form of applied open systems analyses (Lawrence and Lorsch 1967). The 1970s were defined by contributions to a 'theory of practice' (Harrison, 1970) through intervention strategies and team development (Kolb et al., 1971) and 'a proliferation of training approaches to personal growth and empowerment' through self-directed learning (Harrison, 1972). Visioning emerged in the 1980s along with organization culture, systems thinking, and quality management. The 1990s were the decade of consolidation following downsizing and Business Process Reengineering. But the 'greening' of organizations that began in the 1980s has disseminated the idea of values-driven approaches and organizational learning (Senge, 1990; Pedler et al., 1991).

The problem with this 'history' is not that it is inaccurate but that it reflects only one, albeit very prominent, psychological/behavioural perspective on OD. At the same time an organismic, or systemic, sociological definition of the subject emerged using an implicit 'health' metaphor involving diagnosis and organizational health monitoring. For example, Beckhard defined OD as a 'planned change effort' involving 'systematic diagnosis' of the 'total organization' that is 'managed from the top' to increase the 'organizational effectiveness and health' of the overall 'system' (Beckhard, 1969: 9–10). Such definitions reflected the Functionalist thinking of the time and it may be argued that this version of OD has come to characterize the subject more effectively in recent years. It is, however, the often quoted definition by French and Bell that best characterizes the movement away from the social engineering approaches, practised largely by psychologists, who sought to enhance the techno-managerial imperative of the Fordist period. The approach to managing and developing organizations proposed by French and Bell emphasized empowerment through the articulation of the change agent's values designed to facilitate visioning, organizational learning and problem-solving in the interests of a collaborative management of the organization's culture (French and Bell, 1995: 28). Methodologically we are moved a little further away from the inherent positivism of earlier approaches to a humanistic approach that uses Action Research as a mode of enquiry.

There is a tendency in the literature to assume that the discipline of OD emerged inevitably from the internal exigencies of the Second World War production processes and thereafter developed an altruistic concern for people in organizations. These themes are clearly visible in accounts of the historical direction of OD as an emerging discipline:

> Throughout this century, the efforts of managers to cope with and shape their environments, through the way they organize and operate their enterprises, have followed certain identifiable themes. The major theme during the first third of the century was the attempt, through better 'human engineering,' to rationalize the way work was done; the way the work force was utilized to increase the output; and the productivity of the goods and services produced. This theme reached its peak during the Second World War. After World War II, with the considerably improved human condition, working men began to demand that the work environment meet some of their social needs in addition to needs for survival and security. This impelled management to enter into a major search for a strategy to meet

this new requirement. We saw the emergence, therefore, of a second theme: the 'human relations' approach, where the focus was on man's social needs and ways of meeting them to increase motivation and organization productivity. This theme continued into the Fifties. In the late Fifties and early Sixties a new theme emerged for developing people for higher responsibilities. (Beckhard, 1969: 2)

This fascinating interpretation provides a neat linear account of the development of OD but it leaves us ignorant of the circumstances that characterize the delicate tension between control and empowerment that remains the central theme in managing people and enhancing both individual and organizational performance. It is much more a desideratum than a critical discourse since the objective at that time was no doubt to provide a rationale for OD as a distinct discipline.

STRATEGIC HUMAN RESOURCE DEVELOPMENT

As organizations have restructured and downsized, employees increasingly have been required to work in teams. As a result they need to develop new skills such as decision-making, problem-solving and personal skills which include listening, resolving conflict, negotiating and leadership. Team effectiveness has therefore become a critical issue for the development of the organization. For this reason, Human Resource Development (HRD) professionals are required to develop critical facilitation skills.

As working relationships become increasingly focused on the task, employees are less frequently required to act as functional managers. Instead, they operate in a cross-functional manner aided by new technologies in the pursuit of new knowledge. This pursuit of knowledge has transformed HRD by minimizing the role of the training department and refocusing on learning. The emphasis is therefore increasingly on transforming the organization through personal development and management development.

Another trend has been learning and knowledge management which has informed the need to understand performance standards in order to deal with complexity. Feedback has therefore become a necessary condition of organizational learning. As the customer, or client, has been placed centre-stage, the demands have increased on employees to become acquainted with the concepts of quality, benchmarking and continuous improvement. This requires in-house skills and human resources professionals will be increasingly challenged by the need to develop skills of facilitation, action learning, analysis and critical thinking.

It is therefore the changing nature of work and the political, economic and social pressures upon organizations that are forcing them to develop and communicate new corporate strategies; upwardly to develop new human resource strategies and policies; to involve employees, at all levels, in the change process; to determine the most effective and efficient work processes; to build teams with the capacity to learn and become self-managed; and to

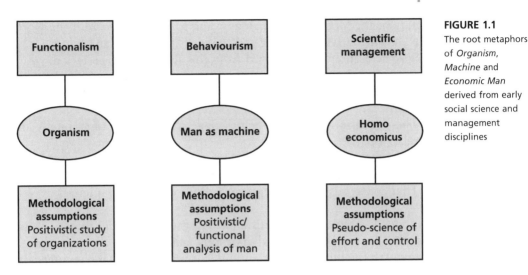

FIGURE 1.1
The root metaphors of *Organism*, *Machine* and *Economic Man* derived from early social science and management disciplines

develop individuals and encourage management development. However, if there is one single issue that needs to be encouraged, it is the need to develop ethical organizations in the pursuit of a better future.

Three central issues, or problematics, which emerged in the first three decades of the twentieth century informed the later development of OD (and were still important by the end of the century). These were: (a) the problem of control and compliance; (b) the application of technology; and (c) the increasing sophistication of organizational analysis.

EARLY TWENTIETH-CENTURY MANAGEMENT AND SOCIAL SCIENCE APPROACHES

Organizational Development emerged from three approaches to the study of organizations, each of which carried certain assumptions about the discovery of social laws (see Figure 1.1) and their application to the newly emerging organizations. These approaches were: (a) Functionalist sociology; (b) Behaviourist psychology; and (c) Scientific Management. Although all three disciplines shared common positivistic assumptions, they each differed in their application.

Functionalism and early industrial sociology

The sociological tradition came to view organizations as organisms in which the analogy with biological systems provided a useful vehicle for assessing the needs of the organization. Functionalism was developed by sociologists to explain social and organizational behaviour and although it can be traced back to the concerns about social and political upheavals of the Industrial

Revolution, the 'organismic' analogy came to prominence with the work of Emile Durkheim, who incorporated the ideas of Darwinian biology.

Specific assumptions emerged from this form of interpretation:

1   The organization has a life of its own, above and beyond the sum of its members.
2   The organization is best analysed as a system of functionally inter-related parts.
3   All organizations have needs which must be met.
4   The act of organizing is based on a consensus about values and goals.
5   That consensus itself emerges as a result of common interests.

The model of a biological organism encouraged a useful but rather one-sided focus on the sources of social harmony and balance. For example, the analogy with the human body is useful since it comprises many inter-related parts which function in harmony for the general health of the whole. Organizations can therefore be analysed in a similar way to the cells of the body. They may alter in relation to their changing needs over time or they may die. Consequently, organizations are considered to have needs and these can be divided into primary needs and secondary needs. Following Durkheim's argument that sociology should search for 'social facts', anthropologists such as Malinowski searched for primary social needs, such as food, shelter, sex, protection in primitive cultures, and the ways in which they encouraged secondary needs such as methods of food distribution, forms of communication, methods of co-operation and control. The early study of organizations progressed in the same way by explaining how every aspect of an organization fulfilled some function or other by associating the primary need (to survive) with secondary needs. This Functionalist interpretation of primary social needs being transformed into secondary social needs has survived, as the following example by Morgan (1986) in Figure 1.2 illustrates. In this example Morgan has transformed Maslow's (primary) needs hierarchy into more sophisticated organizationally based criteria.

If something as complex as a society could be viewed as an organism with inter-related parts (for example, the economic system which produces required goods and services; the political system which makes decisions and allocates resources; the cultural system which provides values for social integration; the ideological system which provides a rationale for legitimizing ideas), then organizations could be explained in the same way. The most sophisticated explanation emerged from the writings of the sociologist Talcott Parsons who focused on the way social systems establish and maintain a state of equilibrium.

Because technology is perhaps the most important cause of organizational change, problems of disequilibrium were explained by reference to cultural lag, which occurred between the technological system and the behavioural system. In other words, while employees may accept changes in technology where they see the benefits, they are less likely to modify their

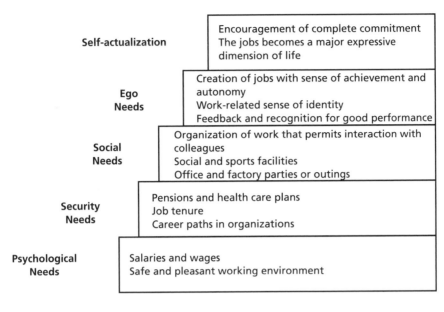

FIGURE 1.2
Maslow's hierarchy translated into an organizational context

Source: Morgan 1986

Self-actualization	Encouragement of complete commitment The jobs becomes a major expressive dimension of life
Ego Needs	Creation of jobs with sense of achievement and autonomy Work-related sense of identity Feedback and recognition for good performance
Social Needs	Organization of work that permits interaction with colleagues Social and sports facilities Office and factory parties or outings
Security Needs	Pensions and health care plans Job tenure Career paths in organizations
Psychological Needs	Salaries and wages Safe and pleasant working environment

norms (attitudes and behaviours), values or beliefs. This may result in a dysfunction (or cultural lag) in attitudes because the behavioural elements of the organization's culture are no longer appropriate to the changes in the technology. Other factors affecting the rate of change include the perceived needs of the organization's members. In this way, organizations were seen to possess needs of their own which required continuous monitoring for potential disequilibrium between the system's parts.

Because the organismic analogy explains social behaviour in terms of the needs of the organization, it ignores the role of human volition within this process. For example, organizations are composed of people who make decisions to which others react. Individual interests coalesce around group characteristics influenced by meanings, motives, and, sometimes, conflicting, values. The strength and popularity of Functionalism was its claim to be scientific by focusing on regularities at an organizational level rather than at individual or group levels.

Industrial sociology has been refined by a variety of researchers who shared a common interest with the 'systems approach' (see Miller and Rice, 1967). This aspect of organizational development 'can be traced through the work of the Tavistock researchers of the early 1950s . . . in particular, the work of Trist and Bamforth' and, 'the work of Joan Woodward and her colleagues in the late 1950s to the work of Burns and Stalker in the early 1960s and culminating in the Aston Studies of the early to late 1960s (Mills and Murgatroyd, 1991: 5). This tradition increasingly came to emphasize the impact of technological structure upon work groups (a good example is the concept of the socio-technical system (Trist and Bamforth, 1951) and the effects of technology upon organizational structure (Woodward, 1965; Burns and Stalker, 1961).

Behaviourism and the emergence of industrial psychology

Industrial psychology emerged from the equally positivistic school of Behaviourist psychology. This sought to apply various psychological techniques to the selection and training of employees and to the promotion of efficient working conditions and techniques, as well as individual job satisfaction. This field of applied psychology first became prominent during the Second World War, when it became necessary to recruit and train the large number of new workers who were needed to meet the expanding demands of industry. Because the selection of employees required the search for 'special aptitudes' and special 'personality characteristics' for a particular job, they became the *cause célèbre* of industrial psychology. Once the worker had been selected, s/he was then trained by means of behaviouristic techniques. This, of course, depended upon the discovery of the most appropriate way of carrying out a particular job. In this sense, the role of the early industrial psychologist was to discover the best way to do a particular job with a minimum of effort. Psychological techniques used included the study of the activities to do a job and the type of equipment used as well as the environmental conditions (such as ventilation, heating, lighting and noise levels) in which the employee works. A good example is the way in which the Human Relations School moved from a search for technological imperatives to the discovery of group norms and other behavioural factors that affected the morale and motivation of the workers.

The work of B.F. Skinner has been the most influential to focus on 'man as a machine'. In his books (1953, 1957, 1972) Skinner has given a functional or causal analysis of behaviour. The objection to investigating inner mental states is that they are irrelevant in functional analysis:

> The practice of looking inside an organism for an explanation of behaviour has tended to obscure the variables which are immediately available for scientific analysis. These variables lie outside the organism, in its immediate environment and in its environmental history. They have a physical status to which the usual techniques of science are adapted, and they make it possible to explain behaviour as other subjects are explained in science. (1953: 31)

In Skinner's Behaviourism change results from selective reinforcement. This works surprisingly well for some things that relate to physiological needs. For example, as Mennell states:

> by depriving a man of water for a period, or by administering a uretic drug, we can increase the probability that he will drink a glass of water. His action can then be explained without reference to his internal state of thirst, which we cannot directly observe. The causal chain consists of three links: (a) an operation performed on the organism from without (deprivation of water); (b) an inner condition (thirst); and (c) a kind of behaviour (drinking). For the behaviourist, any reference to the middle link is redundant to parsimonious theory building. (Mennell, 1974: 10)

The major problem here is that human behaviour is more complex and meaningful than simple examples of physiology. We can, after all, ask people what they think. A critical objection to Behaviourism came from the linguist Noam Chomsky (1959), who argued that human language, rather than observable behaviour, is the essence of the human condition. However, prior to the later debate forcefully articulated by Chomsky, Behaviouristic techniques were applied to the selection and training of employees during the Second World War. By the 1950s similar reductionist psychological techniques were being applied to personality tests and inventories which are used by organizations to select individuals for employment and promotion. Examples include the Eysenck Personality Inventory, the Myers-Briggs Type Indicator and Cattell's 16PF and the so-called 'Big Five' personality dimensions (tendencies to extraversion, emotional stability, agreeableness, will to achieve and openness to experience are designed to reduce complex cognitive processes to simple prescriptive parameters; see Thompson and McHugh, 1995: 247).

SCIENTIFIC MANAGEMENT, FORDISM AND THE ELIMINATION OF UNCERTAINTY

Fordism represented, above all, the shock of the new. It represented a new way of organizing the world through a new type of control over supervision. Fordism represented standardized products, which were machined to a 'T'. Repetition and interchangeability of parts came to shape the twentieth century. By the end of the twentieth century it was not only production processes that were characterized by these features. Services, from hamburgers to hairdressing, also depend on these features. Both Ford and Taylor belonged to the tradition of rationalism which was deeply rooted in the culture of the West, originating with Greek philosophy and gaining scientific momentum from the writings of Descartes to the present. Rationalists believed that the human mind could discover the laws that governed the universe. Fundamental to that belief was the assumption that the discovery of those laws could lead to limitless material progress. Taylor's particular contribution to management theory was in keeping with rationalism in that he assumed that once a law had been discovered, it was possible to write a rule for it. This very task, so he thought, eliminated uncertainty. For Taylor, management should be a science with fixed principles. He thought that because every company wanted to maximize prosperity, the interests of the employer and the employee were inseparable. With this 'unitarist' perspective he suggested that workers feared that greater output would result in fewer jobs. Bad management resulted in workers going slow to protect themselves. Traditional ways of doing jobs were inefficient.

Taylor's Quaker background led him to the study of time and motion. This involved what Braverman (1974) called, 'the science of other people's work', where he developed his four basic principles of Scientific Management. His four principles were:

- the development of a true science of work;
- scientific selection and training;
- bringing together a science of work and the trained man;
- the constant and intimate co-operation of management and men.

His biography also reveals that psychological influences were present in his home background. For example, his childhood was tormented by recurring nightmares of imprisonment by a machine.

Standardization was what Taylor excelled at. To create standardized jobs he found it necessary to observe the operations of workers and make charts of everything they did. Once all operations were timed, he was able to impose strict controls on the work process. In future, the system, not man, would take precedence because of its ability to predict each step in the production sequence. Frank Gilbreth developed these ideas further. Through his photographic images, Scientific Management was applied to all aspects of industrial production. By the end of the twentieth century this very predictability enabled just-in-time flexible employment practices because if it was possible to predict with accuracy when demand for products and services peaked and dropped off, then it became possible to hire staff or lay them off according to the dictates of the supply and demand cycle. This process of organizing the world to solve problems meant that control became the underlying principle.

As a result of the incorporation of Scientific Management within the Fordist work process, however, unfortunate consequences began to emerge. These included: (a) the separation of brainwork from manual work; (b) the way in which the invisible system, once it is constructed by experts and managers, becomes a subtle form of control.

The two major themes of early Organizational Development described above by Beckhard – '*human engineering*, to rationalize the way work was done' and the *human relations approach*, with its focus on 'man's social needs and ways of meeting them to increase motivation and organization productivity' – were heavily influenced by the three root metaphors of organismic sociology, Behaviouristic psychology and the Fordist/Scientific Management approaches to the development of organizations.

THE PROBLEM OF CONTROL AND COMPLIANCE

In reality it is impossible to disentangle Organizational Development from research into organizational behaviour and the latter emerged, by and large, as a reaction to the 'rational', so-called scientific approaches to management. Although it is easy to identify the attributes of control resulting from Fordism, Ford himself was simply applying a technique that had its roots in the development of the Panopticon, and in the Utilitarian philosophy of Jeremy Bentham in particular:

> This identification of factory and prison was, perhaps, quite natural for Bentham. Prison and factory were united in his philosophical mind by the utilitarian conceptions *of* tidiness and efficiency. The root of utilitarianism – this new mode of conduct which Bentham elaborated – is a passion for order, and the elaboration of a calculus of incentives which, if administered in exact measures, would stimulate the individual to the correct degree of rectitude and work. Utilitarianism provided a new definition of rationality: *not the rule* of reason, but the rule of measurement. With it, man himself could now be regulated. When the rule was applied by the engineer – the utilitarian par excellence – not only was work broken down in detail, but it was measured by detail, and paid for in time units defined in metric quantities. (Bell, 1988: 227)

The rational 'scientific' approaches to management that began at the beginning of this century and were informed by such assumptions included: Taylor's Scientific Management (Taylor, 1967[1911]); Gilbreth's motion studies (Gilbreth, 1911); Gantt's task scheduling (Gantt, 1974[1921]); Fayol's principles of management (Fayol, 1949) and Mary Parker Follett's law of the situation (Metcalf and Urwick, 1942). However, it is possible to put a convincing case that Max Weber, although usually placed with the Classical School, was sufficiently unique to represent one of the major social science contributions of his time since his studies not only analysed the nature of the Modernist period (through studies of bureaucracy) but focused on the nature of compliance between managers and subordinates. The other displaced reference points for OD are the problems of alienation associated with the application of production-line technology and the potential anomic effects of 'associational' rather than traditional 'communal' relationships expressed by Durkheim and Simmel.

Important later contributions to the behavioural science of organizations included the Human Relations School and the concerns over anomie and alienation which gave rise to studies of motivation. Thus, although the seminal Hawthorne studies (Roethlisberger and Dickson, 1966) began to focus on the role of informal groups in organizations, other theorists such as Maslow (1965), Hertzberg (1966) and McGregor (1960) began to identify the study of motivation as a solution to the problem of organizational control. Others, such as Merton (1968), and Argyris (1957), began to illuminate the inevitable conflict between bureaucratic organization and adult personality that had, to a large extent, plagued the thinking of Weber. Such personality types were said to be characterized by technicism or the red tape procedures of officialdom. Studies informed by the three root metaphors discussed above considered dysfunctional or 'pathological' personality types to result from excessive *structural over-conformity*.

Writers such as Merton (1968) suggested that such inadequacies involved 'a trained capacity to become dysfunctional' because:

1 Bureaucratic structures demand reliability of response and strict devotion to regulations.
2 Excessive devotion to the rules causes people to lose sight of the organization's purpose which is to serve the client or customer.

Thus, the characteristics that lead to efficiency may cause inefficiency in specific cases. Furthermore, with the passage of time, the original purpose for the rule-guided procedures may no longer be relevant. Such organizations may therefore fail to learn or modify their strategic purpose with the passage of time.

Modernity and the study of alienation and anomie

Modernity is an unusual word because it defines a period of our industrial past. It defines a distinctive time period when machines became paramount and the machine culture, informed by futuristic technologies, dominated a way of thinking. The concept of modernity has affected every walk of life. Design technology and architecture were instrumental in shaping the future of modernity by establishing a devotion to a new machine culture which came to characterize the essence of the twentieth century. In architecture, Le Corbusier's 'house machine' characterized the 'modern' as dynamic, efficient, progressive and above all designed according to scientific principles of form and function. The modern movement seemed to herald the greatest shift in intellectual change in the history of mankind.

The increasingly complex organizations of the twentieth century required control. This emerged in the form of the machine metaphor. The ultimate instructive application of the machine metaphor was provided by Ford's River Rouge plant in which everything was controlled: every resource, every machine part and every human movement was subject to the discipline of machine thinking. Managers became a new breed of decision-makers required by Taylor's principles of Scientific Management, and human labour was engineered to the specifications of the new managers.

The economies of scale created by the development of monopoly capitalism required systems for controlling the complexity of the industrial machine. This was aided by the adoption of military thinking and concepts. Management control and decision-making were characterized by the adoption of military principles (planning, co-ordinating, controlling) and infused with appropriate language (chain of command, lines of communication, leadership, strategic management and strategic planning, authority, delegation, management by objectives, operations management and mission statement).

Complexity had to be planned, organized, controlled and managed with the precision of a military campaign and managers became the officer corps of the modern organization and the workers became the troops. Modernity was characterized by bureaucratic structures, supervisory controls, the separation of ownership and management, national state regulation, a predominant manufacturing base and hierarchical knowledge communicated by a downward flow of information. It also represented a belief in constant linear industrial progress through well-defined stages of development in which products were made for a mass market of undifferentiated consumers.

The central guiding principle of the modern period is that of *rationality*. Rational control was already a general principle of scientific method but with its application to management it gained a new dimension through its focus on systems, procedures, and regulated human activities. As Max Weber observed: 'rational calculation is manifest at every stage. By it the performance of each individual worker is mathematically measured, each man becomes a little cog in the machine' (Mayer, 1956: 127). It is, therefore, no surprise that Ford's River Rouge plant was controlled by its Sociological Department.

The emergence of organizational behaviour and development as a discipline has its roots planted firmly in the soil of modernity. The 'scientific' rationality that emerged ignored the subterranean effects of workers' attitudes, behaviours and social relationships because the work contract itself was seen as the new vehicle of enlightened self-interest which was assumed to be to the benefit of both the workers and employers alike. This can be found in both Durkheim's sociology, in which he discusses the new relationship of 'organic solidarity', and in the very different concerns of Frederick Winslow Taylor and his assumptions that employers and workers shared the same unitary interests.

The study of organizational behaviour and development was a logical consequence of the application of rationalization. The increasing scale and complexity of monopoly capitalism required sophisticated administrative controls. The process of rationalization can be seen as a series of intertwining processes which include: scientific discovery and the faith in progress resulting from the application of the scientific method; the emergence of a managerial elite with technical expertise and able to apply the newly emerging management science; a transformation in power relationships resulting from the rise of the new managerial technocracy. These processes encouraged an instrumental rationality to workplace relationships resulting in an unreflective form of social engineering that came to typify behavioural science. In this way human idiosyncrasies could be subjected to scrutiny so that organizations could be made increasingly effective by the application of methods and procedures that measured time and motion, motivation and job design, leadership and follower behaviours and, finally, socio-emotional behaviours.

Another characterizing feature of modernity is the nature of workplace control. The creation of Fordism as a management system and the application of 'scientific' methods to work behaviours ranged from coercive to utilitarian. Supervision was essentially formal and hierarchical. The state controlled and regulated the economy and was used occasionally as a vehicle of surveillance when industrial disputes affected its interests (examples include the General Strike, the Miners Strike, Wapping). The role of the state is to intervene and regulate the relationship between the economy and corporate organizations in respect of investment, pricing, industrial relations and wage claims. By contrast, the period from 1980 onwards became increasingly characterized by a new set of relationships, which will be discussed later but briefly can be identified by the following:

- the rise of transnational organizations;
- loss of national state influence within the decision-making process;
- the attempt to regulate work behaviours through internal compliance;
- downsizing and the dismantling of bureaucracies;
- the attempt to influence employees' attitudes by appealing to a unitarist perspective;
- change from a manufacturing to a service-based economy.

The application of technology and the origins of organizational behaviour

The roots of Organizational Development are located within the concepts of alienation and anomie. The modernist era of organizational society was characterized by its assumptions of progress. It was an era in which the white heat of technology and the application of rational approaches to organizational life were to transcend politics, ideology and conflict. This new organizational enlightenment had developed mass production and consumption and now had to humanize it. The new behavioural science approaches, including personality and skills testing, were recruited to assist the development of a new type of person who would be organizationally committed (Whyte, 1963) and moulded by the needs of the corporation and whose lives in the organization were routine and largely unemotional (Biggart, 1989: 4). Thus, Fordism, Taylorism and bureaucratic management were assumed to reflect a 'mature industrial society' which retrospectively appears more as a kind of 'ideology masquerading as science than an accurate description of social trends' (Thompson and McHugh, 1995: 4).

Modernity represented unlimited linear progress. The social sciences also adopted the conviction that social laws were discoverable and the early science of organization was located within the positivist tradition that gave rise to the concerns over alienation and anomie. For Marx, alienation was a central problem of industrial society rooted in an exploitative relationship of power between the factory owner and the wage labourer. However, by the 1950s a significant number of empirical studies, driven by the search for technological imperatives, reported alienation not as a power relationship but as hindering the progress of modernity. The most notable example was the original focus of the Hawthorne experiments on the relationship between technology (and alienation) and the social relationships (anomie) that led to effective/ineffective organizational performance. Sociologists such as Blauner (1966) and psychologists such as Eric Fromm (1963) saw alienation as an expression of dissatisfaction or lack of fulfilment that emerged as a direct result of the industrial technology. For such authors, self-estrangement, social isolation in the workplace, and the inability to identify with the products of their labour suggested that alienation was a direct result of technology. Therefore the logic suggested that if the technology was changed, workers would find the work more interesting and fulfilling. The result for the employer was likely to be increased efficiency.

If alienation was the term used to describe either the symptoms of control and exploitation or simply the effects of technology, then anomie expressed Durkheim's original concern that modern society and its institutions was displaying signs of disintegration. The concerns about anomic relationships were transferred to organizational behaviour through the work of Elton Mayo and the research carried out by the Hawthorne experiments. Mayo's assumptions about modern industrial society led him to consider that the external indicators of anomie were liberalism, with its stress on individualism, and the division of labour, required by the Fordist/bureaucratic approach to management. The 'discovery' of group norms in the Western Electric Company led to the rise of the Human Relations movement, which began to focus on motivation and leadership. This had unfortunate consequences, according to Reed, who has argued that the effect was to produce a neutralized and depoliticized reading of alienation (1992: 48). By the 1930s the concept of the social group became a target for influencing productivity within the organization but imaginative sociological studies, such as those by Roethlisberger and Dickson (1966), were beginning to reveal a complex social world in which the concept of 'resistance to change' could not be viewed as the simple instrumental reaction by employees to management actions. Some of these early studies are surprisingly refreshing to read today (Roethlisberger and Dickson and the Hawthorne Studies are good examples of this) and it is surprising to discover just how sophisticated some of them were by comparison to writers today who glibly produce quick fix books on change management and categorize the concept of resistance as if it were a simple formula of management versus worker. Such studies reveal that Taylorist principles and the pursuit of efficiency have become the defining principles by which managers and supervisors come to make moral judgements about employees through arbitrary rules, which carry consequential sanctions for employees:

> This point was illustrated time and again in the Bank Wiring Observation Room. There it was seen that most of the problems encountered by the supervisors were problems of inducing the workmen to conform to the rules of the technical organization. The worker's conduct was considered right or wrong in so far as it corresponded to these rules. The supervisor's success was evaluated by his superiors in terms of how well he succeeded in achieving this objective. Theoretically, these rules were supposed to promote efficiency, and adherence to them was supposed to redound to the

worker's advantage. From the point of view of the worker's sentiments, however, many of them were annoying and seemingly functioned only as subordinating or differentiating mechanisms.

Consider, for example, the unwritten rule that wiremen should not help one another wire. This rule received its sanction from the belief that employees could turn out more work by working only on the equipment to which they were assigned. There would be less opportunity for talking, less likelihood of their getting in one another's way, and less likelihood of their delaying the solderman and the inspector. There was, in other words, no logical reason why workmen should want to help one another in this fashion. To the wiremen, however, this was just another arbitrary rule. Many of them preferred to work together occasionally. It was one of the ways in which they expressed their solidarity; it was one of the integrative mechanisms in their internal organization. Furthermore, they knew that working together did not necessitate slowing down. In fact, the evidence showed that sometimes when they were refused the privilege of helping one another, they became less efficient.

It can be seen that one of the chief sources of constraint in a working group can be a logic which does not take into account the worker's sentiments. Any activity not strictly in accordance with such a logic (and sometimes this means most forms of social activity) may be judged 'wrong'. As a result, such activity can only be indulged in openly within the protection of an informal group, which, in turn, may become organized in opposition to the effective purpose of the total organization. (Roethlisberger and Dickson, 1966: 259)

Such studies make it clear that organizational behaviour needed to search for the underlying dynamics of the situation by examining the internal logic or implicit rules of various groups of managers, supervisors and workers. It is therefore unfortunate that many change management writers lack this training and characterize the nature of resistance by reference to surface appearances and egocentric perspectives.

ORGANIZATIONAL ANALYSIS AS CRITIQUE

Organizational Development absorbed the modernist assumptions of scientific reason and progress from organization theory and as it did so it became a well-defined discipline because it synthesized organismic sociology with Behaviourist psychology. Figure 1.3 illustrates how, as the twentieth century progressed and began to unpack the unintended consequences of the modernist period, the types of interventions made by OD practitioners moved from a predominantly shallow technical focus in which social engineering was predominant to the consideration of deeper socio-emotional behaviours. This history has given rise to various styles of intervention within organizations ranging from the superficiality of the technocratic to the deeper and more probing analysis of individual and team behaviours.

Although it never followed the tradition of Scientific Management, the early focus of OD, on organization-wide change, carried that part of the

The Modern →	Post-modern →	FIGURE 1.3 Key characteristics
1900–1935? Monopoly capitalism Technological determinism Application of scientific method to management Emergence of Fordism, Scientific Management and the Classical School of management	**1935–1970** Socio-psychological concerns with alienation and anomie Hawthorne experiments Discovery of group behaviours Research into leadership, motivation and job design	**1970–2000** Quality Management BPR Empowerment Learning organization Corporate governance	of the modern and the post-modern periods

Control ————————————————→ Empowerment

Characterizing features:	**Characterizing features:**
Bureaucratic structure	Organic structure
Control is external	Control internalized
Separation of ownership and management	Downsizing and teamwork – the global economy
National state regulation	Post-industrial, service economy
Manufacturing base	Information technology
Hierarchical knowledge	Recognition of limits to progress
Constant linear industrial progress through well-defined stages	creates focus on quality
Undifferentiated consumers	Differentiated consumers
Industrial relations as trench warfare	Industrial relations based on inner compliance

rationalist tradition that informed organizational effectiveness. From America, Lewin's (1952) model of change provided a linear destination-oriented journey in keeping with the organismic or health metaphor yet, increasingly, this model of OD came to represent 'an episode divorced from the immediate and more distant context in which it is embedded' (Pettigrew, 1985: 15). Thus, the flowering of OD was to some extent hindered by the paradigmatic constraints of an organizational analysis focusing primarily on organizational structure, on the one hand, and by the parallel nature of psychologistic developments on the other. This led to the division, especially in the USA, into separate areas of study between organization theory and organizational behaviour (Mills and Murgatroyd, 1991: 5).

Later experiments were illuminating. By contrast to the emerging theory on organizational structure from both sides of the Atlantic, T-groups represented the search for authenticity and existential truth in an organizational world characterized by control and exploitation. But T-groups became what Roger Harrison called 'the shadow side of our profession', because they challenged personal defences and damaged members through pressure and attack (Harrison, 1996: 13).

By the 1970s, although there were differences in style, it was reasonable to assume that OD represented a planned programme involving a holistic, systemic approach related to the organization's mission, planned from the top down and representing a long-term linear effort to change the organization through behavioural science interventions and involving collective action. Thus, OD activities are distinguished from a training course or a management workshop because, instead of producing knowledge, skill, or understanding, to individuals, the group or team takes ownership and builds the connections and follow-up change in organizational development programmes. The major target of change is the attitude, behaviour and activities aimed at action programmes (Beckhard, 1969: 15).

By the 1990s organizational learning became a central constituent of OD because practitioners came to realize that simply by increasing knowledge about an activity does not result in personal and organizational learning and growth. As Beckhard put it:

> One does not learn to play golf or drive a car by getting increased knowledge about how to play golf or drive a car. Nor can one change one's managerial style or strategy through receiving input of new knowledge alone. It is necessary to examine present behavior, experiment with alternatives, and begin to practice modified ways, if change is to occur. (1969: 16).

As OD developed its approaches in the 1960s, the idea of organizational health became paramount. Diagnosing the dysfunctions was the key to re-establishing equilibrium. But this meant that a problem had to be identified first by someone in a strategic position who 'really feels the need for change' and where 'somebody or something is "hurting"' (ibid. 1969: 16). A felt need was seen as the catalyst to an OD intervention and such needs were said to form around the pressure to do the following:

1 To change a managerial strategy.
2 To make the organization climate more consistent with both individual needs and the changing needs of the environment.
3 To change 'cultural' norms.
4 To change structure and roles.
5 To improve intergroup collaboration.
6 To open up the communications system.
7 To facilitate better planning.
8 To cope with the problems of merger.
9 To effect a change in motivation of the workforce.
10 To encourage adaptation to a new environment.

Newer forms of organizational analysis increasingly challenged the dominance of structuralist and psychologistic/psychodynamic approaches. The rise of phenomenology, symbolic interactionism and linguistic analysis had been particularly influential in other social sciences but OD had been slower to embrace them since they were not deemed compatible with the dominant paradigmatic ways of viewing organizations (Burrell and Morgan, 1979). Yet these perspectives enabled an appreciation of the way employees as actors view their own organizations.

Thus, interpretative perspectives (Sudnow, 1978; Smircich, 1983) from the late 1970s onwards, began to make an impact and have enriched our understanding of just how negotiable, culturally determined and fluid inter-actions are within organizations. Linda Smircich, for example, in applying this perspective to the notion of organizational culture, views organizations as 'expressive forms, and manifestations of human consciousness' that are 'understood and analysed not mainly in economic or material terms, but in terms of their expressive, ideational, and symbolic aspects' (1983: 347–8).

Interpretive accounts have enhanced awareness of voluntarist action within organizations and in so doing clearly distinguish action and sense-making from structuralist interpretations. Such analyses have challenged the destination-oriented journey metaphor by applying a process-oriented model, allowing for the investigation of previously ignored elements of organizational change dynamics.

More recently, other forms of organizational analysis have been influen-tial in developing OD as a discipline. Morgan's (1986) argument that a variety of metaphors have come to supplement the one-dimensional machine metaphor that had dominated thinking throughout the first two-thirds of the twentieth century has had a major impact on thinking. As a result, recogniz-ing that a more sophisticated diagnostic reading of an organization is required intellectually challenges OD even further. Such readings, or inter-pretative judgements, depend upon the insight gained from various root metaphors that include the machine, the organism, the culture, the brain, and the political system.

A version of OD that remains rooted in the logic and method to the 1960s' definitions would reflect an inherent conservatism in its approach to the subject. The eclecticism thrown up by these newer analyses requires practitioners to re-examine the history of their subject and recognize that subjects as diverse as linguistic philosophy and analysis, politics and anthro-pology, have come to provide a greater depth to the discipline in recent years. And, in recognizing these newer insights we are paradoxically forced to re-examine a wider history of the subject than hitherto.

STRATEGIC HUMAN RESOURCE DEVELOPMENT AS CRITICAL THEORY

Management education and training emerged as an attempt to inculcate technical rationality throughout organizations. In a period when manage-ment was the carrier of reason, progress and modernity this approach to hierarchical management sought the downward flow of information and decision-making according to quasi-scientific principles. In contrast to mod-ernism, postmodern forms of enquiry seek to interrogate organizational practices from a critical perspective in which the concepts of progress and rationality are made politically transparent. While the postmodern label has been applied to a period of history in which organizational society attempts to reinvent itself by challenging the assumptions of Fordism, postmodernism as a form of critical discourse has attempted to challenge many of the basic assumptions that lie behind the rhetoric of the various attempts to bring change to organizations.

Organizational analysis today should enable the Strategic Human Resource Development consultant, or change agent, to find clarity in complexity and deal with ambiguity. In Chapter 5 it is argued that skilful organizational analysis has little to do with the accumulation of facts and should be more concerned with the relationships between them, that is, with interpretation and insight. There are two issues here. First, positivistic enquiry is limited by its inability to explain the relationship between constructs of meaning. Second, it is limited by its attempts to be neutral and value-free. In relation to the first point, because its use of language is not interrogated, it assumes a misleading scientific method for analysing organizations. This is illustrated by Alvesson and Deetz's description of leadership as an example of positivistic enquiry. They point out that the attempt to provide a universal account of leadership, uninfluenced by context, history and people's perceptions, leads it to 'pull together categorically the behaviours, styles, and personalities of quite diverse groups' such as, 'university department chairs, SS officers, US presidents, gang leaders, project managers, non-violence civil rights spokespersons, and students in experimental groups that seem to be spontaneously ascribed higher status and/or more influence than others (Alvesson and Deetz, 2000: 53). In relation to the second point, methods that attempt to replicate the objectivity of the natural sciences adopt a scientifically neutral ability to describe their subject matter by assuming the truthful representations of their subject's responses. This brings us to the problem of respondents' motives and the researcher's ability to reveal transparency through questionnaire design and analysis. Attitude scales that attempt to be universally valid, and these appear to be proliferating in management studies, provide elegant but invalid interpretations precisely because definitions are always tied to context, are always historically and politically defined and are influenced by continually changing shifts in perception.

So far, this defines a critical theory by what it is not rather than by what it is. A critical theory, then, requires certain criteria to enable it to be critical. These are: (a) an activity by which information is transformed into meaning through the process of connoisseurship; (b) a focus that requires a detailed understanding of social context and historical linkages with particular attention paid to political processes in the construction of reality; and (c) a critique which is informed by a humanistic perspective and which seeks to add value to the organization by developing and delivering strategy through its human resources.

Alvesson and Deetz point out that there are actually two strands to critical theory. The first – the critical theorists – belong to a tradition rooted in German moral philosophy. The second are postmodernists who draw upon psychoanalytic theory. Thus, while the first draws attention to ideological critiques about whose interests are being served in a particular situation, the second focuses on the 'communicative processes through which ideas are produced, reproduced and critically examined, especially in decision-making contexts' (Alvesson and Deetz, 2000: 89).

While skilful analysis requires both knowledge of 'conceptual leverage' (Schatzman and Strauss, 1973: 118) and the ability to apply it, it also requires the adoption of a values-driven humanistic perspective. The result might best be described as 'craft knowledge' (Ravetz, 1971; Turner, 1988: 116) which can be understood by other members of the Strategic Human Resource Development community.

Metaphor is seen to be central to the art of analysis and this appears to be the case in science as well as organizational discourse. In science, for example, writers such as Koestler (1969) and Kuhn (1970) have discussed the role of metaphor in the creative imagination of scientists. And, in organizational analysis Morgan (1980, 1983) is the most popularly cited author among the many others now taking an interest in the subject by exploring the metaphorical basis of organization theory.

Reading organizations is like reading a text. This enables managers to learn how to 'read' or analyse their organizations through 'explanatory' (that is, understanding and explaining an organizational problem retrospectively) and 'interventionist' (that is, focusing on a potential course of action) metaphors (Tsoukas, 1993: 33). Metaphors are also prescriptive because they are concerned with (a) how to structure or restructure an organization or part of it (e.g., machine, organism); and (b) identifying existing or preferred behaviours (e.g., culture, political systems, psychic prison) in order to improve customer or supplier relationships.

A central tenet of Strategic Human Resource Development is the promotion of humanistic values. Thus, Cummings and Huse have argued that, 'Values have played a key role in OD, and traditional values promoting trust, collaboration, and openness have recently been supplemented with values for organizational effectiveness and productivity' (1989: 38). French and Bell emphasized empowerment through values designed to facilitate visioning, organizational learning and problem-solving in the interests of a collaborative management of the organization's culture (1990: 28). Tensions arise, however, between humanistic objectives and organizational needs resulting in 'value dilemmas' and 'value conflicts'.

The choice and type of intervention

The way the Strategic Human Resource Development consultant deals with these issues is central to the success of the intervention. For example, one of the problems with some management consultants is their attempt to eliminate resistance to change rather than recognize resistance as a natural and legitimate human process. By contrast, a Strategic Human Resource Development perspective recognizes that resistance needs to be understood and worked with in order to develop ongoing learning experiences within organizations. Although the usual references are to process consultation and

TABLE 1.1 Types and levels of intervention

Type of intervention	Level of intervention				
	Individual	Team	Intergroup	Organization	Society
Acceptant Enters into a contract with feelings, tensions and subjective attitudes that often block a person and make it difficult to function as effectively as he otherwise might	Counselling designed to discharge tensions. For example, dealing with stress, traumas Personal growth and development	Dealing with process, task and maintenance issues, and group dynamics Team building T-groups	Using catharsis at the entire group level to surface emotions, frustration and hidden politics which block the effective management of change	Taking a diagonal slice of the organization in order to get a clear picture of similarities and differences in perspective	Contractual helping relationships facilitated by doctor/ general practitioner, priest, teachers, counsellors
Catalytic By entering a situation the consultant adds something that has the effect of transforming the situation, to some extent, from what it was	Career-planning and development Goal setting Performance appraisal Reward systems	Consultant facilitation for group dynamics Management by objectives Process consultation	Adding something between two groups. In this case the consultant adds a procedure in order to find a resolution to inter-group problems	Intervention by an organizational ombudsman who is empowered to bypass normal channels in order to facilitate a solution to the problem. Today, we can consider organizational learning and management development as catalysts to change	National census Opinion polls

TABLE 1.1 Types and levels of intervention *continued*

Type of intervention	Level of intervention				
	Individual	*Team*	*Intergroup*	*Organization*	*Society*
Confrontation The consultant actively intrudes, usually at the request of different parties in the dispute, into the organizational experience in order to challenge assumptions and paradigms	Understanding alternative perspectives Eliminating conflict and contradiction	Exploration of half-contradictions and discrepancies Inter-action analysis of inter-personal behaviour	The consultant brings two or more groups together with the intention of gaining a shared and realistic perspective	Culture change Challenging strategies and conventions of performance	Government Educational system University Legal system
Prescriptive This is the most forceful type of intervention. Tends to be widely applied by outside consultants who are seen as 'experts' rather than facilitators	Behaviour modification	Team briefing Circulars, memos, agendas, and other various rules that prescribe the conduct of the team	A third party arbiter whose decision is binding on both parties	External diagnosis Organizational redesign Down-sizing Business process re-engineering Mergers and acquisitions	Pressure groups Investigative journalists Newspaper's editorial policy Opinion shapers
Principles, models and theories The intervention is informed heavily by the concept and ideas that have been identified clearly in the literature	Transactional analysis McGregor's Theory X and Theory Y	Diagnosis and feedback of behaviour and processes are formed by a theory and models – for example, Bales' socio-emotional process interaction	Grid Organization Development – based on theory is of inter-group conflict and co-operation. The purpose is to transform current experience with the use of new ideas	Models used by top team to redesign company strategies and values	Bill of rights Separation of powers Rule of law

Source: Modified from Blake and Mouton, 1972.

psychodynamics, critical perspectives have also made an impact on the client–consultant relationship. As Boyce has pointed out:

> A vast literature spanning sociology, philosophy, social criticism, education, and organization studies now exists that advocates a critical perspective (Bowles, 1989; Burrell, 1988; Calas and Smircich, 1992; Clegg, 1990; Ferguson, 1984; Freire, 1985; Giroux, 1992, 1993; Gramsci, 1971; Martin, 1990, 1992; Mills, 1988; Mills and Tancred, 1992; Tierney, 1989, 1993). Some of this work is grounded in modernism and some in postmodernism. Giroux (1993) and Tierney (1993) proposed a blend of these approaches, 'critical postmodernism', which addresses structures and expressions of oppression at both macro and micro levels. Central to a critical perspective is identifying and challenging the assumptions that lie underneath one's work. Taking a critical perspective involves a ruthless and courageous examination and deconstruction of assumptions, norms, expectations, limitations, language, results, and applications of one's work. (1996: 6)

An example of why interventions need to be considered carefully by the Strategic Human Resource Development consultant is provided by Blake and Mouton (1972). In their *Strategies of Consultation* they identify five types of intervention (Acceptant; Catalytic; Confrontation; Prescriptive; Principles models and theories) that may be applied at five levels (Individual; Team; Inter-group; Organization; Society). The important point about this schema is that it forces the consultant to think carefully about the purpose of the intervention (see Table 1.1). The failure to reflect on the motives for the intervention and values that lie behind it will result in methodological problems. While each type of intervention strategy will be agreed with the client system, the choice of intervention will reflect a carefully considered diagnostic position.

There is another reason for thinking very clearly about the type of intervention strategy to be applied. This is described by Roger Harrison in his paper 'Choosing the depth of organizational intervention'. For Harrison, intervention strategies range from deep to surface level. As he states, 'the deeper we intervene, the more we impact core values and self-concepts' (Harrison, 1996: 30). Deep interventions are those that are due to emotional involvement. These require a high level of behavioural knowledge and skill as well as a sensitivity to the client's needs. Furthermore, there are clearly ethical issues which require the willing participation of the client. This is what Blake and Mouton call acceptant intervention strategies. The deepest levels require that 'the target of change is the individual's inner life' when, 'if the intervention is successful, the permanence of individual change should be greatest'. There are, Harrison argues, dramatic reports of life changes as a result of personal development 'in which persons have changed their careers and life goals as a result of such interventions, and the persistence of such change appears to be relatively high' (1996: 19). What makes deep interventions difficult is that the information required becomes more personal, complex and effectively 'less available'. This means that at the deepest levels, the consultant must use more skill and time to uncover information which is hidden, either deliberately or subliminally, by the client. By contrast, surface level interventions, as for example in performance management, normally mean that information is collected through records and quality control systems.

The choice of intervention, for Harrison, depends on a number of factors. These include the following:

1   The degree to which the client is dependent on the competence of the change agent.
2   The extent to which it is necessary to move beyond surface level interventions (and procedures, policies, and practices of the organization) to consider more instrumental behavioural factors such as group norms which ultimately influence the operational performance of the organization's strategy and *modus operandi*.
3   The degree of risk to the client's own value system and personal constructs.

Change events or change processes?

The Greek philosopher Heraclitus, who lived in the sixth century BC, argued that 'everything is flux' by which he meant that opposites, or contradictions have unity. In simple terms this means that argument, contradiction or conflicts of interest should not be avoided since that is how change occurs. It was, for Heraclitus, the very substance of the world. In reality while the world may be perceived as relatively permanent, it is, in fact, always in a state of flux. The stability of objects or 'things' is a fiction because they are like the flames of a fire: they look like objects but they are actually processes. This idea was developed further by Hegel in the early nineteenth century who argued that change is nearly always intelligible. Every complex situation contains conflicting elements within itself. For Hegel, change was always destabilizing. No situation could continue indefinitely. All conflicts must work themselves out until there is a resolution. But this, in turn will bring about a new situation with all the accompanying dynamics for change again. Hegel's dialectic, or law of change, was made up of (a) the initial stage: the idea or event; (b) the reaction provoked by the initial stage and the conflicting elements that comprise the reaction; (c) the synthesis of the two previous stages which also contains the seeds of new conflict. We can therefore draw the following modest conclusions in relation to organizational change.

For change to be organizationally interesting it must do one of the following:

1   Indicate significant transformations in social behaviour, attitudes or regular ways of doing things.
2   Illustrate modifications to patterns of activities, routines or processes.

A more interesting way to think about this is that change is often seen as a series of events, stages, or histories as individuals, groups and organizations transform themselves. But, in reality, this is an illusion in exactly the same way that a historical narrative can give the impression that historical change is like a singular story (the one told by the historian) by ignoring the perspectives or active processes of the actors themselves. In both cases what is misunderstood is that change is much more complex and results from a series of processes which interweave their causality in the same way that a net represents a non-linear flow of information.

Although they are the real motives for change, they are not neutral. Processes are constrained by and also transform the three structures that give form to a seemingly complex reality. These three structures are political, economic and social (see Figure 1.4). Furthermore, while these structures are not rigid, they do have a degree of longevity which makes them appear permanent. In time, of course, the processes which make them cause the structures to be contested and perhaps renegotiated. Organizational change is not, therefore, simply a series of ebbs and flows as they might be described by chaos theory in natural science. These structures represent interests that come into conflict.

A critical theory assumes, then, that there are inevitable clashes of interest in organizations, which are essentially derived from opposing structural (for example, managers/employees, capital/labour) positions. This inevitably means taking care when identifying who the client is (Schein, 1997b).

Taking a critical perspective, according to Alvesson and Willmott, is to adopt an approach that understands management as a political, cultural and ideological phenomenon (Alvesson and Willmott, 1992: 8). The role of critique, therefore, is equated with the adoption of a reflective attitude 'based on asking questions that focus on the influence of the ubiquitous capitalist discourse' and on a critical theory in postmodernity that does not present clear-cut answers, but works towards 'ensuring that the questions that relate to capitalism as a discourse are still being asked' (Grice and Humphries, 1997).

Essentially a critical theory is any position that provides a critique but objects to a positivistic approach. A good example of this is the emergence of organizational culture as a metaphor for organizational analysis, diagnosis and development. The problem, however, is that it was hijacked by positivists who saw it as another variable to be manipulated rather than an analytic tool or approach. White and Jaques have discussed this:

> In the late 1970s, it seemed possible that the concept of organizational culture as a new metaphor for understanding social systems might challenge theorists to contextualize more cautiously the benefits and limits of research modelled on the physical sciences by introducing more interpretive models of inquiry from anthropology and sociology. Very quickly, however,

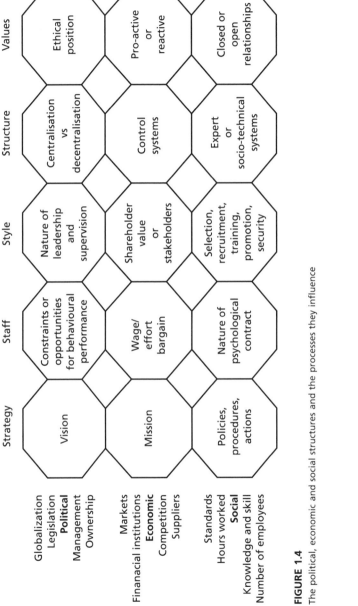

FIGURE 1.4

The political, economic and social structures and the processes they influence

culture began to be absorbed into mainstream theorizing as simply a new 'variable', and its critical potential was seriously diluted or entirely lost (Barley et al., 1988). As early as 1980, Morgan and Smircich (1980) warned of this trend. Smircich (1983) attempted to distinguish between approaches treating culture as a 'variable' and those treating culture as a 'root metaphor'. For the former, culture was simply one more attribute of organizations to be studied using the dominant methods of physical science inquiry. For the latter, culture was something an organization was, an entity not well represented by reductionistic, measurement-centred, hypothesis-testing methods. To conceive of organizations as cultures raised issues of epistemology and social values as well as issues of method. Post-modern theory has been criticized by critical theorists because of its lack of attention to values. (White and Jaques, 1995: 45–60).

The discredited but still dominant functionalist theory placed the culture variable centre-stage, resulting in the loss of its potential for critical debate (Calas and Smircich, 1992; White and Jaques, 1995). Furthermore, in addition to the assumed 'neutrality' of positivism, various topics have become sanitized by the often deliberate removal of their critiques by management consultants who have been responsible for shaping the popular management agenda. As Collins points out, management consultants have played a dual role between providing apparent solutions to problems on the one hand, while on the other plundering the literature and removing the critiques in order to develop their 'booty' of techniques and approaches. Management consultants have become the soothsayers of the modern world charged with near collusion on the one hand and undermining the confidence of managers: 'Hand-in-hand (or perhaps more accurately, hand-in-glove) with the state, management consultants have played a key role in all this; simultaneously bolstering and demolishing management confidence and managerial careers' (Collins, 1997: 23).

Consultants, therefore occupy a privileged position since they create dependency by defining themselves as experts and simultaneously provide templates, recipes and formulae for the organization to follow. The dangers of over-reliance on expert solutions and pre-packaged approaches (discussed in Chapter 5) can lead to the application of simplistic ideas to complex problems that really need to be diagnosed carefully:

> Equally, we could argue that in developing novel solutions to management problems (and in ensuring appropriate rates of product development), consultants have reshaped management thinking, to some degree, by fostering an eclectic approach to management; an approach which happily plunders a range of social scientific disciplines and subject areas. For example consultants have borrowed from areas such as sociology, social anthropology, political philosophy and have acquired such booty as quality circles, autonomous work groups, the concepts of organizational culture and cultural change management, and most recently the notion of worker empowerment. (ibid.: 1997: 23)

Empowerment is another topic that, as Collins suggests, has been removed of its critical scrutiny by many HRM practitioners in the UK by promoting empowerment as a form of individual commitment to the organization and by playing down the political motives behind a preference for individualism rather than collectivism. Thus, the recent political history of the UK (two major recessions, large-scale unemployment, continued structural changes replacing Britain's manufacturing base by foreign corporations and fostered by government policy, the growth in the service sector, the emergence of the flexible firm and the emergence of core and peripheral workers, the challenge to trades union practices by powerful employers and a resultant decline in trade union membership and continual economic turbulence and restructuring) in shaping the British model of HRM is often conveniently ignored. For example Pateman (1983) has argued that the narrow focus of HRM in the UK is essentially about job participation and involvement rather than co-participation and 'a real commitment to allowing workers a democratic voice in the processes of decision making such as that promoted by the Organization Development Institute (1992)'. This is essentially an argument made by Collins (1997) who states that those committed to empowerment seem to face two key issues which appear to pose critical questions that test the value system of OD:

> On the one hand empowering initiatives . . . have been demonstrated often to be initiatives which in denying workers access to frameworks of power, or access to traditional institutions for decision making (such as trade unions), work towards enhancing managerial control over the labour process. Yet on the other hand, it seems that if we simply set about reversing this process (and reversing the trajectory of contemporary politico-economic developments) so that workers operate under a rather more mutual system of decision making – a system less influenced by the operation of management power deployed unilaterally – there would remain the problem that we may, in fact, have done little to democratize the workplace in line with the values of the OD Institute. Under this particular model of empowerment groups such as women, ethnic minorities, older workers or the disabled would tend to remain as dependent and disenfranchised subjects since they would have no real voice of their own to represent their own distinctive needs, drives and orientations. (ibid.: 26)

The extent to which HRM has changed managerial practices has been critically discussed by various authors, many of whom have raised questions about the gap between rhetoric and reality (Keenoy, 1990; Bowles and Coates, 1993). Commenting on what academic researchers can do about this process, Watson, by implication, suggests that the act of reflection is a critical tool in the art of intervention:

> Social science writing generally and management thought particularly is involved in a double hermeneutic. Researchers are not engaged in a one-way process of interpreting the actions of those they study. They are in turn interpreted by their 'subjects', who may be influenced by them. Writers on HRM are not invisible observers behind a two-way mirror. Their utterances may instead act as mirrors in which their subjects examine themselves and

reflect on their practices. And these people may act in the light of the image they observe. (Watson, 1995: 7–8).

The solution is to reposition the place of expertise back in the organization. To develop the role of the internal change agent not only addresses the frameworks of power, it develops the idea of devolved decision-making. In place of recipes and pre-packaged solutions to change, the change agents should engage in a discursive practice when they address their own organizational problems.

Critical theory and the deconstruction of reality

Change management is usually equated with progress and improvement. This perspective tends to assume that instability is the norm and, as the rate of change increases, employees are often consulted over coping strategies. One problem with this received wisdom is the assumption that change related to globalization is natural, inevitable and progressive. Occasionally, however, critical accounts emerge to challenge this assumption. One example is Steingard and Fitzgibbons (1995) who deconstruct what they call 'the four myths of globalization'. In order to do this they employ Derrida's (1967) method of deconstruction which depends upon a structural analysis of opposing linguistic constructs (man/woman, day/night, good/bad, etc.). Thus, in order to 'unpack the subterfuge of globalization' deconstruction enables the possibility of identifying the underlying assumptions.

In this way, the tendency of discourse to naturalize the process of globalization is deconstructed by showing the artificiality of the ordinary and taken-for-granted structures of social thought. As they point out, 'the underlying assumption of deconstruction is that language is far from a value-free component of human communication; language plays a considerable role in constituting the power relations of social reality' (Steingard and Fitzgibbons, 1995: 33). Such an analysis of the language of globalization reveals a *grand narrative* masquerading as neutral scientific and industrial progress along with advances in technology which become available to the world despite differences in wealth or other social barriers. Thus, the language of development is characterized by its assumed opposite – under-development. By viewing 'under-developed' countries as aspiring to developed status the associated processes of 'improvement', 'growth' and 'progress' are naturalized.

In their account, myth 1 – globalization – assumes the need to move to a singular 'healthy' and 'harmonious global culture'. Seen this way globalization is benevolent in its attempt to construct a homogenized world of uniform products. As a result, they argue that globalization, 'as a force in modernity's quest for progress, is sterilizing and silencing the variegated cultures around the planet' (ibid.: 33):

> The homogenization of the world is being facilitated by the standardization of life made possible through the introduction of computers and telecommunications technology. The planetary adoption of the free-market

mentality is engendered by the 'global village' phenomenon outlined by McLuhan (1964). Through satellite communications, the Internet, fibre optics, the fax, digital information transaction, and high speed computers, people around the world are practically neighbours. The values of globalization, transmitted through satellite television and the distribution of worldwide publications, permeate everyone's life. Global marketing, international stock markets, and the availability of nomadic worldwide venture capital complete the scene for the rise of a global market value system. No culture is protected by topography, tradition or just plain disinterest – essentially nobody is out of reach of the extended arm of globalization. (ibid.: 34)

Myth 2 – that globalization brings prosperity to person and planet – ignores the dichotomies of social class, gender, ethnicity and power. This is a cyclical, resource-hungry political and economic system that strives relentlessly for 'global free-market expansionism, consumerism, and the continuous search and manufacture of new markets', this in turn 'leads to the continuous quest for more – more resources, more labour, more needs, more markets'. The twenty-first century is therefore characterized by 'expansion' and 'progress' but it is clearly not a neutral project:

> Most American business free-market expansionist projects do not help other nations start economic initiatives, or preserve, in any meaningful way, their indigenous cultures. They accelerate the transformation of the local culture to an Americanized outpost while making them subservient to the economic and technological system which has been imposed on them. Not only is the American free-market hazardous to the cultural wellbeing of the host country, but it is also detrimental to America itself. The American worker, unemployed by the closing of hundreds of manufacturing plants, now becomes a financial burden to the taxpayers through the need for social support payments. This increases the federal budget, making free-market expansionism even more vital to US economic survival. Thus, the downward spiral continues. (ibid.: 35)

Myth 3 – that the global market spreads naturally – is deconstructed through commentaries of popular magazines, books, newspapers and television accounts. These newsworthy accounts report what are presented as inevitable 'facts' devoid of interpretation. By contrast, Steingard and Fitzgibbons claim that such constructs are ideological: 'We somehow have embraced the distorted ideology that globalization is a natural process or phenomenon which is just happening. Moreover, we have decided to reorient our entire educational, commercial, cultural and governmental systems to accord with its principles' (ibid.: 36).

Myth 4 – that the account of globalization provided by contemporary management literature presents a value-free representation of its subject – is, in reality, not informed by critical scrutiny but by the desire to sell a commodity of packaged conventional wisdom:

Over the last several years, the fields of management and organizational behaviour have become concerned, some would say obsessed, with global-ization. The expansion of democracy and the free-market system on a worldwide basis has called for a radical change in the nature of manage-ment and organizational behaviour education and training. Textbooks, courses, and even degrees are offered in areas like 'international manage-ment', 'cross-cultural business management', 'transnational organizations', and 'marketing in third world countries'. Sweeping globalization has hit the management educator and the business school. Contemporary organiza-tional behaviour and management textbooks are dedicated increasingly to globalization concerns . . . These textbooks offer almost no critical thought as to the origins, moral impact, or cultural considerations connected with the importation to and imposition of globalization on other countries and cultures. (ibid.: 36)

CONCLUSION

Strategic Human Resource Development has the ability to challenge the naïveté of its value-free 'scientific' past by promoting humanistic values and by adopting a critical discourse to organizational analysis. Nevertheless, there are clearly tensions and strains between human benefits and organiza-tion performance resulting in 'value dilemmas' and 'value conflicts'.

The pressures for organizational change reveal themselves through 'increased work targets, threats of job loss, job responsibilities, shifts in the balance of power, and general upheavals that are all features of today's work environment' and all of which constitute sources of job stress (McHugh, 1997). Consultants and change agents working from an understanding of critical debates in social constructionist theory and postmodern discourse are able to 'negotiate' the subjective meanings of these wider historical frame-works by interrogating the complexity of many simplistic accounts in the management literature.

Since people's lives are heavily influenced by their sense-making stories, clients are often helped by looking at themselves and their organizations by locating their problem-focused accounts within a wider framework of mean-ings and understandings. Drawing extensively on the work of Foucault, White (1991) argues that individuals often find themselves in untenable positions because they have unwittingly succumbed to power-laden cat-egories used in societal discourse (Barry, 1997). Labelling theory, for exam-ple, has shown that people often come to internalize the definition of self (although not always in the way intended by the labeller). Thus, 'having been labelled "schizophrenic", "obsessive", and "neurotic" by various experts' people often 'proceed to construct themselves accordingly' and consequently they become 'problematized' (Barry, 1997). This is the new challenge but it is up to Strategic Human Resource Development practitioners to mark out their terrain and rise to the challenge.

FURTHER READING

Reed (1992) provides a clear exposition of the basic theoretical debates that informed twentieth-century management. His treatment of core concepts such as rationality, alienation, anomie and power illustrate the theoretical, methodological and ideological assumptions that lay behind early twentieth-century analysis of organizations. The OD tradition described by Beckhard (1969) is a useful starting point for the reader interested in how the subject came to be defined. A more recent sophisticated account of organizational change and development by Hamlin et al. (2001) is recommended to bring the reader up to date with both academic and practitioner debates. Although not explicitly stated, the idea that organizational analysis should perform a critical function in the debate about organizations is provided by Alvesson and Deetz (2000).

2 Planned strategies for change: the evolution of strategic human resource development

INTRODUCTION

This chapter focuses on six strategies that became central to the development of organizational efficiency in the twentieth century. These strategies – *organizational design, innovation and enterprise, empowerment, strategic downsizing, TQM and BPR, and teamwork* – are identified as precursors to our understanding of the management of change in the twenty-first century. These strategies have transformed our thinking about management from the early twentieth-century blueprint promoted by the Classical School. While the major political driver has been the process of globalization, it has to be recognized that each strategy contains its own ideology for managing change. A central argument is that all change contains its own contradictions and these strategies for change are no exception.

The learning objectives for this chapter are:

1   *Organizational design* which discusses the emergence of bureaucratic procedures and their application to the Fordist production process. The attempt to dismantle bureaucracy is attributed to the Excellence Movement which sought to redesign organizations as flexible structures driven by core values and leadership in the pursuit of excellence.

2   The strategy of the *Excellence Movement* which focuses on the attempt to create permanent *innovation and enterprise*, in organizations that were no longer defined by bureaucratic rules and regulations and where leaders replaced managers, and employees became empowered to meet the needs of increasingly sophisticated customers.

3   The strategy of *empowerment*, which is noteworthy in not only attempting to extend the arguments of the Excellence Movement but in seeking to solve the problems of alienation. Strategies to achieve empowerment may include redefining the nature of supervision or management; reward systems, job design; or even changing the nature of the working environment. The critical determinant, however, is the ability to take control of one's own work situation.

4   The fourth strategy, *downsizing*, was originally developed as a corporate strategy for changing an organization's structure in order to enhance competitive advantage. This was also a tactic driven by the global marketplace. In the attempt to move production-based organizations from high volume goods with low profit margins to niche markets providing high profit margins, downsizing appeared to be inevitable but the strategy came to contradict the very idea that people were resources rather than costs.

5   The fifth strategy – *Total Quality Management (TQM) and Business Process Reengineering (BPR)* – is distinctive enough. While each approach to quality improvement has its own literature and advocates, they all, nevertheless, share the same objectives in seeking an holistic business improvement through a programmed approach to change. Both TQM and BPR sought to achieve quality enhancement through a top-down process of planned strategic change by borrowing fragments from the Organizational Development literature. But each relied, unlike OD, on the expertise of the advocate rather than the joint diagnostic relationship between facilitator and client.

6   The final strategy for change is *teamwork*. Teamwork became one of the fundamental approaches of contemporary management because it offered important positive advantages for organizational development. Yet it was not until the neo-Human Relations theories of the Excellence Movement and TQM that teamwork was adopted as a technique designed to overcome the damaging consequences of the separation of mental and manual labour. If teamwork was a valuable OD technique, it was unfortunately also exploited in the attempt to downsize and delayer the organization.

ORGANIZATIONAL DESIGN AND THE MANAGEMENT OF CHANGE IN THE TWENTIETH CENTURY

Managing change in the early twentieth century was concerned with organizational design. The progressive image for the design of twentieth-century organizations was encapsulated in the metaphor of the machine. This was contrasted with the earlier nineteenth-century image of the wheel:

> Over the literature of work in the nineteenth century broods one image above all – that of the Wheel. We find it already in the description of alienation in Schiller's Letters on the Aesthetic Education of Man of 1795: 'enjoyment is separated from labour, the means from the end, exertion from recompense. Eternally fettered only to a single little fragment of the whole, man fashions himself only as a fragment; ever hearing only the monotonous whirl of the wheel which he turns, he never develops the harmony of his being, and, instead of shaping the humanity that lies in his nature, he becomes a mere imprint of his occupation, his science'. (Meakin, 1976: 19)

By contrast to the image of the wheel, the machine was the image of progress for the twentieth century. Through it, change was seen as positive and forward-looking. This image was consistently contrasted with the negative and pre-industrial organic forms of work and life. The old anti-culture of the organic pre-industrial communities was viewed as a barrier to change that had to be overcome by its destruction (ibid.: 3).

Modern organizations were seen as the social inventions above all others. They came to be defined as social units (or human groupings) that were deliberately constructed and reconstructed to seek specific goals. These were either profit maximization or public accountability. Twentieth-century organizations therefore came to be characterized by:

1   Divisions of labor, power, and communication responsibilities, divisions which are not random or traditionally patterned, but deliberately planned to enhance the realization of specific goals.
2   The presence of one or more power centers which control the concerted efforts of the organization and direct them toward its goals; these power centers also must review continuously the organization's performance and re-pattern its structure, where necessary, to increase its efficiency.
3   Substitution of personnel, i.e., unsatisfactory persons can be removed and others assigned their tasks. The organization can also recombine its personnel through transfer and promotion. (Etzioni, 1964: 3)

Modern organizations were consistently defined as rational because they were much more in control of their nature and destiny than any other social grouping had been throughout history. Bureaucracy became a synonym for modern organizational change. This change focused on producing the following:

1   Standardized products.
2   Interchangeable parts and people.
3   Routinized work processes.
4   Impersonal work relationships.

In the first half of the twentieth century the pacesetters of modernity were 'big business and industry, big government, massive armed forces, and, in recent years, big labor' (Charles Page, in the Foreword to Peter Blau's *Bureaucracy in Modern Society*, 1965). These new organizations resulted from, and in turn stimulated, the 'unprecedented growth in modern society of large-scale formal organisations within which must be developed hierarchical administrative and operating social machinery, if their tasks are to be achieved' (Page on Blau, 1965).

As we noted in the previous chapter, some social scientists became 'social technicians' preoccupied with organizational improvement and efficiency, on the one hand, yet driven by wider concerns about alienation and anomie on the other. The three disciplines (Functionalism, Behaviourism and Scientific Management) informed every organizational design from car assembly lines to the training of the fighting machine – the army, navy and airforce. But unlike many, Max Weber, at least, expressed concern at the reverse side of bureaucratic efficiency: that is, in the moral and political implications of *standardization* and *routinization*, *impersonality* and *interchangeability*. These processes not only led to efficiency, they also presented 'an imposing threat to freedom, individualism, and spontaneity'. In other words, these 'cherished values' of a 'liberal society' were contradicted by man's 'greatest social invention' (Page, 1965: 5). For sociologists in particular, it was necessary to explain patterns of human behaviour in terms of relationships between people and their shared normative beliefs (Blau, 1965: 23). These patterns later became a focus for the more populist writings and pronouncements of the Excellence Movement. The various Excellence writers, as we shall see in due course, were attempting to raise a challenge to the earlier twentieth-century ideas of change management because they came to recognize the unintended consequences of rational change – planned from the drawing board, managed from the centre and leading to a malevolent repression of the workforce. As Clegg noted:

> If organisations are the form of our modern condition, one cannot help but note that this is frequently represented less as an opportunity or benevolent phenomenon but more as something which is constraining and repressive. These elements can be attributed to a pervasive strand of modernist thinking, clearly articulated as a representative experience of modernity in the work of Max Weber and his vision of bondage, of the 'iron cage'. (1990: 2–3)

Although many textbooks on management see Weber as an advocate of bureaucracy, his views were, in fact, in opposition to a more conservative view prevalent in organizational discourse in his time. As he put it: 'the passion for bureaucracy is enough to drive one to despair' because it results in a 'parcelling out of the soul' (Felts and Jos, 1996: 24). Bureaucracy was nevertheless inevitable because the modern forms of human associations were located in the nucleus of the modern state and modern capitalism. It is certain that Weber saw legal–rational authoritative rule as central to all organizations, including those in the private sector, public sector, and not-for-profit organizations. In opposition to the conservatives of his time Weber sought to remove the sacred halo of bureaucracy (Beetham, 1985) and viewed the bureaucrats as a separate power group in society (Felts and Jos, 1996: 24).

Of particular concern to Weber was the issue of power and compliance. Why people obeyed others was the central question for Weber and was reflected in his writings on bureaucracy, religion and politics. Because of the postmodern attempt to go beyond the traditional paradigm of classical management towards flexible organizations, getting work done by others has remained a compelling issue. For Weber the idea that managers in bureaucratic organizations could be leaders was an oxymoron (DiPadova, 1996). The rise of 'managerial leadership' during the course of the twentieth century has, however, challenged certain aspects of the bureaucratic organization by re-engineering the manager's role from a controller of the system to 'corporate stewardship', 'facilitator' and 'entrepreneur'. Such descriptions portray managers as leading actors in a drama with a revolutionary plot. Through the years, while management theorists and researchers have focused on motivation and the influence of managers and leaders to influence subordinates within that process Weber attempted to look at the issue the other way round by asking what it was about the situation that induced individuals to be obedient. One of the problems of bureaucracy, for Weber, was that bureaucratic administrators were not equipped to be leaders: 'Weber's well-known description of the "functionary" who is incapable of forming his or her own ends allows little room for leadership. In a speech given in 1909, Weber lamented the dominance of "these little cogs", whose one preoccupation in life is becoming a bigger cog' (Felts and Jos, 1996: 24).

Fordism came to require bureaucracy since, once employed in organizations, the professional bureaucrat 'is chained to his activity in his entire economic and ideological existence . . . in the great majority of cases he is only a small cog in a ceaselessly moving mechanism which prescribes to him an essentially fixed route of march' (Weber, 1968: 988).

THE EXCELLENCE MOVEMENT: THE ATTEMPT TO CREATE PERMANENT INNOVATION AND ENTERPRISE

By the 1980s Peters and Waterman (1986) argued that bureaucracy alone was ineffective in dealing with the management of people and processes. They cited authors such as Bennis (1968) and Toffler (1980) who advocated 'adhocracy' in order to deal 'with all the new issues that either fall between bureaucratic cracks or span so many levels in the bureaucracy that it's not clear who should be doing what' (Peters and Waterman 1986: 121). By contrast, their idea of 'excellent' organizations were of fluid organizations:

> The concept of organisational fluidity, therefore, is not new. What is new is that the excellent companies seem to know how to make good use of it. Whether it's their rich ways of communicating informally or their special ways of using ad hoc devices, such as task forces, the excellent companies get quick action just because their organisations are fluid. (ibid.: 121)

Their views represented the popular concern at that time that modern organizations were becoming the dinosaurs of the twentieth century because they were slow to make decisions; inflexible in their adaptation to the environment; unimaginative in their thinking; incapable of learning beyond basic stimulus and response processes that failed to question their *raison d'être*; and, most importantly, their command and control style of leadership failed to inspire a sense of corporate community. In 1982 *In Search of Excellence* became a best-seller and the most popular book of its time. By 1990 more than five million copies had been sold. One consequence was 'its ability to create a niche for the money-spinning Excellence Movement' (Clutterbuck and Crainer, 1990: 218).

Both Peters and Waterman's *In Search of Excellence* (1982) and Peters and Austin's *A Passion for Excellence* (1985) were supplemented by others books such as *Thriving on Chaos: Handbook for the Management Revolution* (1987), *Liberation Management: Necessary Disorganization for the Nanosecond Nineties* (1992), as well as a range of his other published works (periodicals, journals, videos). The Excellence debate was enhanced further by arguments for innovation and entrepreneurship (Kanter, 1983; 1989), and the need to think ahead to a Post-Capitalist Society (Drucker 1993). Thus, if stability was a thing of the past, managing change in times of uncertainty and turbulence became the received wisdom. The core of the early work was the famous McKinsey 7-S Framework (see Figure 2.1) which served to demonstrate the interconnectedness of structure, strategy, skills, staff, style and systems revolving around a central concept of shared values.

The investigations by Peters and Waterman led them to challenge the rational model by advocating eight attributes or principles:

1   A bias for action: a preference for doing something – anything – rather than sending a question through cycles and cycles of analyses and committee reports.
2   Staying close to the customer – learning his preferences and catering to them.
3   Autonomy and entrepreneurship – breaking the corporation into small companies and encouraging them to think independently and competitively.

FIGURE 2.1
The McKinsey 7-S
framework

Source: Peters and
Waterman 1982

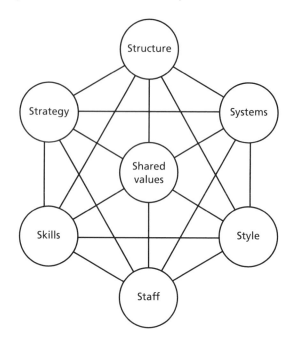

4   Productivity through people – creating in all employees the awareness that their best efforts are essential and that they will share in the rewards of the company's success.

5   Hands-on, value driven – insisting that executives keep in touch with the firm's essential business.

6   Stick to the knitting – remaining with the business the company knows best.

7   Simple form, lean staff – few administrative layers, few people at the upper levels.

8   Simultaneous loose–tight properties – fostering a climate where there is dedication to the central values of the company combined with tolerance for all employees who accept those values.

These eight principles find their way into the later work of Tom Peters. Three things were attacked: the Rational Model of Classical Management; the Human Relations theories; more recent contingency theories. As a result, four themes emerged in the work of the Excellence Movement. These were: (a) a focus on customers; (b) the need for constant innovation; (c) that employees should be regarded as a resource rather than a cost; (d) that leadership should be inspirational.

How can we account for the success of the Excellence Movement? One argument is that such populist literature simply provides busy managers with a shortcut to many complicated issues which are more contentious than they admit.

On the other hand it would seem that the Excellence Movement can be defined by a common thread running throughout their books and other resources. The most repeated theme was the importance of the human side of enterprise. Despite its weaknesses in methodology, the strength of the movement was its ability to capture and critique more than fifty years of management. This led it to challenge the worst attributes of Fordism by advocating a neo-Human Relations movement. This focus on human resources as the driving force behind the other seven principles listed above does not explain the success of the movement in terms of its popularity. The following reasons are provided as a polemic in order to encourage further debate.

First, the Excellence writers tell a story similar to the script-writers of a contemporary soap opera. This is not intended to demean their work but to indicate the mechanics of writing a moving plot. Thus, if the central strategy is the place of humanity in an organizational drama that occurred over the twentieth century and which was essentially characterized by the metaphors *bureaucratic, modern, machine culture* (which we now refer to as Fordism), then this story is told through a simple plot and exemplified through numerous examples that celebrate the plot.

The narrative informing the plot emphasizes the need to understand the service encounter as a qualitative process through which the customer/client needs are not only met but exceeded. This is a reminder that the customer must be seen, not as statistical data, but as a meaningful slice of human interaction that has critical implications for the development of the organization. Attention to customers' needs requires the organization to cultivate an awareness of customer perceptions in a way that could not be achieved by more traditional analyses of market trends. The emphasis on the qualitative dynamics of the service encounter were central to the development of an excellent organization. For example, 'Peters' books are full of examples where bad service or a needless lack of consideration towards the customer has "soured" the customer relationship. *A Passion for Excellence* has a chapter entitled "Mere Perception: On the Irreducible Humanness of the Customer"' (Barter, 1994: 7).

Second, the need for constant innovation emerged out of the debate about customers. To focus on customers required a focus on quality and not quantity and on niche markets rather than mass markets. Therefore, the message was *anticipate customers' needs and differentiate the product or service from that provided by others. In order to do that establish organizational flexibility.*

Third, was the argument that employees should be treated as a resource and not a cost. This people-focused approach to empowerment suggested that empowered employees require a managerial revolution akin to a leap of faith. This was to be achieved by restructuring the organization from a bureaucratic hierarchy to an organic collection of teams with a fluid exchange of internal customer relationships. The difficulty was in dismantling the role conformity and mechanistic attitudes of the bureaucrat in favour of an empowered future. This was the only way, we are told, to create a workplace of experimentation and intrepreneurial activity.

Fourth, leadership was the key to empowerment. In *A Passion for Excellence* Peters and Austin argue that:

> The concept of leadership is crucial to the revolution now under way – so crucial that we believe the words 'managing' and 'management' should be discarded. 'Management', with its attendant images – cop, referee, devil's advocate, dispassionate, analyst, naysayer, pronouncer – connotes controlling and arranging and demeaning and reducing. 'Leadership' connotes unleashing energy, building, freeing, and growing. (1985: Introduction: xvii)

This is interesting given the amount of time that had elapsed between Weber's concerns about the nature of bureaucracy and leadership. For example, Weber argued that while bureaucracy came to represent modernity as technically efficient it was not conducive to effective leadership because true leaders were not likely to make it up the hierarchy because the 'conventions and internal peculiarities of the bureaucratic hierarchy severely impede the career opportunities of precisely such talents' (Weber, 1968: 1414).

For the Excellence Movement leadership was simple. It was about listening, facilitating, and coaching and, above all, reinforcing values (Peters and Austin, 1985: 37).

EMPOWERMENT

Although empowerment lacks a universal definition, the term has come to describe a variety of interventions that give more autonomy and an increase in power to subordinates. Höpfl has argued that in the management literature the term 'appears to have come into general usage in the early 1980s. By the mid-1980s it had become a commonplace expression used in both practical management texts and in the vocabulary of organizations' (1994: 39). One problem, however, is that 'writers on empowerment seem to be quite coy when examining the concept' (Collins, 1995: 29). Thus, the attempt to define empowerment in a universal way is problematic.

Although the term may not have been used until the 1980s, if we see empowerment as the opposite of alienation, then the origins of the process go back to a much earlier period of time. In this case our understanding of empowerment must be located in the international debates – Britain, America, Scandinavia, Germany, Japan – over alienation, on the one hand, and industrial democracy on the other. One thing is certain: that despite the uncertainty of the term 'empowerment has emerged as an idea and focus for organizational change' (ibid.: 32).

The employer/employee relationship during the early phases of industrialization was based, with few exceptions, on distrust between employer and employee. This relationship was regulated through formal control systems such as clocks, fines and supervisory management. One consequence was that industrial unrest remained high since the natural response to the controls employed by employers was the withdrawal of labour. Such direct labour control strategies were enhanced further by the standardization of the work environment. Employees were generally viewed simply as a 'unit of labour'. The emergence of Human Relations Theory, however, seemed to establish a link between employee involvement and productivity levels by studies of organizational behaviour that focused on employee morale and motivation. Studies appeared to suggest that performance would be improved by managers who were able to elicit co-operation by becoming more sensitive to employee needs. Mayo's findings resulted in the displacement of utilitarianism by the more appealing aspects of unitarianism which sought to 'construct relationships within a unity of purpose and ideology between managers and employees in the pursuit of common goals' (Ackers et al., 1992).

The Human Relations School represented a significant shift in organizational theory thus superseding Taylorism in favour of a more democratic and humanistic approach to the management of labour within organizations. By recognizing the importance of employee relationships and environmental influences, management was encouraged to consciously intervene in the informal organization in order to build a new 'moral order' based more on consent than conflict. From these early organizational experiments of the Human Relations School, the social and behavioural sciences became an integral part of organizational management and an extensive body of academic research flourished around the key theme of 'understanding the dynamics of human relationships'.

The later focus on job enrichment and job enhancement schemes were based on Maslow's (1954) earlier work on motivation. Attention was focused on how employees could be motivated to expend effort in particular directions to achieve the organizational goals. There was a recognition that control of the labour process was not possible through coercion or economic incentives alone.

New work practices such as the Volvo experiment with work groups (the Kalmar plant in the early to mid-1970s abandoning the production line and the Uddevalla plant in the mid to late 1980s with a small team building a complete car) attempted to reverse the alienating effects of the Fordist production process by attempting to find more fulfilling ways to enrich emotional, psychological and social needs of employees. Job rotation, as promoted by Sweden and her Scandinavian neighbours, was an attempt to 'redesign work to give workers greater autonomy and more possibility of deriving some sense of satisfaction and achievement from their labours' (Brown, 1992: 173).

In the 1960s the 'Quality of Working Life' programmes were developed in an attempt to establish that performance was linked to 'involvement and satisfaction' (Blumberg, 1968: 123). During this time France appointed a Minister for Job Enrichment, the Swedes set up a Commission on Industrial

Democracy, and the International Labour Organization proclaimed the need to prioritize the humanization of work (Thompson and McHugh, 1995).

While some authors seem to use the terms employee involvement and empowerment interchangeably (for example, Bowen and Lawler, 1992), the latter is focused more on the idea of 'winning commitment' than simply extending decision-making. Empowerment has come to imply a 'moral' commitment at an emotional level within the organization. Seen this way, it is possible to see the Excellence Movement as exemplars of this attempt to encourage managers to reach into the realm of feelings. Thus, requiring flatter and leaner structures is one thing but the management of meanings is of quite a different order since winning the hearts and minds of employees requires a redistribution of power from the top downwards. Such empowerment requires cultural change. For example, if it was possible to draw up a list of characteristics of empowerment we might include a series of items ranging from access to information, involvement in decisions through to actually making decisions, share ownership and a redistribution of rewards. The further we move along the continuum towards a redistribution of rewards, the more empowerment has to mean more to employees than the permission to 'delight the customer', as the Excellence Movement implies.

Empowerment 'has been conceptualised as both a relational and a motivational construct' (Andrews and Herschel, 1996: 180). The relational perspective views empowerment as a function of relationships between managers and subordinates. It is therefore more a function of delegated power or power sharing (Burke, 1986). This has been the focus of the participative management approach from McGregor (1960) and Likert (1961) through to Quality Management, teambuilding and self-managed teams. As Andrews and Herschel point out, 'leaders' intentions and subordinates' perceptions may on occasion differ thus an employee may not desire the responsibility of participating in the decision-making process' (1996: 180). As a function of power, empowerment would be characterized by a concern to accomplish the task rather than by a delegation of formal authority through status: 'Power would be used to get the job done, rather than to stand over others' (Pacanowsky, 1987: 378). Such a view corresponds to Etzioni's (1975) comparison of moral compliance compared to the utilitarian compliance of the wage/effort bargain.

Within the psychological literature empowerment has also been viewed as a *motivational construct* (Andrews and Herschel, 1996: 180) through which individuals are assumed to have a need for power (McClelland, 1975). From this perspective 'an individual's sense of empowerment grows from managerial strategies and techniques that serve to strengthen the employee's feelings of self-determination or self-efficacy' (Andrews and Herschel, 1996: 180). Andrews and Herschel's discussion of Conger's work suggests that to empower is to create 'a process of enhancing feelings of self-efficacy among organizational members through the identification of conditions that foster powerlessness [and by eliminating those conditions]' (Conger, 1986: 474). Thus, factors that contribute to feelings of powerlessness may arise from several sources, including the organizational environment supervisory style, reward systems, or job design. Conversely, the absence of empowerment is characterized by feelings of powerlessness, alienation, and helplessness (Rappaport, 1984).

Finally, it is noteworthy that empowerment has been located as a direct attempt to solve the problems of the alienation datable in the 1950s and 1960s. Thomas and Velthouse (1990), for example, reflect this earlier debate about technological determinists, such as Blauner (1966) by identifying four components of work – *impact, choice, competence* and *meaningfulness* – that relate closely to Blauner's original components of experienced alienation: *powerlessness, meaninglessness, isolation* and *self-estrangement*. Thus, 'impact' (whether accomplishing a particular task or job will make a difference in the scheme of things) addresses problems associated with 'self-estrangement' by involving people in decisions related to work processes; 'choice' (the degree to which personal behaviour is self-determined) addresses problems associated with powerlessness by creating more control over the work process; 'meaningfulness' is a direct corollary of meaninglessness; 'competence' (referring to level of skill) does not appear to have a direct equivalent to Blauner's characteristics of alienation.

STRATEGIC DOWNSIZING

Organizational restructuring – or downsizing – has usually taken the form of closures, mergers and acquisitions. Downsizing has been defined as 'one tactic within a corporate strategy for shifting the organizational structure from what it is now to what it has to be in order to sustain competitive edge and satisfy customers' needs' (Band and Tustin, 1995: 36). Downsizing is also 'one of the most disruptive and dramatic types of organizational change which most leaders are likely to experience' (Drew, 1994: 1). These initiatives are thought to represent 'an early stage of a continuing, long-term, socio-economic evolution. More than simply shrinking the workforce of an organization, much of the change seems to represent a permanent shift in social, economic, and organizational structures' (Lewin and Johnston, 1996: 1; McKinley et al., 1995). Certain environmental pressures are said to lead to downsizing resulting in a paradigm shift from mass production/high volume (from 'bigger-is-better') to niche markets ('lean-and-mean').

But is downsizing simply another name for getting rid of employees in the desire to be increasingly efficient? If so, then this would contradict the aims of the Excellence Movement. However, if it is seen as a strategic organizational objective and involves employees in the process, then it takes on both an ethical and a pragmatic role. This leads Band and Tustin (1995) to argue that: 'If the objective of downsizing should be to raise productivity per head', then

Strategic downsizing can achieve this – layoffs cannot. It is possible to plan to reduce a workforce. In the absence of severe financial and environmental factors, which usually dictate an immediate layoff, downsizing can be carried out with the full commitment of the workforce to the long-term benefit of the company. (1995: 45)

Consequently, it is suggested that employee involvement is possible under certain conditions which, following Cameron et al. (1991) requires that everyone sees the urgency of organizational survival.

When downsizing is viewed as a strategic necessity, it becomes known as rightsizing. Organizational rightsizing therefore seeks to reshape the organization by establishing core and peripheral employees. The flexible firm is then, in theory, able to respond to the flexibility of the marketplace. Two types of employees emerge: core workers with guaranteed job security, and a ring of flexible labour force that expands or contracts as the need arises.

The Excellence Movement was said to be a paradigm shift marking a break with the past. It appeared to become the post-bureaucratic solution by redesigning organizations with 'flatter structures' and 'flexible' ways of working. However, the post-bureaucratic form of adhocracy and fluidity encouraged by empowerment programmes and by the Excellence Movement in particular has also become identified with the problems of downsizing. The latter carry behavioural and perceptual implications detrimental to the aims of the former. Thompson and O'Connell Davison (1995) illustrate these implications as follows.

1   Organizations *decentralize* by breaking up their bureaucracies into smaller or independent units.
2   One solution is to outsource or *disaggregate* to increase 'flexibility'.
3   To replace bureaucratic structures and rational strategic planning in order to deal with unpredictable environments (Kanter, 1989) – *disorganization* – with tactical planning.
4   Delayering to create leaner and meaner organizations that have 'downsized' to the essential core by removing whole layers of middle management.

Each has implications for Strategic Human Resource Development. For example, disaggregation requires a deconcentration of capital thus reversing 'the historic trend towards vertical integration' (Thompson and O'Connell Davidson, 1995). Delayering and downsizing often provide a neutral language to legitimate sacking employees and yet require more effective communication by those who remain through self-managed teams. In addition, career paths and rewards are transformed from an individualized employment relationship to a greater reliance on other collective means for managing each other.

Although the justification for restructuring often takes the form of a discourse about organizational crisis, it also reflects a dimension of organizational change that views efficiency in terms of redefined flat organizational structures and new management strategies based on empowerment. Of major concern is the way in which the 'accountancy' of downsizing – focusing on reducing costs – contradicts the approach sought by the Excellence Movement. The predominance of the debate on cost reduction has led to an unhealthy cynicism regarding the motives for organizational change. Although turbulent environments are becoming the norm, McHugh has stated that 'management within organizations stands accused of looking at the needs of the organization and overlooking the needs of employees' leading to an imbalance between organizational needs and employee needs (1997: 345). The failure rate of downsized organizations appears to be high for a variety of reasons that include: (a) the failure of key decision-makers to estimate the complexity of change issues related to the integration of organizations with diverse working practices and organizational cultures; (b) a significant drain on resources that impairs performance; and (c) an under-estimation of the depth of human issues triggered in a merger or acquisition (Marks, 1997). One estimate suggests that less than 20 per cent of merged organizations achieve their goal of maximizing financial and strategic objectives (Davidson, 1991). Another estimate has reported that 'more than half the 135 major U.S. companies that attempted massive restructuring failed to achieve significant increases in their value relative to their competition' (Tomasko, 1992: 1).

Many factors account for this failure rate including: 'paying the wrong price, buying for the wrong reason, selecting the wrong partner or buying at the wrong time. Another reason, however, that contributes to the high failure rate is managing the post-merger integration process inappropriately' (Marks, 1997). However, many organizations that failed to achieve the desired cost reductions often do so because they fail to consider the human side of the process (Koonce, 1991).

Some of the worst examples of management strategies of downsized organizations result from the 'mafia model' (Stebbins, 1989: 46) in which change is badly planned and executed and carries severe psychological implications both for those who lose their jobs and for the organization's survivors who, in their different ways, suffer insecurity and loss. At an organizational level 'a poorly executed downsizing operation can traumatize a company for years' (Drew, 1994: 1). At an individual level it can lead to mixed feelings of psychological survival in the form of 'survivor guilt' and 'survivor envy' (ibid.). Remaining employees may only marginally feel that they are the lucky ones since downsizing can significantly affect commitment by instilling a sense of insecurity and alienation. Consequently, this may lead to 'distraction, disloyalty and the withdrawing of any form of commitment to the goals and values of the organisation' since those who remain 'may also experience high anxiety as to their own job permanence, guilt from the loss of friends among their co-workers or even deeply rooted anger arising from any insensitivity shown in the downsizing process' (Zeffane and Mayo 1994: 7). An example of psychological survival is provided by Doherty et al.

in their study of survivors at British Telecom. As they point out, the scale of the downsizing was enormous:

> On 31 July 1992, 20,000 BT employees left the company in a voluntary downsizing exercise which cost BT many millions of pounds in redundancy payments and hurt its share price. Since then BT has run annual 'release schemes' each involving over 10,000 people. Twelve thousand more job losses were targeted for the financial year ending in March 1996. BT has cut its workforce from 244,000 in 1989 to 120,000, at a cost of about £24 billion, with further cuts in the pipeline. (Doherty et al., 1996: 53)

In the BT case the survivors had, first, to come to terms with the sudden loss of colleagues and close friends. Second, they had to reconcile themselves to the possibility that they might lose their own jobs at some point in the future. Third, they had to accept an increase in workload that in turn led to increased stress.

A series of contrasts emerged. At the organizational level survivors saw a positive future for the organization, yet at the individual level, survivors expressed 'a marked decrease in motivation' because 'confidence in a personal future with the organization was eroded'. Thus, loyalty to the organization diminished as job insecurity increased. As the work group 'became the focus for BT survivors' their 'friendships with colleagues and support from their line manager became their means of survival'. Line managers in particular suffered from anxieties since 'Not only did they have their personal worries about their own jobs, but they felt they were frequently blamed by subordinates as the cause of their distress' (Doherty et al., 1996: 54). Such experiences demonstrate discontinuity at both the organizational and individual levels. Individuals cope in different ways but such uncertain transitions become 'passages of adjustment'.

PROGRAMMED APPROACHES TO CHANGE: TOTAL QUALITY MANAGEMENT, BUSINESS PROCESS REENGINEERING AND TEAMWORK

Total quality management

The history of quality management has moved beyond its original focus on engineering systems theory to incorporate both social and behavioural science. This has resulted in a hybrid form combining a mixture of the engineering components (quality systems, statistical process control) with behavioural processes (Action Research, Soft Systems theory, team building, and culture management). In the UK, empowerment was introduced in order to facilitate ownership of specific ideas and actions as they developed at appropriate levels throughout the company.

Although there is no universally accepted definition of the concept, the general principles are widely agreed. The concept is aimed at getting the organization, and everyone in it, to concentrate on doing the right things, then finding efficient methods of performance to eliminate faults and constantly seeking more effective approaches to management and more efficient methods for achieving performance. This means that each person must recognize how their individual actions will affect others who depend upon their outputs.

The general concept of quality management evolved internationally from existing management practices. However, the main ideas have been attributed to major Japanese companies who adopted quality assurance principles from American specialists such as Juran and Deming who developed quality improvement programmes in the late 1940s and early 1950s and was a direct result of the Marshall Plan to redevelop the Japanese economy. Juran, for example, introduced the idea of *fitness for purpose* and Deming developed the application of *statistical process control* associated with quality management practices. In recent years a whole range of quality tools and techniques have been introduced for decision-making, problem-solving and data gathering. These include: force field analysis, cause and effect analysis, Pareto analysis, brainstorming, mind mapping and creativity techniques.

The word quality has a variety of meanings which can be a source of confusion. The *Oxford Dictionary* describes quality as 'degree of excellence', 'relative nature or kind or character'. But this definition does not cover all uses of the word and leaves room for further interpretation. For example, from a manufacturer's point of view, quality provides complete customer satisfaction if it matches the agreed specification. From a marketing viewpoint, quality is the ability to provide goods or services valued by customers. From the customer's viewpoint, quality is defined by how well his or her individual needs are satisfied. The British Standards Institute provides guidance for the use of quality. This is shown to be used for several distinct purposes:

- A comparative sense or degree of excellence, whereby products and services may be ranked, or a relative basis, sometimes referred to as 'grade'.
- In a quantitative sense as used in manufacturing, product release and for technical evaluations, sometimes referred to as the 'quality level'.
- In a 'fitness for purpose' sense which relates the evaluation of a product or service to its ability to satisfy a given need.
- For the purpose of quality management the definition used is 'the totality of features and characteristics of a product or service that bears on its ability to satisfy stated or implied needs'.

The predominant history of quality management in the past 20 years can be encapsulated by three major trends:

- Quality assurance, particularly the notion of 'conformance to specifications' which focused on control. Authors such as Shewart, Feigenbaum and Juran provided advice from the 1930s onwards to demonstrate the importance of quantifiable and measurable techniques.

- The amorphous and absolute definition of excellence provided by the Excellence movement.
- The service characteristics of quality which originally emerged from the service marketing literature but has more recently been driven by the European Quality Foundation.

The main vehicle for continuous improvement, however, was not so much the tools and techniques but the application of neo-Human Relations theories. These focused mainly on teamwork, leadership, motivation, and culture management. In the West, however, in the eager attempt to catch up with the progress of Japan's leading manufacturing industries of the 1970s and 1980s, the quality management agenda adopted the ideas of planned change from the discipline of Organizational Development. Unlike the Japanese concept of *kaizen*, quality management was more like a transformational and messianic movement that needed to introduce a whole raft of techniques through new behavioural and attitudinal lenses.

As a result, quality management became a planned change intervention which sought to do the following:

1 Obtain an organizational consensus about values regarding political interests as unitary. This was reinforced by a central philosophy that sought a unity of purpose for all employees. This became difficult to sustain in the face of differences in physical conditions, earnings, pay and rewards.

2 Identify the sequence (or steps) of change leading from the current dysfunctional state to one with enlightened quality practices. Change therefore represented, in the Lewinian sense, sequential linear stages beginning with (a) unfreezing of the present state moving to (b) a transitional state represented by the internalization of the quality programme to (c) refreezing the new state of normality represented by enlightenment. Unfortunately quality came to be seen more as an event despite its often cited use of the rhetorical journey metaphor characteristic of OD.

3 Use the organization's culture as a technique to manage attitudes, behaviours and work practices. The advantage was the attempt to move the locus of control from classical bureaucratic approaches with their heavy emphasis on supervision and managerial mindwork to neo-Human Relations approaches of empowered teams who came to control their own activities and behaviours. One of the major problems, however, was the top-down, paternalistic and democratized consensus required by this type of culture change programme.

These assumptions are common to all planned Organizational Development approaches and have their origins in the application of the planning models of Lippitt et al. (1958) and Kolb and Frohman (1970).

A number of problems are evident in these assumptions which include the following. First, the requirement to achieve value consensus fails to address key political issues such as, who makes the decisions? How much transparency exists in the decision-making process? Whose interests are served? The assumption that organizational values are unitary rather than pluralistic leads to an unhelpful intervention that fails to deal with the organization's dynamics. Thus, to recognize the importance of social and interpretive dynamics in change situations is fundamental to the skills and activities of the change agent. A second problem is the formulaic way that quality management has often been introduced to organizations. In such cases consultancy packages are installed in different types of organizations with different external and internal operating environments. Consequently, they may fail to deal with (a) different contingencies and (b) the specific needs of the client system. A third major problem has been the tendency to view change as an event leading to the illusion that once introduced, quality has been successfully achieved and can be demonstrated through quality assurance. Consequently, such an approach may be inflexible and fail to deal with critical management and operational processes required for continuous improvement. Finally, there is often a tendency, especially in the public sector, to view quality as simply another administrative control mechanism rather than a highly dynamic learning orientated process. Public sector organizations such as hospitals, universities, local authorities, etc. often spend too much time demonstrating the traceability of the quality system rather than continuously improving organizational effectiveness. This may be catastrophic when it causes people to satisfy the needs of the system rather than the customer. This is not only a contradiction in terms, it also represents a return to the problems originally identified by Robert Merton in the 1950s with his critique of bureaucratic dysfunctions.

Business processing reengineering

Business Process Reengineering (BPR) emerged in 1990 from a paper on business process redesign by Davenport and Short (1990). The term became referred to as BPR as a result of Hammer's (1990) paper 'Reengineering Works: don't automate, obliterate' in the *Harvard Business Review*. In the 1990s BPR became the most cited technique for organizational transformation despite the fact that results were not tried and tested over time. By the late 1990s disillusionment had set in:

> To most business people in the United States, re-engineering has become a word that stands for restructuring, layoffs, and too-often failed change programmes. At a recent Boston forum, in fact, Michael Hammer gathered a group of business journalists to explore why re-engineering had become such a tainted term . . . The rock that re-engineering has foundered on is simple: people. Re-engineering treated the people inside companies as if they were just so many bits and bytes, interchangeable parts to be re-engineered. But no one wants to be re-engineered. (Deakins and Makgill, 1997: 81)

These views are reminiscent of the earlier critical debate about Scientific Management. Whether intended or not, the technique was adopted in a

FIGURE 2.2
A typical BPR
programme

Establishing the vision and cascading the concept
from the top of the organization in order that employees understand the purpose and rationale of the initiate. This process requires top management to demonstrate commitment to the process.

Identification of key business processes in need of redesign
By establishing project teams who identify measurable objectives for redesigning the critical processes.

Evaluation of the problems and benchmarking for improvement
The project team clarify the critical problems and identify opportunities to be gained from redesigning processes.

Transformational actions
Which should begin in a small controlled environment moving sequentially through the process chain. To be successful the transformational actions are seen to require critical management processes of leadership, training, redeployment of technical and human resources and motivation.

Evaluation of the programme
In order to identify the extent to which the objectives have been achieved.

highly mechanistic way with little or no regard for the unintended consequences that would affect the subjects of BPR. People became increasingly suspicious of the motives, techniques, and objectives of BPR.

Although BPR was initially viewed as pioneering by addressing organizational change through process activities and work redesign, BPR interventions, in practice, lacked humanistic values, focused on short-term financial gain, and lacked an agreed methodology. Like TQM, the transformational stages tend to follow those represented in Figure 2.2.

BPR has become synonymous with downsizing, layoffs, and viewing people as expendable costs. It was this last point, in particular, that made it different from the claims of the Excellence Movement, and TQM which viewed people as assets or human resources to be cultivated and developed. BPR in the 1990 came to represent the return of Leviathan despite the original intentions of its advocates. In its worst manifestations BPR encouraged a return to social engineering, so reminiscent of the first half of the twentieth century, which resulted in people being seen as costs. The concept of change management became tainted with failure.

In the USA, for example, a survey of 1,468 restructured companies conducted by the Society for Human Resource Management estimated that more than half reported that employee productivity either stayed the same or deteriorated after layoffs resulting from BPR (Guimaraes and Bond, 1996). Reasons for failure include:

• processes applied to intangible targets;
• root causes of business problems inadequately defined;

- too radical and fails to establish positive organizational learning during the transitional state;
- changes fail because attitudes, behaviours, and values are not addressed effectively;
- the pressure to produce quick results leads to a failure to identify unintended consequences of actions;
- alienation of employees;
- creation of a less friendly working environment;
- loss of expertise becomes expensive to company;
- survivor syndrome in which remaining employees are more introspective and risk averse and distrust management.

While organizations do report some benefits in improved productivity, quality, profits, customer satisfaction, down time, etc., on average, surveys reveal that as an intervention strategy, BPR seems disappointing.

Teamwork

Teamwork has become one of the fundamental approaches of contemporary management. Teams have been promoted and popularized because they are seen as a focus for unification and as a means of making the organization more efficient and productive. Countless books and articles have been written on the virtues of teamwork and numerous consultants have earned their living from the courses, books and packages they have sold to clients. Teams have proliferated to include task forces, cross-functional teams, action teams, steering committees, problem-solving teams, self-managed teams, etc. Teamwork is a relatively recent phenomenon, but one that has been driven by four of the six key strategies identified in this chapter – *Excellence, innovation and enterprise; empowerment; downsizing; TQM and BPR.*

The psycho-dynamics of groups have long been the subject of investigation by OD practitioners and by Tavistock researchers in particular. Yet it was not until the neo-Human Relations theories of the Excellence Movement and TQM that teamwork was adopted as a technique designed to overcome the damaging consequences of the separation of mental and manual labour designed on the drawing board of Frederick Winslow Taylor.

During the past 20 years or so, the use of teams within organizations has grown dramatically. The experimental origins of teams go back to the 1960s with the development of the T-group and most authors attribute the functional development of teams in organization with the Volvo Kalmar plant that reduced defects by 90 per cent in 1987. Quality improvement became popularized by quality circles in almost every industry but their effectiveness was doubtful. Like many other quality initiatives they 'started with a great fanfare and then fizzled' (Bounds et al., 1996).

In the attempt to reverse the problems of alienation typified by high volume mass production lines of earlier periods, autonomous self-managed work teams emerged in the 1990s and sought to link employee involvement to decision-making. They sought to empower teams by abolishing the role of supervisors and acquiring all managerial functions such as being accountable for their actions, and planning and scheduling of tasks. According to Sexton:

> the study of autonomous work groups continued from a socio-technical systems perspective . . . and was also incorporated into job design studies as 'self-regulated' or 'self-managed' work groups. The members of the group had the authority to handle the internal processes as they saw fit in order to generate a specific group product, service, or decision. (1994: 46).

In so doing, it moved the locus of control away from the manager or supervisor, who previously had responsibility for planning, record keeping, and scheduling of tasks to the team.

If teamwork was a valuable OD technique, it was unfortunately also exploited in the attempt to downsize and delayer the organization. This has also led to charges of teamwork as neo-Taylorism. For example, it has been argued that the incorporation of teamwork into programmed approaches to managing organizations, such as quality management and BPR, has led to an ideology of empowerment which sought to alter the mind-sets, values and culture of the organization in the attempt to utilize the 'same tired manipulation and productivity agendas which fill the diary of modernist business history' (Boje and Winsor, 1993: 57). As a result, what really has changed according to this argument is not a real increase in empowerment but a self-imposed control by the team. It has even been suggested that teamwork may perpetuate surveillance and control and that employees become their own 'thought police' with the team gaze representing Bentham's Panopticon (Steingard and Fitzgibbons, 1993: 32). While there are wholehearted advocates of teamwork, it is important to recognize that the critics are more critical of the rhetoric and ideology of late twentieth-century capitalism than teamwork *per se*.

Advocates argue that teamwork facilitates collaborative efforts to solve quality-related problems by placing responsibility for quality improvement with the team. From the perspective of quality management it is claimed that it permits greater sharing of information and facilitates greater co-operative approaches to continuous improvement (Oakland: 1989). The benefits of teamwork are usually said to include: (a) increased employee motivation through enhanced employee involvement; (b) increased productivity by teams creating synergy; (c) increased employee satisfaction through collaborative interactions rather than individualistic self-interest; (d) increased commitment to goals because of the social pressures exerted by the team; (e) expanded job skills and organizational flexibility through multi-skilling, job rotation; and (f) the creation of a more customer-focused culture that improves communication and the quality of service provided to the customer. Against this, it can be argued that in recent years, the introduction of teams in most organizations has been associated with cuts in staff in the form of downsizing with fewer people doing more work.

The dangers of teamwork also need to be stated and as Drew and Coulson-Thomas argue, teamwork is not risk free:

> There have been notable disappointments and critical re-evaluation of teamwork since . . . the . . . 1980s. For instance: although Florida Light and Power was the first non-Japanese winner of the Deming prize for quality in 1989, with 1,900 quality teams involving three-quarters of employees, in 1990 CEO Jim Broadhead abandoned most of these quality process teams, citing a loss of customer focus and excessive rigidity as the reason for his decision. Others have also cautioned against transplanting notions of teamwork from observation of Japanese firms to the more individualistic cultural and social setting of North America or the UK.
>
> High-energy team effort has enormous potential for promoting change. However, it is rapidly becoming an overworked nostrum – the benefits are all-too-often exaggerated and the difficulties underestimated . . . Despite the instances of outstanding success by empowered and self-managed teams, there are numerous (but less well publicized) disappointments. (1996: 8)

The recent preoccupation with teamwork can lead to a collective amnesia about the creative ability of individuals who do not work in teams. Furthermore, there is some evidence that individuals operating within a loose network or coalition regularly achieve more effective results than formal teams (ibid.). But rather than see teamwork as a universal solution to a variety of problems, it may be better to consider alternatives such as 'communities of practice' (Marshall et al., 1995) that relate to knowledge shared by loose coalitions of people who develop their own tacit knowledge and methods for doing things. This is more common among certain professions such as lawyers, barristers, GPs, or academics whose conduct is regulated by professional associations and who share a similarity of attitudes and conventions.

The self-managed work team is associated with the more pro-active organizations that have moved away from the need to maintain management or supervisory control over the team. It has, on the one hand, been defined as the productivity breakthrough of the 1990s (Sexton, 1994). The most popular reasons cited for the development of the self-managed team include: quality improvement, cutting service errors and reducing defect rates.

Self-managed teams have been implemented to improve quality, productivity and quality of work life. They can be defined as teams of interdependent members who self-regulate their behaviour (Cumming and Griggs, 1976; Goodman et al., 1988) through (a) face-to-face interaction (Goodman et al., 1988); (b) the inter-relationship of tasks and responsibilities in the co-production of a service and/or a product; and (c) discretion over decision-making of tasks, methods for achieving them and work scheduling (ibid.).

Unlike quality circles, self-managed work teams move responsibility for quality down to the point of production. This creates a tension between the needs of the productive system and the needs of the social group. For example, if the purpose of the self-managed team is (a) to improve the quality of the working life of its members by meeting their socio-psychological needs on the one hand and (b) to increase organizational effectiveness and productivity by restructuring working relationships, on the other, then a balance between the two will inevitably be a movable feast.

The claims for effectiveness of such teams are based on the assumption that changed behaviours and attitudes will lead to increased productivity. These changed behaviours and attitudes include empowered decision-making; self-regulation and self-control; control over the quality of working life and other change-related issues affecting the team (Manz and Sims, 1987). In addition, commitment is related to the traditional issues of job design identified by Hackman and Oldham (1975). This includes job enrichment through task variety, autonomy, identity, significance and feedback. Other writers have argued that team members perform more effectively by sharing power and rewards (Lawler, 1986).

While we are attempting to dismantle some of the problems of a Fordist past, we fail to recognize a whole series of control mechanisms that contradict the spirit of co-operation underlying teamwork. Many companies introduce teams to develop talent, and ideas in order to encourage shared knowledge throughout a workplace. But they may also fail to provide adequate mechanisms for self-management and performance appraisal. Consequently, teams may get tangled up in a web of contradictions between control and empowerment. Thus, 'Initiatives to increase worker commitment through increased autonomy have clashed with efforts to standardize work methods in the interests of achieving process control' (Donnellon, 1996: 34).

The increase in mergers, take-overs and international collaboration has led not only to increases in flexible teamworking methods but also to an increased emphasis on interpersonal communication between people of different cultures. International teams are seen to be more complicated than those composed of a single nationality. New challenges emerge because, while 'Mixed nationalities in a team can bring richer and more appropriate solutions' they can also 'bring increased communication difficulties, interpersonal conflicts and substantially higher costs' (Canney Davison, 1994).

CONCLUSION

Weber's analysis of the bureaucratic machine and his concern about its negative implications for the spiritual/values-oriented aspects of human life appeared to find an echo in the popular writings of the Excellence Movement. In the attempt to restructure bureaucracy, the Excellence Movement successfully promoted a simple solution, to focus on interpersonal relationships with the customer and employees. In some respects they went beyond the simplistic assertions of various quality management programmes by arguing that employees were more than a set of internal customers with exchange values. Indeed, they celebrated achievement and entrepreneurial activity. And then came strategic downsizing. The flexible firm met the flexible marketplace and the movement towards empowerment in organizations was challenged by the accountancy of cost reduction. As the twentieth century drew to a close the empowered solutions that sought to redress the problems of Fordism (by implication, bureaucracy with coercive physical and psychological controls resulting in alienation) were in retreat.

In one way or another each of these interventions were highly prescriptive. They invariably result from the interventions of management consultants in conjunction with chief executives or other senior managers. All of these interventions are planned by an 'expert' in the form of plans, recipes and formulas for the organization to follow. Each involves changing the structure of an organization in some way to make it more flexible. Some of these interventions are, however, more political than others. Where the concepts of *empowerment* and *excellence* carried through the implications of Human Relations theory to develop and work with people, downsizing, by contrast, was driven by the increased competition of the global marketplace.

Those interventions that are politically prescriptive lack transparency. They become policies defined and secretly exploited by a small cadre of senior executives. By 2001 senior managers of two giants of British and American industry – Marconi and Enron – had not only deceived their employees, they had also deceived shareholders, wrecked their companies yet managed to pay themselves excessive bonuses and fringe benefits for doing so.

FURTHER READING

Weber's (1968) text is essential for its description of sociological concerns related to modernity. Blau's (1965) re-evaluation of Weber's text discusses the 'dysfunctions' of bureaucracy that Weber did not foresee. The third classic text is Etzioni (1964) who discusses the power dimension of modern organizations. The critiques evident in each of the classic texts are redrafted and redefined for management practice by Peters and Waterman (1982) who argued that bureaucracy alone was ineffective in dealing with the management of people and processes. The text by Peters and Austin (1985) clearly adopts Weber's concern with the decline of leadership where it is argued that managers should be replaced by leaders. A useful critique of empowerment is Ackers et al. (1992). Bounds et al. (1996) provide a useful descriptive text on quality and Davenport's (1993) text on BPR is usefully supplemented by an account of its decline in Deakins and Makgill (1997).

3
Analysing culture

INTRODUCTION

Chapter 2 identified six strategies that were precursors to our understanding of the management of change in the twenty-first century – organizational design, innovation and enterprise, empowerment, strategic downsizing, TQM and BPR, and teamwork. It was noted that each strategy contained an ideology for managing change. Each type of intervention strategy was described as essentially prescriptive for two reasons. First, because it sought to change the structure of an organization in some way in order to make it more effective. Second, each requires an expert, sometimes with guru status, to design the plans, recipes and formulas for the organization to follow. We also noted that while certain change strategies were more political than others and offered a formula for success, each contained internal contradictions that limited the success of the change. By contrast, this chapter recognizes that all change contains its own contradictions and that the wise thinker or skilful change agent must strive for the goal of enlightenment. Let me explain this further.

All the change strategies previously mentioned involve the manipulation of an organization's culture in some way. Most strategies sought to radically transform an organization with a new formula for change. Most, therefore, required the organization to reinvent itself with a new ideology of meaning and purpose reinforced by tools and techniques. But a new approach, such as the adoption of a new technology, requires a careful diagnosis of the organization's culture. The failure to recognize this places the change agents in a precarious position because they unwittingly become the storm-troopers of change management. Such tactics rarely transform the hearts and minds of employees. So, how does one engage the willing co-operation of employees? How does the vision get successfully transformed into the mission and critical success factors in such a way that it becomes a valued activity for all?

The starting point for this process is to acknowledge what we have learnt from the planned strategies of change discussed in the previous chapter. Essentially, we have gained tools and techniques in organizational design, innovation and enterprise, empowerment, strategic downsizing, TQM and BPR, and teamwork. These are all extremely useful. To move beyond this we must engage with a process of continual learning and discovery. And, to do this, we need to analyse the capability of the organization through its culture.

The learning objectives for this chapter are:

1   *Approaches to analysing culture*: the history of organizational culture as an analytical concept derived from anthropology but popularized and reconstructed as a management tool.
2   *Functional analysis* of an organization's culture which is said to be composed of traits, patterned behaviours and social relationships that must be fully integrated to achieve an effective organization.
3   *Interpretive approaches* to culture which regard cultural integration as problematic, temporary and a continuously negotiated arena of volatile social interactions. The use of the drama metaphor discussed further in Chapters 5 and 6 is particularly useful as a device for observation.
4   *The analysis of cultural codes* which reveal activities that range from formal to deeper levels of meaning. The latter are usually expressed elliptically through metaphoric codes. By observing these linguistic codes we can analyse semantic rules which inform people's perceptions.
5   *Developing organizational cultures* that question in what circumstances we should attempt to manage culture. Other issues addressed are: whether culture change is always manipulative, the need to develop a robust safety culture, changing attitudes to workplace harassment, bullying, stress and discrimination.

APPROACHES TO ANALYSING CULTURE

Organizational diagnosis requires the change agent to assess how well the culture of the organization fits its purpose. In the private sector, for example, the purpose will be defined by market trends and the ability to exploit opportunities in the face of competition. In the public sector, the purpose will be defined by political policies that demand effectiveness, efficiency and accountability for the public good. An examination of the organization's culture is the key to this process.

In recent years it has become acceptable practice to talk about organizational culture as the expression of rituals, stories, sagas and myths. Such expressions of culture provided a discourse of Eastern promise by offering the potential for organizational improvement and Western salvation (Hickman and Silva, 1987) and by inviting a cultural analysis of organizational life. The popular discovery of ritual accomplishments and stories of success promoted culture management as the vehicle for enhanced performance (Peters and Waterman, 1986; Deal and Kennedy, 1988). Consequently, 'the concerns of the organization studies avant-garde became redefined from systems and structures to culture and symbolism' (Jeffcutt, 1994).

Despite provocative questions being asked about the legitimacy of culture management (Silver, 1987; Thompson and McHugh, 1995) and about the effectiveness of culture on bottom-line performance (Lim, 1995), management rhetoric has focused its discourse of organizational restructuring on post-bureaucratic transformations (managing chaos, disorganization, disaggregation, delayering etc.) by presenting a recurrent theme of turbulent times (Thompson and O'Connell Davidson, 1995). Much of the rhetoric adopted a democratized, top-down concern with culture change and culture management: defined by the employer rather than the employee.

Organizational culture is a relatively recent conceptual tool for managers. This was due largely to the popularity of the Excellence Movement and by Peters and Waterman (1982) in particular who influenced the thinking of managers by suggesting that corporate success required a strong culture. As a result, organizational culture became the route to competitive advantage. A second source of popular interest emerged from writers on Japanese methods of work. Writers such as Ouchi and Jaeger (1978) influenced the 'Japanization' of Western organizations by arguing that Japan's economic success and meteoric economic development resulted from their strong corporate cultures. The concept of organizational culture as an issue for organizational analysis and development is therefore of recent origin. The reasons for the development of the concept appear to be twofold. First, is the recognition that classical quantitative and 'scientific' approaches were no longer as appropriate as they had been thought to be earlier in the century. Second, is the realization that the world's first industrial nation, Britain, and the world's most successful and prolific nation during the twentieth century, the USA, were being overtaken by Japan.

Such differences were explained in cultural terms by researchers making comparative studies. Hickman and Silva (1987), for example, saw this as the replacement of Fordism, with its emphasis on systems and control to 'complexity management' which, by contrast, emphasizes (a) shared perspectives between different stakeholders; (b) creativity; and (c) social relationships.

Studies of organizational culture emerged in management literature from earlier Structural–Functional anthropological and sociological origins. However, the more recent interpretive approaches were largely ignored. As a result, the culture concept became infused with sound-bite clichés such as 'strong', 'empowered', 'power', 'task', 'role', 'the way we do business around here' that promised more than they could deliver. These similes of gross over-simplification are intended to portray the layers of complexity that characterize the corporate culture. For example, one is almost tempted to say that the recipe becomes: if you want to manage the corporate culture think of it 'like an onion'.

Despite the superficiality of popular writings, the study of organizational culture has the potential to provide a penetrating analysis. In the interests of this debate we need to redress the balance by rediscovering the roots of the concept where we will find a more meaningful definition of culture.

The earliest and most succinct is the anthropological definition by Edward Tylor in 1891: 'That complex whole which includes knowledge, belief, art, morals, law, custom, and any other capabilities and habits acquired by man as a member of society' (Tylor, 1891: 37). Organizational culture may be defined, therefore, as the sum total of the learned behaviour traits, beliefs and characteristics of the members of a particular organization. The key word in the above definition is learned, which distinguishes culture from behaviours that result from biological inheritance. Consequently, learned behaviour is the one factor that distinguishes humans from other animals. This requires the ability to communicate at a highly sophisticated level. The human faculty for symbolic communication facilitates the acquisition of culture and makes it possible for humans to transmit culture between generations.

Communication is what makes culture. Humans communicate with symbols in four basic ways. The first is spoken language, patterns of sounds with meanings attached to each. Spoken language facilitates learning and communication. The second method of communication is written language, the graphic recording of spoken language which facilitates the preservation of learning and the legacy of culture. The third is body language which denotes the exchange of meanings through gestures and body postures. Finally, humans communicate through artefacts. The study of this is known as semiotic communication.

FUNCTIONAL ANALYSIS

The modern study of culture began with the application of functional analysis originally outlined by Emile Durkheim. For Durkheim, analysis of social life required the study of 'social facts'. In his *Rules of Sociological Method* (1938) he suggested that it was necessary: (a) to find the causes of social facts; and (b) to find the functions (that is, the part they play in establishing order) of social facts.

The study of social facts required a search for antecedent social facts and for the functions the facts fulfil in the maintenance of the social system but they should not be reduced to biological or psychological components. Although Durkheim was concerned to explain phenomena at the level of society, the study of organizations would reveal the possibility of studying the precise characteristics that produce consensus or social solidarity. These would include the symbols, ceremonies, or rites of passage that reinforce a cohesive group.

Just as Durkheim argued that religion was functional for society because it reinforced the moral unity, various anthropologists such as Malinowski and Radcliffe-Brown extended his functional analysis to show how order was constructed. For example, Malinowski studied how the antecedent social facts of 'basic needs', such as food, shelter, sex, and protection in primitive culture gave rise to secondary needs such as the distribution of food, communication, co-operation, control of conflict, etc. These secondary needs were satisfied by the development of language norms and rules. In this way early anthropology progressed by studying how every aspect of culture was fulfilling some function. A good example was Radcliffe-Brown's study of joking relationships. In 'primitive' society a joking relationship allows one person to 'insult' another who is not allowed to take offence. This is a relationship of 'permitted disrespect'. Thus, to understand its function it is necessary to see it in the context of respectful relationships. That is, it reinforces cohesive relationships.

The sociological development of functional analysis was taken further by Robert Merton (1968) who was critical of many functionalist accounts. As a result, Merton qualified functional analysis and suggested that it should be reserved for *observed consequences* of social events which enable the adaptation, or adjustment, of a given system. Thus, patterns of behaviour can be studied to show the functional properties of a component part to the system as a whole. For example, families are said to be functional for society by enabling the socialization of younger members, thereby creating stable personalities. In this way, individuals become competent role players. Similarly, organizations can be said to perform a function by integrating the activities of all their members through processes of secondary socialization such as selection, recruitment, training, and so on. Figure 3.1 illustrates a functional analysis of organizational culture in which the parts are integrated. The functional integration or fit of activities requires careful analysis. As Merton suggests, functional analysis should be reserved for observed consequences of social events which enable the adaptation, or adjustment, of a given system. Patterns of behaviour can be studied to show the functional

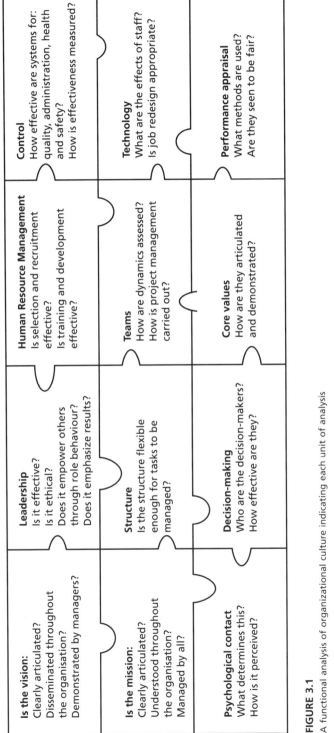

Is the vision:
Clearly articulated?
Disseminated throughout the organisation?
Demonstrated by managers?

Leadership
Is it effective?
Is it ethical?
Does it empower others through role behaviour?
Does it emphasize results?

Human Resource Management
Is selection and recruitment effective?
Is training and development effective?

Control
How effective are systems for: quality, administration, health and safety?
How is effectiveness measured?

Is the mission:
Clearly articulated?
Understood throughout the organisation?
Managed by all?

Structure
Is the structure flexible enough for tasks to be managed?

Teams
How are dynamics assessed?
How is project management carried out?

Technology
What are the effects of staff?
Is job redesign appropriate?

Psychological contact
What determines this?
How is it perceived?

Decision-making
Who are the decision-makers?
How effective are they?

Core values
How are they articulated and demonstrated?

Performance appraisal
What methods are used?
Are they seen to be fair?

FIGURE 3.1

A functional analysis of organizational culture indicating each unit of analysis

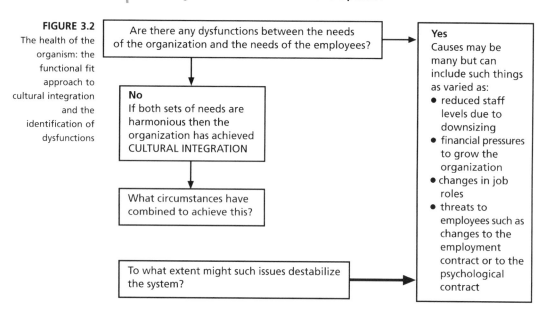

properties of a component part to the system as a whole. From this perspective managers would ask: what are the functions of each of these components and how effective are they in achieving their aims?

For Merton, functionalist analysis needed refining in various ways. His first critical point was to argue that not all practices were functional for the entire cultural system. It was important to recognize that certain activities may be functional for some members but not necessarily for others and it was therefore necessary to locate the *unit of analysis* rather than assuming universality of function for the entire system. In Figure 3.1 the unit of analysis is indicated by the function it serves. Mission, leadership, decision-making and so forth are all functionally related but we can ask if each component is functional for everyone. For example, decisions made in one area may not be functional for another. Furthermore, we might see how an activity may be functional for one group (for example, shareholders) but not for another (for example, employees). It is therefore not possible to say that ceremonial activities are functional for all members of an organization; they may well unify a group who share one set of values but they may be equally counterproductive to others.

The second critical point he raises is that not all activities fulfil positive functions. Historically they may well have done but with the passage of time an activity may have outlived its usefulness. Therefore some activities may become *dysfunctional* because they carry negative rather than positive consequences leading to the destabilization of the system. Merton's solution is to identify positive and negative functions when analysing a particular activity before deciding if they are functional for the entire cultural system. In this way, the health of the organism can be ascertained. This is illustrated in Figure 3.2. A good example here is his discussion of the dysfunctions of bureaucracy. In particular he discusses *retreatism* – when an individual retreats behind the role rather than dealing with a problem identified by a client or customer; *ritualism* – where an employee displays a rigid adherence to a rule thus undermining the relationship (again it is not difficult to see how the dissatisfaction of the client or customer could lead to dissatisfaction); and *rebellion* – when the bureaucratic procedures themselves may lead to rebellion or lack of co-operation from clients, customers and staff alike.

A third critical point from Merton is his insistence that no activity is indispensable. Therefore we should recognize that for many social practices there may be functional alternatives. The final critical point is his distinction between *manifest* functions (those which can be easily recognized and are obviously intended by the individuals involved) and *latent* functions (the unintended and unrecognized consequences of social behaviour). Thus, members of an organization may hold values that are counterproductive to the organization. For example, a sales person may not realize that her non-verbal behaviour contradicts the verbal statement made to the customer. We can therefore look for both latent functions and dysfunctions when observing an activity. In this way we can 'look behind' the behaviours and activities of individuals and groups of people in organizations.

From a Functionalist perspective, an organization's culture is composed of a series of traits that combine to form a cultural complex of organized, patterned, social relationships. A cultural trait refers to the smallest unit of a culture; it may be a phrase, an object, a gesture or a symbol. When such units of communication become patterns, they begin to form expectations and behaviours that become predictable or normative. A cultural norm is therefore an established standard of what a group expects (or approves of) in terms of thought and conduct. Cultural norms take many different forms, some of which can be defined as values, habits, behaviours and customs. For example, if we focus on values and customs, we can note the following:

1   Values are the deep-seated sentiments shared by members of an organization that will often dictate the actions and behaviour of its members.
2   Customs carry significant implications of right and wrong. Customs may change through both an unconscious, unplanned, and non-directed process, or by enacted change which is planned and deliberate. One approach to detecting an organization's customs is to investigate its regulative and constitutive rules.

This approach would seek to analyse cultural integration by asking the extent to which people share the goals of the organization. This may not be difficult to ascertain and may well be a valuable activity. It becomes much more problematic, however, when deeper questions are asked pertaining to employee commitment. It is possible that if the organization carried out a survey of its culture in these terms, then it might discover that while people understand the business strategy and corporate goals, they may give a negative response to questions of commitment. This can be approached in one of two ways. First, the organization regards the negative responses to commitment as dysfunctional (which, of course, would be a dangerous judgement) or, second, it accepts that people are committed to many things which may on some occasions be aligned while on other occasions may conflict. For example, in a large NHS Trust it is likely that all staff may respond positively to strategy and goals but differ in respect of the values and interests (financial, material, cognitive) they hold. This is because there are many professional and occupational groupings in the health service comprising consultants, junior doctors, nurses, physiotherapists, occupational therapists, radiographers, pharmacists and others whose values and interests are likely to be influenced by various factors such as occupational (rather than organizational) interests related to the market situation or their attitudes acquired through role socialization. Thus, when planned organizational change occurs, the various professions may act defensively to protect their members' interests.

The problem with the pursuit of cultural integration is that different occupational groups rarely share the same interests or values except, that is, on the most general of levels. The *functional fit* view assumes that cultural integration is the central purpose of the organization. These ideas were popularized in the 1970s and 1980s by Peters and Waterman (1982), Deal and Kennedy (1988) and others in the Excellence Movement to emphasize the need for harmony and equilibrium. Problem-oriented approaches, or the search for dysfunctions, are thus characteristic of attempts to bring the organization back to health or stability. The alternative is to consider the limits of integration and manage the meanings that emerge and change over time. This will be discussed in the next section.

THE INTERPRETIVE APPROACH: CULTURE AS NEGOTIATED MEANING

By contrast to the Neo-functionalist views, an *interpretive* (phenomenological) approach argues that cultural integration must be viewed as problematic since agreement is a temporary and continuously negotiated arena of volatile social interactions. For example, some larger organizations contain subcultures. A subculture is a group within an organization that is related to the larger culture in the sense that it accepts many of its norms, but it is also distinguishable because it has some norms of its own that mark it out from the others. A further distinction can be made with the concept of counter-culture. A counter-culture is made up of groups that sharply challenge and reject the norms and expectations of the dominant culture. Under such circumstances it is common to find significant gaps between the regulative rules (the written policy statements and formal rules of the employment contract) and the constitutive rules (the conventions and practices that often contradict the regulative rules). In this sense, the meaning of a situation is potentially variable depending upon the values and background expectations of a particular subculture. Various writers have suggested that significant subcultures arise from occupations within complex organizations.

The symbolic interactionist approach

Merton began to modify many of the issues that appeared to be problematic in functionalist analysis. Another problem with the Structural–Functionalist approach was the appropriation of specific metaphors and language of natural science in order to investigate immutable laws rather than interpretations of a socially constructed organizational reality. This was the fundamental difference between the emergence of the various phenomenological accounts and the previous positivistic approaches. By comparison, Symbolic Interactionism did not view organizations as problematic or prone to dysfunction. Situations were imbued with flux and uncertainty because they were negotiated by individuals and groups who managed scripts, adopted roles, and consciously performed in skilful and meaningful ways the motives that were not always apparent to observers. Nor was there a focus on the 'health' of the organism. Symbolic Interactionism offered an interpretative perspective that assumed appearance to be superficial because we could not observe motives and, while this was not a problem for the Positivist or Behaviourist, it was *the* problem to be investigated for the Symbolic Interactionist.

The very notion of order was precarious and in this sense it was possible to argue that organizations – the epitome of order in the modern world – only appeared orderly to us as casual observers. Therefore if we really wanted to analyse organizations, we needed to go beyond the façade of appearance, simplistic observations and imputed motive. Research required the analysis of the webs of meaning, values and motives created by people in their everyday activities rather than seeking to observe a fixed entity – a thing-like quality waiting to be discovered. Furthermore, if meaning was contextual and continuously negotiated, then the focus should be the 'fictions', or artful constructions that people place upon their activities. In order to do this, the notion of the 'actor' became an essential device for understanding one of the key metaphors of Symbolic Interactionist analysis. This *dramaturgical analysis* contrasted sharply with functional analysis because it was founded upon an epistemology that explained social phenomena more accurately.

The dramaturgical metaphor brings all public performances into sharp focus. Therefore, to view all organizational activity as drama requires a very different form of analysis than the discovery of functions typical of the organismic metaphor. The dramaturgic metaphor by Goffman (1966) has been an extremely useful device for understanding social interaction. It has since become a feature of Symbolic Interactionist studies and the application of 'grounded theory'. More recently, studies in organizational behaviour have began to explore this approach essentially because it provides a vocabulary to explain the subterranean world of organizational activities. For example, although we often assume that decision-making is a rational process, it is in fact limited by incomplete information, psychological and sociological processes, and the decision-maker's cognitive ability (March and Simon, 1958). We often assume that meetings exist to solve problems but they may serve other more fundamental symbolic purposes, many of which enable participants to develop their own strategies to influence the course of action that best serves their own interests. As Bolman and Deal (1994) point out, meetings as theatre help 'individuals become clearer about their roles in the organizational drama and to practice and polish their lines'. An example of the drama metaphor is illustrated in Chapter 6 with the case study 'The graveyard of ambition'. This is also discussed in Chapter 5.

Geertz's interpretative semiotic approach

The anthropologist Clifford Geertz is the best-known exponent of such an interpretative exposition of culture. For Geertz (1975a), situational analysis required 'sorting out the structures of signification' by (a) identifying the various frames (actors' strategies) of interpretation; and (b) moving on to show how and why at that time and in that place their co-presence produced a negotiated outcome. Geertz's mixture of ordinary language philosophy, Symbolic Interactionism, ethnography and cultural semiotics led him to suggest that seeing beneath the surface requires 'thick description'.

Analysis requires the skilful ability to understand a 'multiplicity of complex conceptual structures, many of them superimposed or knotted into one another' (ibid.: 10). The analysis of culture is therefore the analysis of signs which emerge from behaviour, artefacts and from talk. All signs, furthermore, draw their meaning from the role they play in an ongoing pattern of activity. Reporting on analysis may well reduce its complexity to a simpler form in order that the reader may make sense of it, but such interpretation should not lose its ability in 'tracing the curve of a social discourse', by 'fixing it into an inspectable form' (ibid.: 19). Geertz's reference to a semiotic analysis requires the ability to read signs and by this he means the discovery of meaning in both artefacts and language. This moves us beyond simple observation by requiring the researcher to *analyse relationships between motives, values and actions*. There are two obvious ways of doing this. The first involves the analysis of what the socio-linguists call 'linguistic competence' – the recognition that all utterances are tied to a context. The second is based on a different approach to language known as Structuralism or semiotics.

Geertz takes issue with versions of culture that view social behaviour as complexes of observable behaviour patterns (Positivism and Behaviourism). Instead, he urges us to view culture as 'control mechanisms'. That is, as 'plans, recipes, rules, instructions (what computer engineers call "programmes") for the governing of behaviour' (ibid.: 44). The reason for this is because, as Geertz points out, man is the animal most dependent on 'extragenetic, outside the skin' programmes for ordering behaviour. Although he does not specify how to analyse culture, the most precise way of viewing this is as a series of codes acquired when one enters a culture.

For Geertz, learning to read a culture is like learning to read a text. Thus, while it is possible to teach the functional characteristics of a text and the appreciation of basic skills such as genre, grammar and syntax, it is much more difficult, if not impossible, to teach the art of connoisseurship. Similarly, while it is possible to teach musicology, a musician will only become a virtuoso by their own effort to understand and appreciate the relationship between musical conventions and their ability to communicate emotional and psychological qualities to an audience. For example, a musician may be highly skilled but may fail to give personality to the music.

It is possible to provide a tentative framework for the analysis of organizational culture. Following Geertz, the analysis of culture requires the ability to read codes like a text. All codes rely on common agreement among their users about both the content of an expression and about *the way it* was expressed and communicated. In other words, we learn how to apply meaning to expressions by learning the rules. And just as reading more sophisticated texts requires readers to appreciate how various codes are over-laid on top of each other (for example, aesthetic, psychological, emotional), then an organization's culture is not only layered with multiple levels of codes, its analysis requires the ability of the reader to unpack and explain them.

THE ANALYSIS OF CULTURAL CODES

At the risk of over-simplifying the message, there are three principal ways of illustrating the cultural codes within an organization (see Table 3.1). While Geertz does not explicitly refer the reader to semiotic codes, one useful and simple way to apply this to organizational analysis is by referring to: (a) conventional codes; (b) explicit codes; and (c) metaphoric codes. By observing the combinations of these codes we can analyse semantic rules which influence a particular course of action for individuals as well as for the organization. Examples of semiotic codes are provided below, followed by the final section on the analysis of organizational culture.

Conventional (dynamic) codes

Convention refers to unwritten expectations derived from shared experiences by members of an organization. These might include sharing the highs and lows of a common history such as a take-over, delayering, celebrations of

TABLE 3.1
Analysing
organizational
discourse

	Conventional (dynamic) codes	Explicit (static) codes	Metaphoric codes
Type of discourse	Emphasises informal verbal shared expectations	Formal and written	Transformational images. Symbols that carry new meanings into a situation by turning the conventional into the unconventional Holistic iconography giving rise to a rich variety of symbolic constructs Language games play with reality
Type of message	Narrowcast message Implicit/elliptical	Explicit with sanction	Highly ambiguous and transformational language games play with reality
Purpose	To regulate the expectations or concerns of ingroup Articulates methods for dealing with threats: aggression, exploitation, negotiation Security against economic, political, or psychological deprivation (Harrison, 1996) The pursuit of one's own growth and development where this may conflict with the immediate needs of the organization (Harrison, 1996) To challenge values through covert whistleblowing	Regulation of formal activities Meaning is not negotiable Prescribes the appropriate relationships between individuals and the organization Indicates what kinds of controls are legitimate and illegitimate Internal integration and co-ordination of effort toward organization needs and goals, including the subordination of individual needs to the needs of the organization (Harrison, 1996) To establish values	Attempts to transform meaning through cognitive and affective attitudes, behaviours and *modus operandi* Seeks to transform relationships Emphasises that meaning is negotiable

success as when a ship is completed in a shipyard. It might also reflect shared experiences *vis-à-vis* managers or shareholders, etc. Such conventions will give rise to expectations that people will act in a particular way because it relies on common experience. Agreements made between people are usually unstated. For example, most organizations have a dress code. While this can vary according to the requirements of the organization or the dictates of the manager, there are always boundary rules which distinguish the 'acceptable' from the 'unacceptable'.

Perhaps a better way of explaining this methodological problem is the phrase used by Umberto Eco (1965) in which he refers to 'aberrant decoding'. When a clear message is sent (encoded) to a discrete audience who share the same meanings it can be seen as a 'narrowcast message' because their interpretation of it (decoding) will be reasonably precise. However, if the message is observed by a member of a different culture or subculture, then that observer may not be able to understand the meanings that lie behind it. Such a statement is highly metaphorical in the sense that in order to 'read' the linear expression of the message, the ability to decode the connotations is required. To miss the metaphor is to miss the message. Conventions also determine the nature of the psychological contract and, as Handy (1985) has pointed out, this is implied, 'usually unstated' and exists 'between the individual and the organization'. In this sense conventions lead to expectations and analytically it is worth exploring this relationship to test the degree of congruence between groups of employees and managers within the organization. While Handy refers to the correlation between psychological maturity in an individual as an expression of their motivational calculus and the amount of effort they seek to expand in the attainment of a particular goal, it is very difficult to identify, assess or measure it. By contrast, a better way of analysing the psychological contract is to identify the congruence or incongruence of conventions in the organization (see Table 3.2) between conventional and explicit codes.

Language is critical to the analysis of culture. Key features include the language used by group members about the extent of shared meaning and common phrasing to describe group events and actions. Language establishes a set of boundary rules in relation to the culture or subcultures to which individuals belong. It does so by invoking particular language games (as Wittgenstein observed) and in so doing it indicates both the cognitive dimension of thought and the affective judgements of the subculture. As a result, language not only helps to establish order, it maintains the emotional climate (Mills and Murgatroyd, 1991: 37). Of particular interest is the way talk establishes ideological boundaries yet it is common for them to go unrecognized by managers and administrators as the cause of conflict in organizations (Harrison, 1996).

Harrison's work in this regard has been overtaken, at least in the UK, by the descriptions that Charles Handy gave to organizational culture. As Harrison observes, ideological differences are often a root cause of conflict which 'are recognised only when they are blatant and the lines of struggle are drawn, as in labor–management relationships. But by then, the conflict may well have developed to the point where a constructive resolution is virtually impossible' (Harrison, 1996: 150).

For Harrison, although the term *organization ideologies* is ambiguous, it at least characterizes 'the systems of thought that are central determinants of the character of organizations' (Harrison, 1996: 150). Thus, an organization's ideology will affect the behaviour of employees and this will, in turn,

TABLE 3.2
Analysing
organizational
discourse in one
organization

	Metaphoric codes	Transformational language games play with reality
Example	There is the impression that they walk on water. I'll tell you what it's like, ethnic cleansing. That's what people say about it.	Analogy with Bosnia is a performative device that refers to the intensity of feeling about the lack of career progression because of merger.
		A language game that exposes ideological differences in this organization between the old and new management.
Example	These new 'change agents' go around to make sure they pump flesh and talk to the guys yet we know that if we don't perform then they'll take my head off.	Ruthless Machiavellian abuse of power.
	That's what drives the top cats.	
Example	If you don't keep climbing you're a failure. There is a kind of attitude of: 'move to Malaysia or lose your career'.	Self-interest and exploitation.
		Language is not a mirror reflecting experience. It is a social activity in which organizational members construct the meanings of events important to them. In the brief examples of an unfolding story of acute ideological differences career progression is determined not by a person's experience and capabilities but by demonstrating the right 'attitude'.

create a cycle of increasingly negative reactions between managers and others. As a result, the organization will fail to meet employee needs and they, in turn, will fail to meet the expectations of the organization. Furthermore, as Harrison argues, 'much of the conflict that surrounds organization change is really ideological struggle (an idea that is certainly not new to political science but one about which behavioral scientists have, until recently, been curiously quiet)' (ibid.).

Following Harrison, the six most obvious functions that an organization's ideology performs include how it does the following:

1   Specifies the goals and values toward which the organization should be directed and by which its success and worth should be measured.

PRIMARY INTERESTS OF PEOPLE
1 Security against economic, political, or psychological deprivation 2 Opportunities to voluntarily commit one's efforts to goals that are personally meaningful 3 The pursuit of one's own growth and development, even where this may conflict with the immediate needs of the organization
PRIMARY INTERESTS OF ORGANIZATIONS
1 Effective response to threatening and dangerous complex environments 2 Dealing rapidly and effectively with change and complex environments 3 Internal integration and co-ordination of effort toward organizational needs and goals, including the subordination of individual needs to the needs of the organization

FIGURE 3.3
Six reasons for ideological tension and struggle

Source: Harrison 1996: 150.

2   Prescribes the appropriate relationships between individuals and the organization (that is, the 'social contract' that legislates what the organization should be able to expect from its people, and vice versa).

3   Indicates how behaviour should be controlled in the organization and what kinds of control are legitimate and illegitimate.

4   Depicts which qualities and characteristics of organization members should be valued or vilified, as well as how these should be rewarded or punished.

5   Shows members how they should treat one another: competitively or collaboratively, honestly or dishonestly, closely or distantly.

6   Establishes appropriate methods of dealing with the external environment: aggressive exploitation, responsible negotiation, pro-active exploration.

As organizations increase in size and their operations become more complex, they experience conflicting messages and rapid change in many of the environmental domains in which they operate. Harrison therefore identifies six interests which are the subject of ideological tension and struggle. Three of these are primarily interests of people, and three are primarily interests of organizations. These are illustrated in Figure 3.3.

Explicit (static) codes

Many agreements in organizations are explicit. These agreements include contracts of employment, mission statements, financial statements, quality control policy, recruitment policy, equal opportunity policy, training plans, marketing strategy, etc. These are the official rules by which the organization attempts to regulate its activity. As such, these documents attempt to appeal to logic. That is, they are codes which seek to regulate agreement because they are explicit, defined and often carry a sanction. Meaning is not negotiable since it is contained in the text itself and, whereas meaning is open-ended in conventional codes, explicit codes are less dynamic and less susceptible to change. Such codes can only change by explicit agreement. To get the full flavour of such codes, it is necessary to consider Max Weber's concerns with 'legal–rational authority' which links modernity with bureaucracy. Thus, while legal–rational authority is the ultimate standard of modern democratic practice, epitomized essentially by the rule of law, it can also be used to stifle and wear down initiative and innovation.

Metaphoric codes

Metaphor is more likely to exist within conventional codes than explicit codes since the latter seeks to avoid ambiguity. However, a metaphor or trope can occur either as an utterance between two or more speakers or it can occur as a product or artefact. In the latter sense its analysis is semiotic. Metaphors can be regarded as symbols that carry meaning by association. However, such associations are transposed from one plane to another, turning the conventional into the unconventional. Organizations are replete with metaphors pretending to be literal descriptions. Thus when we notice this we can often recognize a style of discourse. For example, the literature of change management is littered with descriptions of change as a journey: 'seven steps to success' and change agents are seen as 'corporate navigators', 'riding the waves' of change. Organizations are arenas where people do all sorts of identity work. They define their social identities through their work; they learn about gender rules; they express emotion and celebrate their individuality and collective identity. The speech acts represent the things that cannot really be said in literal discourse because communication is not open. You can feel the power of this by asking what these people are doing with language. Metaphoric codes enable people to do identity work. Because metaphoric codes are elliptical, they can also express references to emotions such as how people feel, how they define their social identities through their work, their gender and collective identity. Metaphoric speech acts can also represent the things that cannot really be said literally because communication is not open. To do so may therefore be dangerous for the individual (see Table 3.2). Whistleblowing, for example, often reveals organizational activities that are couched in elliptical language. Gossip and moral opprobrium often do this also. Metaphors can also be used in a more deliberate and thought provoking way when they are employed skilfully as an intervention strategy by the change agent. As a form of discourse designed to transform meaning the change agent can enable organisational members to identify a forward looking iconography through either the construction of images or stories. In this way, a transformation in values, attitudes and working practices can be achieved (see table 5.2 in chapter 5).

ANALYSING DISCOURSE: SPEECH ACTS, METAPHORS AND ORGANIZATIONAL CULTURE

The values of an organization's culture are never transparent. While numerous references to culture management exhort us to identify and change the values of the organization in the interests of achieving a strong culture (for example, Deal and Kennedy, 1988), it is often difficult to identify existing values because they are underground. However, the analysis of tropes represents one type of speech act which enables the observer to identify an organization's value system by examining the way language expresses the continuous flow of experience (Tsoukas, 1991).

Taking discourse seriously requires an appreciation of metaphor as a fundamental linguistic device for defining and enriching reality. Morgan (1986), for example, has provided a framework for 'imagizing' an organization through a series of metaphors. However, little has been said about the uses of metaphor and tropes by members of an organization in relation to their emotional experiences. Thus, the way the story is told by members of an organization conveys a rich picture expressed both cognitively and emotionally. As Tsoukas has pointed out: 'Unlike other sign systems, language possesses an inherent quality of reciprocity: it establishes a "conversation" between thinking and acting' (1991: 567). Metaphors convey neologism and therefore make language dynamic. They do this by transferring information 'from a relatively familiar domain . . . to a new and relatively unknown domain' (ibid.: 568). The most important aspect of metaphor, following Tsoukas, is its ability to *prescribe* meaning rather than describe it: 'Metaphors, similes and analogies, more than literal assertions, do not simply describe an external reality; they also help constitute that reality and prescribe how it ought to be viewed and evaluated' (ibid.: 570).

The following criteria are offered as reasons to search for tropes as expressions of feelings and values in an organizational context:

- Live metaphors are provided by people as substitutes for literal utterances in order to express intensity of feelings and emotions in a manner not possible with literal discourse.
- As live metaphors figures of speech draw out an analogy between relationships by transposing values from one field to another.
- Figurative naming and classifying create a perceptual frame which guides action.
- The analysis of figurative speech acts reveals the existence of regulative and constitutive rules. Regulative rules seek to regulate interpersonal behaviour while constitutive rules tell listeners the meaning of a particular reference. (Schall, 1983; Pearce and Cronen, 1980; Farace et al., 1977)

The analysis of language, then, is fundamental to the view that people socially construct their organization 'in a process of ongoing learning by narrating their experiences in ways that produce and reproduce dominance and submission', thus 'the storytelling collective is a community of many different and often opposed interests. The story builds up a series of alliances and counter-alliances' (Boje, 1994: 436). However, one of the reasons why a discourse represents the way a story is told is that certain types of utterances represent performative speech acts related to identity. Thus, for Austin, who was the first to draw attention to the functions performed by language as part of interpersonal communication, utterances may go beyond simply communicating information by conveying a new psychological or social reality. Examples include statements such as: 'I apologise', or, 'I promise' or 'I name this ship', etc.

Performatives are therefore very different from statements that convey information (constatives) because they are neither true nor false. Students of organizational analysis are therefore more concerned to study the effect of the utterances on the behaviour of the speakers and listeners. Analysis is therefore separated into (a) the recognition that a communicative (locu-tionary) act has taken place; (b) the nature of the action (e.g., promising, warning, threatening, questioning, etc.) or illocutionary act; and (c) the effect the speaker's utterance has on the listener (is he amused? angry? persuaded? etc.) – the perlocutionary act. While there are thousands of possible ill-ocutionary acts, Searle's (1976) classification into five basic types is useful. These are:

1   *Representatives* (or assertives or claims) by which speakers commit themselves to the truth of a proposition by affirming, believing, conclud-ing, denying, or reporting.
2   *Directives* (or requests) by which speakers attempt to get the listeners to comply by responding to a question, challenge, command or request.
3   *Commissives* (or promises) whereby speakers commit themselves to a specific course of action by guaranteeing, promising, swearing or vowing.
4   *Expressives* (refer to the affective state) through which the speakers express an attitude by apologising, deploring, congratulating, thanking, welcoming, etc.
5   *Declarations* by which the speakers alter the condition of an object or situation by resigning, firing, declaring war on, etc.

Speech acts can represent a conflict of ideologies. When the organization's need to deal rapidly and effectively with change in a complex environment clashes with the individual's voluntary commitment to goals that were personally meaningful, this can result in a conflict of ideologies, as Figure 3.3 illustrates. The statements in Table 3.2 reflect the conventional dynamic codes as they are decoded by understanding the social and political contexts to which the metaphors refer. These are restricted codes and can be con-trasted with the formal elaborated codes of the explicit or static codes. The performative utterances taken together create a picture of this organization where senior management have emerged as the dominant victors of a successful corporate take-over. The original management team perceive the new team as a cadre of Machiavellian managers who ruthlessly exploit a situation for their own short-term advantage. At the heart of this is the clash of two ideologies – the old, very successful company that has nurtured its development and is at the forefront of creativity and development, and the new financially powerful corporation that, having made a successful take-over bid, installs its own mechanistic controls and mind-games.

Organizations exert a powerful influence upon their members. They can enable people to express their emotions or they can severely constrain the social identity of individuals by placing pressures upon them to outwardly conform to organizational requirements (Goffman, 1966). Mainstream debates in organizational behaviour tend to restrict discourse about the self to politically neutral agendas such as learning behaviour, organizational socialization, or personality variables. Yet organizations are arenas where people do all sorts of identity work. They define their social identities through their work; they learn about gender rules; they express emotion and celebrate their individuality and collective identity. The tropes represent the things that cannot really be said in literal discourse because communication is not open. The use of discourse is a critical element in reinforcing the status quo or in enabling people to change their attitudes and behaviours to gain ownership of change. Rather than seeing discourse as something that occurs in the change process, it is more useful to recognize that change can result from discourse. This is discussed further in Chapter 5.

This is similar to Geertz's (1975b) description of deep play (which he borrowed from Bentham), as play in which the stakes are so high that it is irrational for people to engage in it at all. To express such an opinion outright leads to the recognition that employees with less power are in over their heads and risk too much by way of disciplinary retribution or outright dismissal. In some situations, then, values are suppressed precisely because they are more likely to be affective.

DEVELOPING ORGANIZATIONAL CULTURES

Developing organizational cultures is controversial since it raises the vexed question of whether organizational culture can be managed at all. Trends in 'culture management' during the late twentieth century attempted to identify how organizations sought to develop cultures in the interests of organizational improvement. In order to understand this attempt to develop organizations through people management, it is necessary to begin by asking two critical questions. First, why manage culture? This is essentially about the circumstances under which we may recommend culture management. Second, can it be managed? This question touches on epistemological debates about the extent to which organizational culture is subject to control. Both of these questions will be the subject of the next two sections.

Why manage culture?

Essentially, organizational culture was seen to be a relatively recent attempt to influence organizations by suggesting that corporate success required a strong culture. This was due largely to the popularity of the Excellence Movement and Peters and Waterman (1982) in particular who influenced the thinking of managers. As a result, organizational culture became the route to achieve competitive advantage. A second source of popular interest emerged from writers on Japanese methods of work. Writers such as Ouchi and Jaeger (1978) influenced the 'Japanization' of Western organizations by arguing that Japan's economic success and meteoric economic development resulted from their strong corporate cultures.

The search for superior performance therefore challenged bureaucratic control (or rather the 'rational model' as Peters and Waterman called it) by seeking to replace it with innovative, knowledge-based organizations that tore up the rule books, focused less on procedures and regulations and more on the development of core values. By doing so, organizational culture became aligned with organizational structure and business strategy. Managers were therefore encouraged to change their organization's culture in order to achieve competitive advantage by being the best. Since this represented the challenge to bureaucratic rules and regulations, it also implied a challenge to the old Fordist methods of control: management by systems was out and management through people was in. Corporate culture was designed to replace management through systems with a heightened sense of employee commitment and involvement by increasing the sense of collective identity. The vehicle for doing this was the core values of the organization.

The argument that culture could be managed in this way is based on certain assumptions that often remain unchallenged in the change management literature. One of the major problems, however, is that culture change is often viewed as the prerogative of senior management leading to old-style 'leader-centred', charismatic, transformational and radical change strategies. New programmes such as TQM and BPR are 'launched' through the goal of culture change. A number of questions need to be raised therefore when considering the desire to develop cultural change. For example, if organizations are more accurately characterized as arenas in which ideas, values and emotional loyalties are continually contested and negotiated (as suggested by pluralists), then this raises questions about the role of the leader in attempting to recommend a homogeneous culture. The failure to recognize that in complex organizations there are different subcultures which often become the source of change through their very diversity of ideas may lead to an unhealthy outcome (Meek, 1988).

Another difficult problem that tends to be glossed over in much of the change literature is the extent to which values can be manipulated or altered. As Woodall has pointed out, value change 'is one of the unsolved mysteries of the social sciences', yet it is often assumed that 'changes in behaviour signify value change, and that formally espoused values will actually influence behaviour' (1996: 28). This question as to whether culture can really be managed has previously been raised (Fitzgerald, 1988) but remains a source of some academic concern.

In comparison to the recent change management literature, Strategic Human Resource Development is concerned to develop an ethical position in the development of organizations. Woodall illustrates this 'yawning gulf between this and the approach to culture change in which the sole stakeholders are the senior management team and the financial markets, with the rest of the workforce unaware of what is being contemplated, and without any say over their own involvement' (1996: 29). She refers to the ethical position of OD by citing French and Bell who point out that change agents need to do the following:

- select interventions that have a high probability of being helpful in the particular situation;
- ensure that a consultant does not use interventions that exceed his or her expertise;
- inform the various stakeholders or 'client system' as far as practicable about the nature of the process;
- establish the values of the consultant to avoid working with personal or hidden agendas;
- observe commitments to confidentiality;
- avoid coercion by getting employees to divulge information about themselves or others;
- avoid unrealistic promises made to the client in respect of outcomes.
(French and Bell, 1990; Woodall, 1996)

One problem appears to be that senior managers tend to see change as a strategic weapon and as a result fail to develop the sophistication required because they manage change programmes as they would a war game: by 'identifying potential sources of resistance, monitoring where it appears, and above all [by] "neutralizing" it' (Woodall, 1996: 29). By exploring Brown's (1995) critique of the common misuse of Lewin's process model of unfreeze–change–freeze, Woodall argues that regular misuse occurs at each stage. For example, at the unfreeze stage, two issues of integrity emerge. The first concerns who it is that defines the dysfunctions. This is a clear reference to those senior leaders in positions of power who may, either unwittingly or deliberately, abuse their positions when they provide their 'view from the bridge'. The second issue is related to the first and refers to the pseudo-science of techniques such as Gap analysis or SWOT analysis that 'can create the illusion of scientific rigour' masking a 'naive pragmatism' (Woodall, 1996: 29). As a result, it is possible to suggest that critical questions at this stage should include:

- the method of data collection;
- the source from which it was obtained;

- the integrity of the researcher/consultant to stay close to the data and to explain any difficulties with the analysis.

Further problems occur at the refreeze stage when senior management seek to install values yet expect the workforce to 'own' the change. These criticisms, however, should be seen as dangers alerting change agents to the sensitivity of change. Whether culture can be managed depends upon the definition of culture employed and whether it can be managed strategically from the top of the organization. For example, if culture is seen to operate at a subliminal level, then it could be argued that it is the very intangibility of culture that makes it inaccessible to manipulation, control or modification. If, on the other hand, culture is expressed through tangible forms – that is, through the artefacts, the rituals, and the symbols and myths of everyday organizational life – then culture, for practical purposes, is amenable to influence and development. A number of well-known authors take this approach from Peters and Waterman (1982), Deal and Kennedy (1982), and Schein (1985). Authors such as Beer and Walton (1987), Gagliardi (1986) and Dunphy and Stace (1988; 1990) put the case even more forcefully by suggesting that under certain circumstances, such as organizational crisis and destruction and where the only option is change to survive, coercion may be the only strategy available.

Drawing on the work of Lundberg (1985), Schein (1985), Gagliardi (1986), Watson and D'Annunzio-Green (1996) have argued that there are four common themes that emerge in the change literature:

- a reliance on the notion of crisis;
- the view that leadership is crucial;
- agreement that perceived success is important;
- acceptance that change constitutes a form of relearning.

A series of modifications by Schein (1984), Beyer and Trice (1988) and Isabella (1990) to Lewin's original work (Lewin, 1952) 'identifies some of the complex cultural processes likely to be associated with organizational change. It thus provides a micro and detailed view of what may be occurring in organizations experiencing cultural change' (Watson and D'Annunzio-Green, 1996: 26). Thus, human resource policies and practices such as job design, recruitment, selection and socialization, appraisal, training and development, manpower flows, reward systems, and communication systems become levers for change.

Organizational culture is both a subliminal process and yet is amenable to influence through the activities of change agents. Any attempt to influence change may have positive or negative consequences for the organization but this depends upon the ability of the change agent and on the demands of the situation as described below.

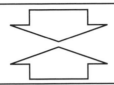

THE ROLE OF THE CHANGE AGENT

- To diagnose organizational problems
- To identify appropriate stategies of consultation
- Process consultation

THE DEMANDS OF THE SITUATION

- The nature of the crisis
- Shared agreement that success is important
- To recognize that change requires a process of relearning

FIGURE 3.4
The ability to influence a change in an organization's culture will depend on the competence of the change agent and the demands of the situation

Is culture change always manipulative?

At the beginning of this chapter it was stated that the themes identified in Chapter 2 were, to a greater or lesser extent, manipulative in some way. Is it possible, therefore, to identify any strategy of change that is not manipulative? This partly depends upon the integrity of the change agents and their willingness to be transparent by declaring their intentions and actions. But it also depends on the desire of organizational members to recognize the need for change. However, there may be circumstances when changing the culture of the organization is the only solution to organizational transformation. In other words, when change in behaviours, attitudes, values and processes is a progressive force. In this case, the ability to influence a change in an organization's culture will depend on two things: (a) the competence of the change agent; and (b) the demands of the situation and the extent of agreement among shareholders about the appropriate course of action. This is illustrated in Figure 3.4.

Cultural change cannot be considered to be manipulative when the demands of the situation are recognized by all stakeholders and agreement is reached about the course of action. However, there are two other situations that require change interventions that may be prescriptive or, manipulative, in some way. These involve (a) the need to develop a more robust safety culture, and (b) the need to avoid the problems of workplace harassment, bullying, discrimination or stress. Although these may well be prescriptive it is not necessarily unethical to talk about managing cultural change.

The need to develop a robust safety culture

That changing the culture of the organization is the only solution to progress is illustrated when safety is compromised by systems failures resulting from

FIGURE 3.5

Newspaper
headlines
illustrating a
problem of safety
culture

Rail companies warned on safety
The Guardian, 29 June 2001
Rail safety chiefs have written to 10 rail companies ordering them to take urgent
action to improve their performance and reduce the number of signals passed at
danger on their lines, it emerged today.

Lamentable failures that claimed 31 lives
The Guardian, 20 June 2001
Charges of corporate manslaughter are being considered against Railtrack and
Thames Trains following the Paddington rail crash, in the light of a scathing
report yesterday by Lord Cullen which condemned the entire industry for
'institutional paralysis'.

Air safety under scrutiny after near misses
The Guardian, 19 June 2001
The strains on safety and air traffic controllers at Heathrow are to be urgently
considered at a meeting of senior air safety administrators, it was announced
yesterday.

Maintenance firm guilty over fatal air crash
The Guardian, 7 December 1999
An aircraft maintenance company was found guilty of violating air safety rules
last night, three years after a crash in the Florida Everglades in which 110 people
were killed.

Nuclear weapons secrets vanish from Los Alamos labs
The Guardian, 13 June 2000
Computer hard drives holding some of the United States' most sensitive nuclear
weapons secrets have vanished from a vault at the Los Alamos research
laboratory, in New Mexico, the US Department of Energy admitted yesterday.

How BNFL deployed dirty tricks arsenal
The Guardian, 13 April 2000
A large number of internal documents have been leaked from British Nuclear
Fuels Ltd revealing that the public relations department was involved in a series
of 'dirty tricks', in dealing with hostile ministers and MPs in Ireland and the UK.

Nuclear leak worse than first feared
The Guardian, 2 February 2000
Japan's worst nuclear accident exposed nearly five times as many people to
radiation as was originally thought, the government said yesterday.

Sellafield shipment rejected by Japan
The Guardian, 17 December 1999
British Nuclear Fuels was humiliated by its biggest customer yesterday as Japan
rejected a controversial consignment of plutonium fuel from the Sellafield plant
and accused the company of being untrustworthy.

inappropriate behaviour, attitudes and decision-making. In such cases, culture becomes the vehicle to manage change in order to avoid disasters. This is
illustrated by the newspaper headlines reported in Figure 3.5.

Researchers in this area have noted that failures often result from
the social contexts in which decisions are made rather than simply from

technology failure. Issues such as perception, commitment, communication, decision-making, analysis, etc., may all contribute either to errors or to the efficient avoidance of them. When systems fail, it is often the predominance of human factors that contribute to failure. Many incidents are too insignificant to be noticed yet over time incubate the potential disaster.

Turner (1989) has commented on the role of organizational learning in safety management by attempting to go beyond appearances to understand how organizational processes lead to certain outcomes. Central to this is (a) the appreciation of the processes and (b) the multiple perceptions of the organization's members. Referring to the failure of socio-technical systems Richardson points out that 'Business disasters begin well before, and [are] often distant from, the final triggering event. They also continue to generate costs long after the catastrophe has subsided' (1994: 44–6).

The other characteristics of socio-technical disasters defined by Richardson include the involvement of stakeholders 'who play a part in either precipitating the disaster and/or in contributing towards its resolution' (for example, the Hillsborough disaster) and a number of key players who 'will "intervene" in each of the three phases of the disaster', each of which 'will inevitably bring with them their own "cultural web"' leading to a potential for negative interactions. Consequently,

> strategists need to identify and get to know those stakeholders who are likely to be important to the effective management of each of the phases of particular potential disasters since identification and knowledge of these important contributors can then act as a springboard for collaborative activity towards a more effective avoidance or management of potential or actual disasters with which they might be associated. (Richardson, 1994: 55)

Elliott and Smith (1992) in their study of sports stadia disasters refer to the cultural web – stories and myths, symbols, power structures, organizational structures, control systems and routines and rituals – defined by Johnson and Scholes (1988). This draws out the subconscious shared assumptions and beliefs that are often difficult to change because they are 'hedged about and protected by a web of cultural artefacts' (Johnson, 1992). This has enabled managers to 'confront the culture of their own organisation' and 'to understand the difficulty of changing it' (Frosdick, 1995). This reference by Johnson (1992) is clearly about habits, cultural practices, behaviours and attitudes and as such it deals with some of the central problems of a safety culture.

Developing a safety culture is not the same as developing a corporate culture since the former 'must be capable of mediating between "best practice", norms of conduct and good order and, at the same time, create an environment which is receptive to multiple sources of information, one which protects itself from its own delusions and which problematizes learning' (Höpfl, 1994: 55).

Changing attitudes to workplace harassment, bullying, stress and discrimination

Another reason to influence a change in culture would be to address the problems of workplace harassment or bullying. Some examples are illustrated in the newspaper headline shown in Figure 3.6.

Changing organizational culture in order to deal with harassment is illustrated by Deadrick et al. who refer to the need to prevent workplace harassment by developing a workplace culture based on mutual respect for difference:

> We contend that a more effective approach to preventing harassment involves developing employee responsibility for maintaining a harassment-free work environment, thus developing an environment of mutual respect where individuals take it on themselves to monitor and eliminate harassment from the workplace. When harassment prevention is examined from this perspective, the critical issues involve how to increase employee awareness about harassment in the workplace and get employees themselves to enforce a culture of mutual respect. This type of organisational change approach to preventing harassment is consistent with the current literature on diversity management, which focuses on culture versus legal mandates as the mechanism for change. (Deadrick et al., 1996: 66)

This 'cultural' approach to dealing with harassment in the workplace seeks to engage employees in mutual respect at both an individual and group level. At the individual level, developing culture involves 'motivating employees to take on "prosocial" behaviours that demonstrate respect for individual rights and allegiance to the needs and interests of co-workers' while at the group level, it involves attempts to encourage shared understanding through a 'bottom-up, joint problem-solving, approach to organization and culture change'. This requires: (a) the need to recognize the problem; (b) employee learning and development; and (c) evaluation of change effectiveness.

Problem recognition at the organizational level requires the need to assess the effects of anti-harassment policies and procedures. At the individual level, it requires an assessment of employees' attitudes and behaviours. Employee learning and development involve 'creating a desire to change, soliciting input about how to change, and designing development programmes to implement change' (Deadrick et al., 1996: 70). Evaluation of change requires feedback about the effectiveness of the change effort in relation to behaviours 'that either promote or violate the mutual respect culture' (ibid.: 72).

CONCLUSION

This chapter has looked at the emergence of organizational culture from its Functionalist origins and in its more popularized form through the neo-

FIGURE 3.6

Some newspaper headlines illustrating the problems of workplace harassment, favouritism and bullying

Harassment victims are forced to quit
The Guardian, Thursday 30 August 2001
Alarming evidence of young workers being forced out of their jobs by the predatory sexual advances of company directors and line managers is revealed today in a report by the Equal Opportunities Commission. Analysis of employment tribunal cases over the last three years found that more than 90% of staff who were victims of sexual harassment lost their jobs or resigned as a result of the experience. Most of the victims were young women who started receiving unwanted sexual advances within a year of joining the firm. They tended to be in low paid occupations, such as shop workers, carers, office staff or factory workers on shift work.

The boss's pet
Favouritism at work can be very divisive
The Guardian, Monday 30 July 2001
For many people, the realization that favouritism exists starts in the playground, the moment they twig that getting picked for the netball team has little to do with sporting ability and everything to do with being friends with the captain.

Are you in their line of fire?
The Guardian, Saturday 10 March 2001
You'd recognize a psychopath if you were unlucky enough to come across one, wouldn't you? Don't be so sure. The media may portray the psychopath as a crazed serial killer – the stuff of nightmares and horror films – but the reality is chillingly different. Not all psychopaths are violent criminals and fewer still have a desire to eat you for dinner. Many are highly successful businessmen and women, lawyers, academics, politicians, doctors and teachers. Psychopaths wear suits too . . . in fact, there could be one in your office.

Insecurity 'fuels job bullying epidemic'
The Guardian, 15 February 2000
Long hours and growing job insecurity have helped fuel an epidemic of workplace bullying, with one in four employees saying they have been bullied in the past five years, according to the first comprehensive study of the problem, published yesterday.

Submissive worriers' the likely victims of bullying at work
The Guardian, 7 January 2000
Conscientous workers who worry about their professional ability and are shy and submissive among colleagues are the most likely to suffer workplace bullying, research revealed yesterday.

Bullies add cost to balance sheets
The Guardian, 1 December 2000
If you were sent 42 memos in one day detailing your supposed faults and failures, would you feel managed or bullied? This is what happened to Alan, a senior manager, whose boss used this tactic to control, threaten, and ultimately destroy his workers.

Human Relations theory of the Excellence Movement. Figure 3.1 encapsulates a Functional analysis of organizational culture. This focused on identifying the normative characteristics of how well the various component parts of an organization are integrated. Although Figure 3.1 identifies what change agents try to influence when they seek to change components of the organization's culture, against this is the recognition that such changes are not always in everyone's interests. In reality, this happens only in rare circumstances when the survival of the organization is threatened.

By contrast to the functional fit thesis it was argued that interpretive analyses of organizational culture created more sophisticated insights into organizational behaviour. These were illustrated in Tables 3.1 and 3.2 where the ability to recognize interpretive or semiotic codes becomes a critical ability of the change agent in coming to terms with the hidden reality that creates the flux and potential conflict inherent in much of organizational life. Yet, while Functionalist analysis sought the management of culture, interpretive analysis has generally argued that culture cannot be managed since it is not a component of the organization but rather, culture *is* the organization. From this perspective, cultural control is therefore seen to be manipulative and not in the interests of those seeking purely to analyse and describe what goes on. This argument was seen to be wanting in three respects: (a) when the demands of the situation are recognized by all stakeholders and agreement is reached about the course of action; (b) when a safety culture is of paramount importance; and (c) to avoid the problems of workplace harassment, bullying, discrimination or stress. In such circumstances, it is not necessarily unethical to talk about managing cultural change.

FURTHER READING

Organizational Development adopted the view that cultural integration is paramount to organizational success. This functional fit thesis was popularized by Peters and Waterman (1982). Other texts, such as Schein's (1985) focused more on the cultural processes. An interpretive understanding of culture is illustrated by the Bolman and Deal (1994) text where the reader will recognize the importance of viewing the organization as theatre. Handy's (1985) reference to psychological contract is useful because it formulates the expectations associated with conventional codes and Harrison's (1996) account of ideological differences as a common cause of conflict is worth pursuing. The importance of language is illustrated by Tsoukas (1991) with his reference to metaphor as coded speech and Boje's (1994) account illustrates how organizational storytelling either reinforces or challenges the status quo. Woodall, (1996) provides a useful reminder that culture change is an intervention that requires the adoption of an ethical position by change agents.

The emergence of strategic human resource development 4

INTRODUCTION

By the end of the twentieth century OD had developed a mature perspective for managing change. This perspective had become more flexible than the planned change programmes of the 1970s. It remained experimental and forward-looking but, above all, influenced by interpretive analyses, it had become much more aware of the behavioural dynamics that influenced change. There is a problem, however. As organizations changed by flattening hierarchies, downsized and delayered, the responsibility for change management was passed on, down the line, to middle managers, supervisors and team leaders armed with pre-packaged programmes for managing change at a variety of levels throughout their organizations.

Prescriptive programmes based on half-baked theories, lacking analytical awareness, organizational diagnosis, and methodological rigour were driven by the myopic vision of a garden pruned and maintained by managers looking for a quick technical fix. Cultivating the organizational garden requires more than a set of pruners. It requires the ability to develop its potential through the application of imagination, appropriate knowledge, skill and care. It is in this sense that the case for Strategic Human Resource Development has now emerged in order to progress a more enlightened, methodological, and ethical change management that puts human resources back where they belong – at the forefront of the change agenda. Strategic Human Resource Development combines three things: (a) an awareness of the complexities of change management; (b) a desire to rescue the concept of Human Resource Development from a mundane existence in the depths of training programmes; and, (c) a refined OD perspective to provide direction for the twenty-first century.

The learning objectives for this chapter are:

1   *Approaches to change* which contrast the Organizational Development approach to change with programmed approaches to change. This discussion provides the starting point for the development of Strategic Human Resource Development.

2   *The reasons for failed change programmes* which explores why many change programmes have little impact. These are generally related to lack of vision and commitment, ineffective integration with other systems and processes, and ill-conceived implementation plans but lean production methods and a naïve behaviourism embedded in simplistic consultancy models are also identified.

3   *Change, world competition and the revival of the managerial agenda* whereby the world economy became the catalyst for further rationalization in the 1990s. By the end of the decade, there had been a revival of the managerial agenda for quick fix solutions to quality improvement, BPR and downsizing. Analysis of the trends suggests an increased dependence on rigid training methods and an over-simplified view of change management. Highly structured recipes reflect the six strategies identified in the previous chapter although the degree of dependence results from changes in capitalism.

4   *Critiques of planned change interventions* which challenged the rational models of change produced by the Strategic Management theorists and the client–consultant relationships of the OD approach. This highlighted the need to pay attention to historical, processual and contextual issues that inform the underlying dynamics of the organization.

5   *The birth of Strategic Human Resource Development* which emerged from the OD tradition. Strategic Human Resource Development combines three things: an awareness of the complexities of change management; a desire to rescue the concept of Human Resource Development from a mundane existence in the depths of training programmes; and, finally, a refined OD perspective which provides direction for the twenty-first century. Strategic Human Resource Development promotes

a more enlightened, ethical and skills-focused change management that puts human resources back where they belong – at the forefront of the change agenda.

6   *The triggers for change influencing Strategic Human Resource Development* which emerged as a result of two pressures: first, the new climate of disorganized capitalism and, second, from the internal developments and debates within Organizational Development. This general direction sought to replace overt control-oriented cultures with organizational cultures characterized by creativity and learning.

7   *Strategic Human Resource Development and the drivers of change* which was informed by four debates that force us to recognize the importance of pro-active change to organizations in the twenty-first century. These debates are the contingency perspective; the labour process approach; the flexible specialization thesis; and the strategic choice approach.

8   *Strategic Change and Learning* which illustrates how new learning strategies have been developed to respond to the increasing rates of turbulence. There are four basic types of response: strategic planning, emergent strategy, intrapreneurship, and strategic intent. These are discussed in relation to four central characteristics of Strategic Human Resource Development.

9   *Four central characteristics* which are at the heart of the Strategic Human Resource Development. These refer to the need to see HRD as business strategy; the need to devolve responsibility to line managers; the need to replace the concept of training with learning and the need to emphasize workplace learning.

APPROACHES TO CHANGE

During the past 20 years the idea of managing change has become part of the received wisdom of turbulent environments and has often emerged through commercial programmes such as Total Quality Management or Business Process Reengineering. As a result, a series of change initiatives has emerged that has tended to borrow fragments of the OD approach. This has had both positive and negative consequences. On the positive side, it has made aspects of OD more widely known. On the negative side it has tended to misunderstand and misapply much of the underpinning theory, methodology and intervention practices of OD. These differences between the old OD and programmed approached to change are outlined in Table 4.1.

Table 4.1 is an over-simplification and tends to generalize programmed approaches to organizational change as extremes on a continuum. Nevertheless there are differences which deserve a brief mention. By the end of the

TABLE 4.1
Comparison of OD
and programmed
approaches to
change

Characteristics	Organizational development	Programmed approaches
Methodology	Action research	Task-focused
Approach	Joint diagnostic involving stakeholders	Expert
Interests	Pluralist	Unitarist
Development	Personal and organizational learning	Training
Culture	As analytical tool	A variable to be managed
Values	Promotes humanistic values	Promotes instrumental values
Mode of intervention	Process-focused	Task-focused

twentieth century six essential characteristics informed OD (see Table 4.1). These were:

1 A methodology informed largely by action research – a term coined by Kurt Lewin in the 1940s (see for example, Peters and Robinson 1984: 9–24).

2 A recognition that effective change required participation through a stakeholder approach to collaborative action (according to Steadman et al. (1996) the concept of stakeholders was developed in the organization theory, strategic planning and corporate social responsibility literatures).

3 An awareness of the political processes that either progressed or limited change efforts and the adoption of a pluralist frame of reference in place of the unitarist framework. The pluralist view of organizational reality is founded on the awareness that different groups of people (stakeholders) are attracted to organizations that satisfy their aspirations and that because different people want different things from the organization, 'conflict and "politicking" are natural aspects of organizational life' (Nwankwo and Richardson 1996: 43).

4 The increased emphasis on personal and organizational learning by contrast to training and as a logical development of collaborative action (see Revans 1984).

5 An appreciation of organizational culture (Pettigrew, 1979; Potter, 1989).

6 An approach that embraced humanistic values (Cummings and Huse 1989).

Apart from these characteristics the most enduring metaphor bequeathed by OD was that of the 'journey'. The idea of a journey has traditionally been viewed as a destination which itself is the very rationale for the nature of change. Thus, Lewin's (1951) three stages of change – unfreeze, change, refreeze – reflects the essence of the traditional OD approach through which a clear goal or destination is identified and cascaded to the organization's members. Originally the very idea of the journey depended on a linear model of change (Marshak, 1993) which tended to omit the 'untidy parts of the process that did not fit neatly into Lewin's framework' (Inns, 1996: 23). Today, however, processual dynamics have come to be recognized that were not apparent to earlier OD practitioners. A recognition that this OD journey itself has changed and that the new practitioners will be a variety of people throughout the organization requiring the limited development of skills and knowledge suited to their current task has driven the need for Strategic Human Resource Development.

The differences between the approach adopted by Strategic Human Resource Development and programmed approaches to change are listed below in more detail.

Methodology

Strategic Human Resource Development is informed by a variety of research methods from the social sciences ranging from quantitative to qualitative approaches. However, action research remains the central approach and, as such, it requires the systematic collection of data on organizational problems. Since analysis frames the focus of the problem in the first place, we can identify some of the root metaphors described by Morgan (1986) and distinguish between those with explanatory and interventionist applications (Tsoukas, 1993). Thus, interventionist metaphors (machine, organismic, culture, holographic and political) inform our judgements about what needs to change. Since each represents one aspect of organizational reality, we can understand their representations as follows. First, for machine, we mean control systems (for example, quality control, administrative control, control of health and safety). For organismic, we mean open systems. For culture, we mean attitudes, behaviours and values informed by a series of interpersonal rules. For Holographic, read learning, and, finally, for political, read interpersonal influence and control (or leadership) and organizational structure.

By contrast the programmed approaches of TQM and BPR tend to lack both analytical depth and sensitivity to basic processes (contracting; data collection; diagnosis; feedback; design/action planning; change interventions and evaluation) of action research. The methodology of programmed approaches is essentially driven by the task.

Approach

As a result of the methods used, Strategic Human Resource Development is informed by a joint diagnostic relationship between the consultant or change agent and various stakeholders in the organization. This enables the problem to be understood from multiple perspectives. By contrast, programmed approaches tend to see the change agent (internally this is the quality manager or equivalent position and externally it is the consultant whose expertise is bought in) as the expert whose role is the identification of task-related changes.

Interests

Strategic Human Resource Development views the main activities of the organization – the human processes – to be prior to the task itself. This means that in order to redefine the task, it is necessary to redefine the human processes. However, this requires a recognition that the organization is, in reality, a 'negotiated order'. This requires knowledge of the interpretive approaches that underpin the analysis of culture. By contrast, the programmed approaches tend to adopt a unitarist position by assuming that there should be a single source of authority and loyalty within the organization. Because Strategic Human Resource Development views organizations as pluralistic rather than unitaristic, it sees agreement between various subcultures as a state of permanent negotiation. Since this is a central issue for Strategic Human Resource Development, the skills and competencies of the change agent are critical to successful change and the holding together of federations of different interests. By contrast, the programmed approaches tend to see the role of the transformational leader as the agent driving change in the common interest.

Development

Strategic Human Resource Development sees its role as the development of people and organizations. Thus, learning rather than training has become the central characteristic of change. Individual and organizational learning therefore characterize Strategic Human Resource Development. Contrast this with the many programmed approaches to change which, because they are defined by the expert, are task-focused, unitarist and depend upon training to cascade the downward flow of task-related changes.

Culture

There are essentially two ways to view the concept of culture: (a) as an analytical device or (b) as a variable to be managed. One useful approach to analysing organizational culture is the drama metaphor. In this way, the social construction of organizational reality becomes clearer and we come to see behind the façade of rationalist assumptions of order and decision-making. In addition, the need to focus on discourse is a critical skill for the change agent. Thus we learn to recognize that situations are ambiguous and uncertain and in a constant state of flux. In addition, we recognize that symbols become the vehicles for staging reality and creating direction. By contrast, programmed approaches view culture as a variable to be managed (Bate, 1995). This became, for example, the view promoted by the Excellence

Movement as well as by various authors on Japanese methods (for example, Ouchi and Jaeger, 1978; Ouchi, 1981). This approach was also adopted by various writers on TQM and BPR.

Values

Strategic Human Resource Development promotes humanistic values. The approach to OD proposed by French and Bell emphasized empowerment through values designed to facilitate visioning, organizational learning and problem-solving in the interests of a collaborative management of the organization's culture (French and Bell, 1995: 28). According to Cummings and Huse, 'Values have played a key role in OD, and traditional values promoting trust, collaboration, and openness have recently been supplemented with values for organizational effectiveness and productivity' (1980: 38). Yet there are clearly tensions between humanistic objectives and organizational needs resulting in 'value dilemmas' and 'value conflicts'. Unfortunately, this attempt to find a balance between more empowered solutions on the one hand and organizational needs on the other, has become a major dilemma for the OD consultant (Greiner, 1980; Margulies and Raia, 1990; Church et al., 1994). Nevertheless, Strategic Human Resource Development recognizes how an ethical framework helps change agents perform a positive role of facilitation. Ethical issues tend to arise around the following issues: (a) choice of intervention; (b) use of information; (c) withholding of services; (d) client dependency; (e) choosing to participate; and (f) client manipulation.

In the light of recent trends including increased global competition, downsizing, the creation of core and peripheral workers and the flexible firm, Strategic Human Resource Development professionals have various value-driven problems to contend with. For example, various writers have suggested that current priorities of the marketplace, or of capitalism itself, have undermined the traditional goal of a values-driven approach. In a rapidly changing business environment driven by global competition, 'where downsizing is commonplace and productivity is often the number one priority for clients, there is significantly increased pressure' on the Strategic Human Resource Development professional 'to focus less on humanistic values and more on activities which have a direct impact on the organization's bottom line' (Waclawski et al., 1995: 12–13). Consequently, many change agents and managers appear to be driven increasingly by the demands of the global marketplace resulting in a tendency to concentrate on radical change strategies.

Mode of intervention

Strategic Human Resource Development is concerned with processes which lead to tasks. This is in contrast to many programmed approaches which are task-focused. This means that Strategic Human Resource Development views its role as a dynamic process of modifying patterned behaviour consisting of four styles:

1   an initiative;
2   this initiative requires change to critical organizational processes;
3   these critical organizational processes influence individual behaviours;
4   individual behaviours impact on organizational outcomes. (Dehler and Welsh, 1994)

THE REASONS FOR FAILED CHANGE PROGRAMMES

In recent years many organizational failures have been reported. One criticism notes that many 'popular trends in management organizational consulting' such as 'business process re-engineering, total quality management and the learning organization represent systematic methods . . . for responding to and channelling effectively the forces of change. Unfortunately, the vast majority of improvement initiatives undertaken by organizations, even with the best of intentions, are destined to have little impact' with success rates, in some industries being as low as 10 per cent (Church et al., 1996: 98). The failure of many programmes has been linked to a variety of factors such as 'lack of vision and commitment from senior management, limited integration with other systems and processes in the organization, and ill-conceived implementation plans' (ibid.: 1996). Other factors include the development of lean production systems leading to a desire for quick technical fixes in the form of recipe knowledge; top-down information flows cascaded down through layers of managers; change seen as episodic rather than processual; and naïve behaviourism permeating the change management literature resulting in simplistic consultancy models.

The development of lean production systems and the desire for quick technical fixes in the form of recipe knowledge have been cited as a reason for failure. For example, Garvin (1993) has argued that failure of TQM programmes results mainly from organizations failing to understand that TQM requires a commitment to learning. Others have argued that: 'Like ISO 9000, TQM has been oversold as a stand-alone package, and the high level of failed programmes has led to a search for the "missing ingredients" and to some disenchantment with TQM' (Chelsom, 1997: 140).

It has also been pointed out that in such areas 'failed programmes far outnumber successes, and improvement rates remain distressingly low. Working on style, improving communications and the like still do not seem to be getting anybody anywhere. Is it surprising that people get a bit cynical about all these quick-fix solutions and flavours of the month?' (Granville, 1996: 39).

Perhaps the reasons should not be surprising. Reductions in lead-time, the attempts to enhance services, cost minimization, value creation and stock reduction 'are all enticing business goals' (ibid.: 39) of lean production. But these require new arrangements which ultimately means that such companies can only develop by reducing labour to 'half or less of the human effort, time and overall cost' (ibid.: 39). Interestingly, failure to achieve the desired performance is often seen as a failure of the task itself thus requiring some new, previously unrecognized activity and is rarely seen as a deeper OD problem requiring entirely different solutions of participation and involvement. For example:

> Good as these experiences may be, they should have made us realize that applying lean techniques to discrete activities is not the end of the road. If individual breakthroughs can be linked up and down the value chain to form a continuous value stream, the performance of the whole can be raised to a dramatically higher level. (ibid.: 39)

The third major problem is the method of the intervention with cascaded top-down information flows, through layers of managers, resulting in problems of understanding and commitment. A fourth and related problem is that change is seen as episodic rather than processual. A good example of these problems is illustrated by the National Health Service which has undergone significant changes over the past 20 years and provides us with some interesting examples of change management from TQM, BPR, patient centred care, etc. As Edmonstone points out, 'Most change which has taken place in health care has been "programmatic", that is, it has been episodic, project-based and with a clear and distinct beginning, middle and end' (1995: 16). However, if the health service is typical of programmatic change, it tends to reflect older OD thinking of top-down information flows cascaded in a procedural manner through layers of managers operating at the level of strategies:

> Change programmes and projects have been seen to be distinctively different from the ongoing process of managerial life. 'Bracketing-off', a problematic aspect of management into a change programme with different management arrangements, has been seen as the conventional wisdom. Taking place in large public bureaucracies, it has embodied and enacted many bureaucratic assumptions. Thus, change has proceeded typically in 'cascades' from top management to middle management, through junior management and then to the workforce. It has also focused on 'infrastructure' matters (policies, structures and systems). Finally, it has assumed (in a good democratic tradition) that change is best brought about by 'normative/re-educative' strategies, whereby individuals (most usually through education and training experiences) are encouraged to re-examine their values and attitudes, change them and hence modify their behaviour at work. (ibid.: 16)

Another problem is the simplistic thinking that lies behind the implementation of change programmes resulting in a type of naïve behaviourism. The management literature reveals various simplistic consultancy models which naïvely see resistance as problem behaviour. According to Edmonstone, various assumptions are made about employees' problematic behaviour. These include assumptions that (a) individual problematic behaviour can be 'isolated' and 'changed'; (b) the primary target for change should be the content of ideas and attitudes; (c) behaviour can be influenced by altering formal structures and systems; and (d) promulgating organization-wide change programmes such as mission statements, TQM, culture change programmes, etc. will be effective.

As a result, Edmonstone criticizes these by arguing that: (a) they tend to focus on global and longer-term issues which are not always perceived to be in the short-term 'critical path' of the organization; (b) they rely heavily on education and training methods which encourage representational learning (through acquiring a new management language, complete with jargon, catchphrases, etc.) rather than behavioural learning (through doing); (c) they are too often driven by an exclusive core group who are seen to be the sole or main owners of the problem (and therefore of its solution); (d) such groups are often insensitive to the history, culture and priorities within sub-parts of the organization; and (e) all this serves to set up a tension between the 'rhetoric' and the 'reality'.

CHANGE, WORLD COMPETITION AND THE REVIVAL OF THE MANAGERIAL AGENDA

One of the major problems for OD since the 1980s appears to have been that the world economy became the catalyst for further rationalization. In picking up the arguments of Pfeffer (1994) and Argyris (1990), Alpander and Carroll have argued that:

> The global orientation that characterized OD was replaced during the 1970s with more specialized efforts at improving organisations . . . The 1980s witnessed even more specialization. Organisations focused on the narrow use of single approaches, such as teambuilding, survey-guided development, performance management, process consultation, action research, socio-technical systems analysis, grid analysis, goals management, and re-engineering. These approaches are by no means exhaustive of all OD approaches but are representative of the most widely used OD techniques. (Alpander and Carroll, 1995: 4–5)

A major criticism of many programmed approaches to change (from the perspective of OD) is the recipe approach to knowledge and learning caused by consultants, or change agents, who use rigid formulas for changing the organization. This mechanistic 'how to' approach hinders the synergy of cognitive and behavioural learning in complex situations for two reasons: first, it focuses on training methods that are constructed as toolbox formulations of recipe knowledge; second, it is driven by a small and unrepresentative cadre of problem definers. Examples are cited by Werr et al. (1997) in their investigation of methods used in Business Process Reengineering (BPR) projects undertaken in five large consulting companies who developed highly structured methods and tools for bringing about organizational change. Their study indicated that there was no evidence of positive effects of these 'structured methods' on learning and that such rigid methods of programmed approaches may support uncritical action because they are based on an over-simplified view of management and organizations. As they put it, highly structured programmes with recipes and methodological toolboxes may, on the one hand, 'create a feeling among their users of security' but this can counteract reflection and learning (ibid.: 305). The implications of this research is that consultants transform a process into a product which becomes their vehicle for engaging with the host organization. A second problem emerges when 'less capable' change agents are not equipped to translate the product into a process of cognitive and behavioural learning.

Similar remarks have been made about the more formulaic encounters of OD consultants in healthcare organizations. In an account that criticizes the reductionism thinking of many change agents Edmonstone and Havergal (1995) have remarked that the healthcare sector has become 'sanitized' and 'made safe' from critical challenges. It has become 'the terrain of the problem-page agony aunt' by promoting inappropriate people to the position of internal OD consultants and by adopting the safety of the recipe book:

> As a result of this, OD becomes a supporter of the status quo of conformist innovation (incremental change within prescribed ideological boundaries), rather than deviant innovation (concerned with reframing the status quo, with the leading-edge and with 'what comes next'). As a result, a multitude of people claim to be 'doing OD' (a safe activity) – human resource directors, training managers (who overnight become transformed into OD managers!), quality facilitators, etc. This process is accelerated by a growth in the number of 'recipe books', which, while helpful in demystifying some of the more arcane aspects of OD activity, also portray OD as the application of problem-solving tools and techniques . . . This newly-sanitized and 'safe' OD creates a further problem. The OD function is seen as the custodian of the softer organizational values – the terrain of the problem-page agony aunt. Having provided satisfactorily a place within the structure for such unbusinesslike behaviour, the rest of the organization permits itself to become even less concerned with 'people' and the ratchet tightens further. (ibid.: 31)

This can lead to the celebration of rhetoric under the banner of OD to give it credibility. This is what Edmonstone, and Havergal (following Morgan, 1993) refer to as the 'deer-hunting' approach 'where the trophies of the multiple change programmes (BS 5750, Investors in People, National Train-ing Award, etc.) are flaunted to interested parties' (Edmonstone and Havergal, 1995: 31).

While the authors provide seven reasons for the death of OD in healthcare, none can be as culpable as the 'neo-unitary revival' of the managerial agenda through a 'whole range of management initiatives and actions (communications audits, organizational audits, TQM programmes, etc.)' that 'have all sought to foster a set of shared (market) values which favour: a single authority source, general management; a single loyalty focus, the employer, not the profession; common objectives, through mission statements, business plans, performance appraisal, etc.; integration of functions, through restructuring and team building' (ibid.: 31).

CRITIQUES OF PLANNED CHANGE INTERVENTIONS

Since the late 1980s there have been various, albeit fragmented, challenges to the older OD approaches of planned change. These are related to what Pettigrew (1985) identified as the concern with constant innovation rather than stability. This is clearly an echo of Burns and Stalker's (1961) research from a contingency perspective suggesting that organic structures require the management of more dynamic processes. This has affected an increasing number of organizations as they struggle to survive in a global marketplace. As a result, the planned change approach has come under increased scrutiny. For example, Pettigrew (1985) argued that while there were many issues of complexity in the change literature in need of greater consideration, two central problems emerge consistently to limit the literature on the management of change. The first is the limitation of rational models of change produced by the Strategic Management theorists who tend to view change as a series of strategic episodes in which each element of change has a specific beginning and a finite end. The second is the problem within the OD literature to limit the diagnosis of change processes to a relationship between the consultant and client. What they both shared in common was a 'limited frame of reference' which viewed organizational change to be purely concerned with the mechanics of change in an organization thus ignoring the historical, processual and contextual issues that inform the underlying dynamics of the organization.

Since the concerns expressed by Pettigrew in the mid-1980s there have been attempts to address these problems by focusing on processes. The most notable empirical examples have been Pettigrew (1985), Dawson (1994), and Pettigrew and Whipp (1993). The emerging alternative to planned change models has been dubbed the 'emergent change model' (Burnes, 1996b) and 'processual change' (Dawson, 1994). Dawson argued that change should not be treated as a series of linear events but as a complex, temporal, iterative and non-linear patchwork of unfolding processes, and Dawson and Palmer (1995), noted in their study of TQM programmes into a number of companies that unforeseen critical events during the change process could serve to impede, hasten or redirect the route to change. Pettigrew and Whipp (1993) also observed how managers had to make assessments, choices and adjustments to change initiatives continuously which were outside of the scope of the original planned change initiative.

It is clear that the critiques are increasingly influenced by the turbulent environments in which many organizations are required to operate. In relation to turbulence, Burnes appears to argue that where the environment is less predictable then the processes will be more dynamic:

> Although not always stated openly, the case for an emergent approach to change is based on the assumption that all organisations operate in a turbulent, dynamic and unpredictable environment. Therefore, if the external world is changing in a rapid and uncertain fashion, organisations need to be continually scanning their environment in order to adapt and respond to changes. Because this is a continuous and open-ended process, the planned model of change is inappropriate. To be successful, changes need to emerge locally and incrementally in order to respond to and take advantage of environmental threats and opportunities. (1996b: 14)

As a result Burnes has suggested that the 'main tenets' of the emergent change approach are: (a) that it is characterized by a continuous process of experimentation and adaptation in order to match the organization's capabilities to the uncertain environment; (b) that it is best achieved through a complexity of incremental changes which occur over time and which can themselves 'constitute a major reconfiguration and transformation of an organization'; (c) that the role of managers is one of facilitation not the planning of change initiatives. This means that the focus is on developing a cultural climate which 'encourages experimentation and risk-taking'; (d) that key organizational activities are 'information-gathering – about the external environment and internal objectives and capabilities'; 'communication – the transmission, analysis and discussion of information and learning; and 'the ability to develop new skills, identify appropriate responses and draw knowledge from their own and others' past and present actions' (ibid.).

An alternative approach to change has increasingly emerged, founded on a different set of basic assumptions to those of the planned change models. These are:

- Change is devolved down the organization and results from learning by groups rather than by the cascaded expertise of senior management.
- The focus of change should be tasks, skills, ideas and values.
- A solution to 'a one best way for all' to organizational excellence contingent issues determine whether (a) the organization's culture needs to change or (b) whether to introduce change to fit the organization's culture (see, for example, Burnes' (1996b: 16) reference to Schwartz and Davis (1981) 'cultural risk' approach to change which alerts us to the danger of under-estimating the resistance that may arise when proposed changes clash with existing cultures).
- Organizational change must expose its ideological underpinnings by identifying whose interests the change serves – shareholders, citizens, customers and internal stakeholders? – rather than carrying implicit ideas about the direction of change while remaining silent about its

potential consequences. In other words, whose interests are served and whose point of view is expressed?

There is a distinction to be made between the more fashionable aspects of managing change and organizational development as seen, for example, in the difference between programmed approaches to change such as TQM and BPR. The differences are related to methodology, approach taken, the analysis of interests groups, the nature of development in terms of learning or training, the approach taken to organizational culture, promotion of values and the mode of intervention. There is a significant amount of literature on failed programmes which appears to have some bearing on the approach taken. Many public sector programmes appear to reflect more of a concern to collect trophies than to engage in OD work and, to a large extent, this may reflect the skills of the internal consultants. Finally, it is obvious that a number of critiques of planned change have emerged. Various writers are drawing on this literature and developing an 'emergent change model'. This requires more research related to differences in epistemology and approach (all contributions to this debate welcomed).

By the twenty-first century, change has been seen as: (a) a process of exploration where the destination is unknown (McLean et al., 1982); (b) a continuous process involving the management of chaos (Smith, 1982; Wheatley, 1992; Marshak, 1993); and (c) carrying consequences for other inter-related sub-systems (Wheatley, 1992; Marshak, 1993). This brings into question the very predictability of change. If predictability is challenged, then so is the ability to control the destination. The more recent process-oriented models of change enable previously hidden elements of the journey (uncertainty, circularity, exploration, unpredictability) to come to the fore (Inns, 1996: 25). This approach has recently been informed by 'alternative' non-Western perspectives, such as Taoism, which views the agents of change as 'helpers, guides, mirrors, dragons, mentors and ritual elders' in place of the individualistic, hierarchical and control-driven modernist (Cheng, 1994). This moves the focus of the debate away from top-down, destination-oriented planned change models to a recognition that change moves in small circles through processes that are hard to define in advance.

THE BIRTH OF STRATEGIC HUMAN RESOURCE DEVELOPMENT

The subject of this book has emerged as the logical development of the OD tradition. Strategic Human Resource Development promotes a more enlightened, ethical and skills-focused change management that puts human resources back where they belong – at the top of the change agenda. The journey metaphor has already been adopted by the HRM literature although it has been significantly modified as indicated below.

Human resource management and the journey of inner commitment

HRM has been described as the application of OD through an organization's policies and procedures:

> The overlap between HRM and OD can be interpreted in two ways. Both interpretations suggest that OD consultants have significantly contributed to the growth of HRM. First, it can be argued that it is inevitable that OD consultants, as change agents, are likely to use what they consider to be the best tools to effect change. Often these tools will be akin to HRM policies and practices and this reflects the apparent similarities between OD and HRM. The argument can be taken further in that many HRM policies and practices could be seen as a subset of existing OD techniques, or that the roots of HRM can be traced back to OD, i.e. HRM policies and practices were available as OD techniques some time before HRM itself arrived on the scene. The second interpretation of the overlap is that HRM appears as something new and innovative and that it has a potential to improve competitiveness. (Grant 1996: 193–4)

While it is clear that OD and HRM have similar aspirations because they each share the same aim – to develop the organization through its people – significant differences exist between the skills, knowledge and experiences of the OD and HRM practitioners. For example, not all HRM practitioners would claim to be knowledgeable about strategic issues within their own discipline and many may not possess a social science or behavioural background. Furthermore, OD and HRM practitioners may not share similar values-driven assumptions. Nevertheless, strategic HRM carries its own metaphor of journey in its attempt to replace the old industrial relations or 'trench warfare' approach with the metaphor of the 'wagon train' symbolizing a journey of inner commitment rather than external control (Dunn, 1990). This approach is more concerned with rearranging the politics of change than it is with dealing with complex OD issues. The attempt to move the locus of control towards greater internal compliance (more enlightened employers and more empowered employees) is due not only to political, economic and legislative developments but because of the emergence of increasingly 'disorganized capitalism' (Lash and Urry, 1987; Rose, 1994). Rose suggests that the underlying causes of macro economic change are: (a) the increasing trend towards globalized markets and multinational organizations which shift the balance of power from national markets; (b) the decline of class politics and collectivism and an increase in individualized industrial relations; (c) the emergence of an underclass and low-paid, non-unionized work force; (d) the restructuring of organizations into smaller plants with a flexible, often feminized and casualized, labour force; (e) the demise of occupational communities and regional economies; and (f) the emergence of a post-modern culture in which social identity is no longer bound up with occupational communities but with individualized, consumer leisure identities.

Human resource development

HRD has so far been seen as an umbrella term that carries vague and multiple connotations (Garavan, 1997). This was even more problematic because it carried different practical emphases in various countries. In Belgium, for example, attention focused on training and development, whereas in the UK the characteristics and language of organizational change appear to be the central focus. In Northern Ireland more attention focused on evaluation. In Italy HRD emphasized strategies and plans (Nijhof and de Rijk, 1997).

In the UK, writers on HRM described the purpose of HRD as 'training', 'learning', 'development' and 'education' (Reid and Barrington, 1994). Despite its lack of emphasis it was becoming a strategic weapon in maintaining competitiveness in the international arena (Garavan, 1997). Some writers concentrated more on the need to see HRD as strategically focused organizational development (OD) by emphasizing the turbulent nature of the external environment and the need to concentrate on continuous change and development (Church and McMahan, 1996).

While these debates have moved us in a variety of uncertain directions, it has become increasingly necessary to recognize Strategic Human Resource Development as an appropriate response to two things: (a) globalization, world competition and the revival of the managerial agenda; and (b) the need to move OD down the organization to line managers and other employees who are themselves responsible for dealing with change processes and who are required to engage with learning by doing.

Human Resource Development has lived in the shadow of OD. The most promising search for an HRD model emerged from the contemporary arguments between Swanson and McLean. Their images reflect a battle of minds between a three-legged stool (Swanson, 1995; 1999) and an octopus (McLean, 1998). Swanson argues that HRD is best conceptualized as a three-legged stool with each leg representing a main foundation of economics, psychology, and systems theory. McLean, on the other hand, argues that this 'simplistic' model should be replaced by either a centipede or an octopus. McLean's 'octopus' suggests a representational model of HRD in which the historical foundations are more varied than Swanson's three-legged stool.

What is important about this debate is that both Swanson and McLean see OD as the central component, as Swanson's retort to McLean makes clear:

> When someone asks me what HRD is, I respond by presenting a HRD definition and noting the core HRD process: HRD is a process of developing and or unleashing human expertise through organisation development and personnel training and development for the purpose of improving performance at the organisational, process, and individual/group levels. (Swanson, 1999)

As the debate unfolded, OD became recognized as a key player in a Wittgensteinean card game holding some very promising cards.

The role of the HRD professional

Garavan (1995), who has suggested that two models of HRD management tend to dominate the HRD agenda, has explored the role of the HRD professional. These are: (a) the *single sovereign model* of HRD management in which 'the right and power to manage the HRD function is vested in a single ultimate authority – the HRD specialist'; (b) the *steerer model* of HRD management which requires the HR specialist to steer a course for equilibrium among the competing interests by forming coalitions. Because Strategic Human Resource Development requires the involvement of employees, it can be argued that the HRD professional must have some of the skills required of effective change managers. These skills are invariably qualitative and require knowledge of power relationships within organizational theory as well as experience of those relationships within a particular workplace.

It is argued here that since OD sought to challenge traditional training as a result of the Industrial Training Act of 1964 (Leitch and Harrison, 1996) and replace it with organizational learning, HRD might be described as a search for the mechanisms of the approach through the HRD specialist who is able to synchronize personal and organizational learning with the organization's strategy. HRD can be seen as the drive to deal with contemporary issues in order to develop intrapreneurialism, promote a long-term focus, instil a learning-oriented culture, and focus on high quality products and services. Thus, Stewart and McGoldrick (1996) identify HRD as a specific type of subject located more at the learning end of the OD continuum. This is similar to the position identified by Nadler and Nadler (1989) who see HRD as organized learning experiences provided for the purpose of improving job performance and personal growth and development, and Harrison (1992) who views HRD as fundamentally concerned with developing people as part of an overall human resource strategy.

Referring back to Table 4.1, HRD specialists are likely to be located somewhere between the quasi-professional and the practitioner/manager because of their focal concern for organizational learning. The competence of the HRD change agent is likely to be more limited than that of the OD consultant but will, at the very least, include *knowledge* of: (a) the organization's strategic direction; (b) change management; and (c) organizational learning; the internal environment (its size, structure, traditions); the external environment (organizational trends and developments, international and national economic changes, technological change, influence of national cultures, industry sector characteristics, actions of competitors). Like the OD consultant, humanistic values are central to the role. The *experience* of the HRD professional is likely to result from knowledge of HRM strategy and managerial expertise with cross-functional responsibilities for line management.

Strategic Human Resource Development has a promising future as a vehicle to promote personal and organizational learning. Central to this development is a better operational understanding of organizational strategy, on the one hand, and an understanding of the knowledge and skills of OD practitioners, on the other. Strategic Human Resource Development will develop its true potential when it identifies its core knowledge and skills. One way of doing this is to identify the skills and knowledge of the Strategic Human Resource Development professional by focusing on the role of the internal agent of change. The journey metaphor inherent in OD is also critical to the development of Strategic Human Resource Development as a form of internal organizational intervention.

STRATEGIC HUMAN RESOURCE DEVELOPMENT: THE TRIGGERS FOR CHANGE

Strategic Human Resource Development has emerged as a result of two pressures. First, the new climate of disorganized capitalism and, second, from the internal developments and debates within Organizational Development. This general direction seeks to replace overt control-oriented cultures with organizational cultures characterized by creativity and learning.

One of the most recent images to emerge is that of the knowledge-centred company in which personal and organizational learning is central to the future growth and development of the organization. The knowledge-centred company is based on the claim that information, knowledge and learning are central to organizations operating in a more sophisticated marketplace and with employees whose needs and aspirations are more demanding than hitherto. For example, it is argued that:

> One of the key characteristics of the debate on the evolution of the socio-economic environment of business in advanced industrial economies at the end of the twentieth century is the progressive emphasis on a knowledge-centred culture in which learning is central to the survival and growth of all organisations. (Leitch and Harrison, 1996: 31)

A major reason for this is that the 'relentless change in market expectations and the demands for new products have seen the gradual replacement of capital and labour intensive firms by knowledge intensive firms, and routine work by knowledge work' (Tenkasi and Boland, 1996: 79; Starbuck, 1992). Consequently, it is argued that 'knowledge work involves the creation of new understandings of nature, organisations or markets and their application by a firm in valued technologies, products or processes' (Boland and Tenkasi, 1995). While we can observe the nature of knowledge work in high technology environments, various writers are beginning to comment about the need to apply the knowledge-intensive/learning metaphor to all organizations because of the increased complexity of operating environments (see, for example, Drucker 1988). Others have argued that the reasons for the emergence of the knowledge-intensive firm will require a post-HRM solution to the flexible organization. For example it has been argued that 'to consider knowledge a mere variable will keep HRM locked in increasingly obsolete models of organisation, to the detriment of HRM practitioners and their organisations. The evidence suggests that organisations are fast becoming knowledge communities and HRM must broaden its perspective to keep pace' (Despres and Hiltrop, 1995: 10).

HRM, as it emerged in the 1980s, was increasingly challenged by the demands of the knowledge-intensive organization, precipitating a deeper consideration of many issues related to the flexible firm, including the need to ensure an adequate supply of knowledge workers; the need to identify, develop and evaluate knowledge workers and their outputs; the ability to motivate and reward knowledge workers in order to maximize productivity and enhance quality; the ability to structure the organization in order to facilitate change transitions to new organizational forms (ibid). The emergence of Strategic Human Resource Development can therefore be seen as an organizational solution to strategic issues which include the importance of new technology, the drive for quality, internationalization of business, the need for more flexible and responsive organizations, and the supply of resources (Garavan et al:, 1995).

Strategic human resource development and the drivers of change

A Strategic Human Resource Development perspective is informed by four debates that force us to recognize the importance of pro-active change to organizations in the twenty-first century. These debates have not only informed our history, they will shape our future. First, is the argument that internal changes to an organization should be considered in relation to key contingencies and from technology in particular. This is the *contingency perspective* of which the work of Burns and Stalker (1961) and Woodward (1965) are classic examples. Second, is the argument that change results from the internal dynamics of pluralistic organizations in which different interest groups seek change that maximizes their own interests and resist changes that minimize their interests. This is the *labour process* approach. Third, is the argument that change today is driven by enlightened consumers whose insatiable appetites have forced organizations to replace mass-produced goods and services with niche products. This is the *flexible specialization* thesis. The fourth view is represented by the fact that organizations are managed by key players (managers) who make decisions. These decisions appear to be rational but that rationality is itself circumscribed by political boundaries. This is the *strategic choice* approach (Figure 4.1).

FIGURE 4.1
The drivers of
change

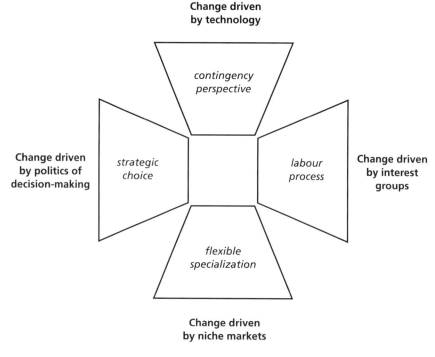

The contingency approach emphasized technology as the most important variable in modern organizations. Success was seen to depend upon the usual open systems assumptions about adaptation except that the organization structure was seen to be determined by the requirements of the technology. Thus, successful management depended on the degree of integration between the various systems. For example, between technology (as the productive system) and organizational structure (as the management control systems). Thus automation, which was characteristic of the high period of modernism, required impersonal management control systems to be designed into the technology. This type of 'productive bureaucracy' therefore required the monitoring, rather than involvement of the activities of the workforce.

By contrast, the labour process approach challenged the assumptions that technology, *per se*, determines change. Rather, organizational change was seen to result from the attempt to control the labour process. As a result, management control systems emerge as a direct result of management intervention in the inevitable contest between the interests of capital, on the one hand, and labour, on the other. Thus, whereas technology was the main determinant for researchers such as Joan Woodward, researchers from a labour process perspective, such as Harry Braverman, saw the key determinant as control of the workforce with technology viewed as a mechanism in this process. When new technology is used, it is used as a strategic weapon in the struggle to maximise profit, principally through the deskilling of job content and secondarily by the attempt to remove control over the execution of tasks by workers themselves. The classic example here was, of course, Fordism.

The flexible specialization thesis viewed change as a result of transformations in markets and products. The use of technology was therefore seen as a way of enhancing design and ultimately profitability. This approach viewed technological innovation as an attempt to disentangle the unintended consequences of Fordism and mass consumer goods by replacing them with relatively low volume, niche markets. Perhaps the central assumption here was the attempt to solve the adversarial politics of the workplace that had emerged as a result of the Fordist work process with its machine-like characteristics. As McLoughlin and Clark (1994) have argued:

> According to the thesis, during the late nineteenth century and early twentieth century major economies such as the USA and Britain experienced a shift from a craft mode to a Fordist mode of industrial organization, based around the provision of high volume standardized products to a mass market using relatively inflexible production technology and work organization. The workplace characteristics of a detailed division of labour, low-skilled jobs and tight management control promoted adversarial types of industrial relations. In the late twentieth century changes in product markets and production systems are stimulating developments which suggest that a 'second industrial divide' is taking place. Here, in response to the saturation of mass markets, and using the capabilities of new computing and information technologies, innovative firms are developing more differentiated products for consumption in specialized markets. These are being produced at low volume and cost through the combination of flexible technology and flexible modes of working. Jobs are reskilled and industrial relations more cooperative. (1994: 62)

The assumptions of the strategic choice perspective differ from the other three perspectives because of its methodological orientation. Although largely phenomenological, it originated within industrial sociology during the 1960s and with the action perspective of David Silverman in particular. Since then it has developed through symbolic interactionism and other phenomenologically driven approaches to the social world of work.

The approach was effectively named by John Child (1972) who, according to McLoughlin and Clark, made an important early contribution to this social action approach and 'introduced the concept of "strategic choice" as a means of emphasizing the role of managerial choice, rather than technology, in shaping work and organization' (McLoughlin and Clark, 1994: 56). This suggests that the major focus should be with the process of decision-making in organizations although, as Child suggests, decisions may be informed by any of the factors previously discussed by other perspectives, especially those of the labour process theory. The value of the strategic choice perspective is that:

> it draws attention to the question of who makes decisions in organizations and why they are made. This is a useful antidote to the perspectives discussed above, which tend to portray technological change, and forms of work and organization, as though they were independent of the goals and

objectives of organizational actors in particular cases. Child argues, in contrast, that decision-making is a political process whereby strategic choices on issues such as long-term organizational objectives, the allocation of resources and organizational design are normally initiated and taken by a 'power-holding group' or 'dominant coalition' within the organization. (McLoughlin and Clark, 1994: 56-7)

Strategic choice suggests that an organization's strategic choices are made in three general areas: (a) domain (e.g. type of industry, market, competitors, suppliers and, more generally, the limitations and constraints facing their organization, (see Porter, 1980); (b) structures and systems (refers to choices made about how centralized, standardized and specialized an organization's activities will be. Thus the structure may be organic or mechanistic and decision-making systems may be participative or authoritarian, (see Dyck, 1994); and (c) performance standards (which partly determine the extent of flexibility an organization has within its economic environment. For example, 'performance standards based on market share will lead to the creation of market share data and competitor monitoring; performance standards based on innovativeness will lead to familiarity with technological literature and R&D; and performance standards based on reducing costs will lead to the development of cost controls' [Dyck, 1994]).

It is particularly in the area of performance standards where, as Dyck (1994) suggests, unacceptable performance based on these standards may lead to the old dominant coalition being succeeded by the new guard.

Taken together, these three strategic choices constitute what here will be called an organization's 'strategic configuration' and once 'a particular configuration has been chosen it is very difficult to transform and the organization tends to experience extended periods of equilibrium' (ibid.: 48). This has significant implications for organizational change since 'the only changes that do occur are convergent changes which are consistent with, and serve to fine-tune, the interrelationships among the sub-components within the configuration. Therefore it is difficult to add transformational "sustainable development" to one component without transforming the entire configuration' (ibid. 48).

STRATEGIC CHANGE AND LEARNING

Managing strategic change has been transformed by the economic climate since the end of the Second World War and three influences can be identified. Up to the mid-1960s, competition was limited to local and national borders. By the late 1960s and 1970s, many companies became more selective about the markets they would invest in and diversified to enhance future growth. Consequently, strategy became even more adversarial (Porter, 1980). Until relatively recently the critical variables of market size and the number and size of the key competitors in a given industry could be identified. During the late 1980s and 1990s, however, globalization and the geopolitical upheavals that have overtaken former communist countries have created flux and uncertainty. Managing strategic change has therefore become a movable feast. For example, Boisot has raised a number of questions about the uncertainty of the future driven by new formations of capitalism:

> Are we still moving towards a global economic order as predicted by many strategy gurus, or are we reverting to competition in territorial units even smaller than the nation state itself, i.e. the Crimea, Serbia, Moldavia, Catalonia, Corsica, Scotland, etc.? Or, more perplexing still, are we moving towards both situations simultaneously? Underlying such questions are more basic ones. Of what strategic value is forecasting or competitor analysis in the face of geopolitical discontinuities of such seismic proportions as the disintegration of the former Soviet Empire? How helpful are these analytical tools in coping with turbulence? (1995: 32)

Following Boisot, strategists appear to have responded to the increasing rates of change or turbulence by adopting four basic types of response: *strategic planning, emergent strategy, intrapreneurship,* and *strategic intent* (ibid.: 32).

Strategic planning, for example, is a legacy of the relatively stable past 'when the environment was changing sufficiently slowly for an effective corporate response to emerge from methodical organizational routines' such as the collection of large quantities of data 'on a periodic basis from the base of the corporate pyramid and sent towards the top for processing'. The top then 'extracts a pattern from the data that tells it what is going on both within the firm as well as in the external environment' then, 'on the basis of the pattern it perceives, it . . . decides on a course of action that is subsequently transmitted downward towards the base of the organization for its implementation.' (ibid.: 33).

Emergent strategy describes an organization-wide process of incremental adjustment to environmental states that cannot be discerned or anticipated through a prior analysis of data (Mintzberg and Waters, 1985). A single coherent picture constructed at the top of the organization is therefore not available because the operating environment has become increasingly complex with analysis and decision-making potential decentralized to meet speedier responses to customer needs. Thus, 'the strategic level of the organization cannot act like an all-seeing central planner because threats will emerge which have to be dealt with incrementally in ways not originally foreseen by the strategy' (Boisot, 1995: 33). One reason for this is that

> the data needed for dealing with them will not necessarily be located at the strategic level but may be found at any location within the organization. If time does not allow for the upward transmission of data through the prescribed channels, an adequate response to it may have to be formulated and often in an *ad hoc* way, with the rest of the organization adjusting to such local behaviour only subsequently. (ibid.: 33)

Intrapreneurship appears to be a strategy more likely to be used when the environmental turbulence facing the company is high and when incremental adaptation is not a viable option because the company becomes less integrated and 'threats and opportunities emerge that have to be dealt with locally, but now with little or no understanding of how they may affect the organization as a whole' (ibid.: 33). The strategy is therefore a high-risk solution in the attempt to solve the problem of vulnerability:

> Here, of course, we are at the polar opposite of the strategic planning process: not only can environmental turbulence not be reduced through analytical means, but action has to be taken at whatever point in the organization has the capacity and the willingness to act on very partial and ill-understood 'noisy' data. With intrapreneurship, the world is purely Heraclitan; all is flux and the top of the firm has no privileged insight into what to do since any intended strategy it may have pursued has all but been submerged. Of necessity, then, the firm must decentralize and operate as a loosely coupled system. Intrapreneurship can only be effective where the opportunistic behaviour it requires of particular individuals can be placed at the service of the firm as well as those individuals themselves. This is not always easy to achieve since an equitable matching of risks and rewards between individuals and firms cannot be ensured. Often intrapreneurship works at the expense of the firms that try to foster it. It requires a degree *of trust* between the players that cannot be taken for granted and that is continuously being placed under strain by the very turbulence for which it is designed to compensate. (ibid.: 35)

Strategic intent describes a process of coping with turbulence 'through a direct, intuitive understanding, emanating from the top of a firm and guiding its efforts' (ibid.: 36). Thus because a turbulent environment 'cannot be tamed by rational analysis alone . . . it does not follow that a firm's adaptive response must be left to a random distribution of lone individuals acting opportunistically and often in isolation as in a regime of intrapreneurship'. Strategic intent relies on an 'intuitively formed pattern or *gestalt* – some would call it a vision – to give it unity and coherence' (ibid.). Strategic intent creates a potential solution by enabling all employees to identify with the vision or mental image of an intended future state. This appears to be more like a process of corporate benchmarking in order to develop the company at the expense of the opposition (Hamel and Prahalad, 1989).

The major benefit of this strategy appears to be the coherence given to the image and the energy employed by employees to bring about the changes to corporate strategy:

> To counter the centrifugal tendencies that plague the decentralized intrapreneurial firm, the one operating in a regime of strategic intent can use a common vision to keep the behaviour of its employees aligned with a common purpose when it decentralizes in response to turbulence. Intended strategy then gets realized in spite of any turbulence. It succeeds by remaining simple and intelligible and by avoiding a level of detail that might quickly be rendered obsolete by events. (Boisot, 1995: 37)

FOUR CENTRAL CHARACTERISTICS OF STRATEGIC HUMAN RESOURCE DEVELOPMENT

At the heart of the Strategic Human Resource Development approach are four main characteristics. First, is the need to see HRD as business strategy. Second is the need to devolve responsibility to line managers. Third, is the need to replace the concept of training with learning. Fourth, is the need to emphasize workplace learning, see Figure 4.2.

Strategic human resource development as a strategic intervention

Strategic Human Resource Development views the development of human resources as a strategic advantage. Through business strategy both organizational and employee development are facilitated. Organizational change is driven at three levels: at the organizational, at the group and at the individual level. However, Strategic Human Resource Development does not just reflect the strategy of senior managers. Senior managers may be informed equally by the internal development of products or of service design. This means that the mission may be influenced as much by internal developments from teams or from individuals as much as, or perhaps more than, by external market trends. The role of senior management is to extract a pattern from the data to ascertain the internal and external drivers for change. Then, on the basis of the pattern detected, to decide on a course of action. The strategic level of the organization can no longer act as an all-seeing central planner because threats will emerge which have to be dealt with incrementally in ways not originally foreseen by the strategy.

Devolved responsibility to line managers

Line managers are required to facilitate change by developing individuals and teams. This necessitates the development of key skills, the acquisition of appropriate knowledge, and the ability to be driven by values and an ethical responsibility. Each is reinforced by their application to the workplace. As facilitators in the development of their staff, line managers are required to stimulate and develop creativity either as mentors or as change agents. This is a pro-active organization-wide process of incremental adjustment. It requires decentralized decision making to meet speedier responses to customer needs. Where time does not permit the upward transmission of data, then *ad hoc* adjustments will have to be made with information passed on subsequently to inform changes to strategy.

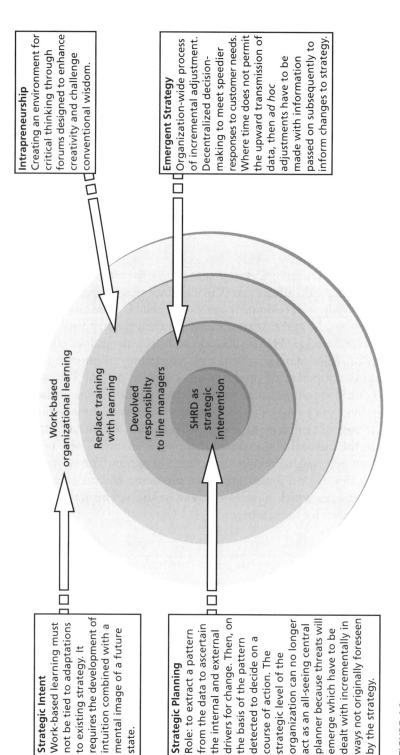

Intrapreneurship
Creating an environment for critical thinking through forums designed to enhance creativity and challenge conventional wisdom.

Emergent Strategy
Organization-wide process of incremental adjustment. Decentralized decision-making to meet speedier responses to customer needs. Where time does not permit the upward transmission of data, then *ad hoc* adjustments have to be made with information passed on subsequently to inform changes to strategy.

Work-based organizational learning

Replace training with learning

Devolved responsibility to line managers

SHRD as strategic intervention

Strategic Intent
Work-based learning must not be tied to adaptations to existing strategy. It requires the development of intuition combined with a mental image of a future state.

Strategic Planning
Role: to extract a pattern from the data to ascertain the internal and external drivers for change. Then, on the basis of the pattern detected to decide on a course of action. The strategic level of the organization can no longer act as an all-seeing central planner because threats will emerge which have to be dealt with incrementally in ways not originally foreseen by the strategy.

FIGURE 4.2
The four central characteristics of Strategic Human Resource Development

Replacing training with learning

Learning, in this sense, is required to go beyond the passive stimulus and response principles of training programmes. It follows from the previous point that the development of the imagination, the intellect and the collective synergy of groups or teams will be focused on creativity. This will occur either as new product or service design or as creative problem-solving. The most important criterion is the need to challenge the conventional wisdom. By its nature this will involve many experimental ideas to fire up the intellect and the imagination.

Work-based organizational learning

Work-based learning (WBL) is already central to HRD. However, a much greater emphasis is needed on the development of organizational learning. That is, on the continuous development of processes and activities within the organization. At the very least the idea of development would require the establishment of a culture of creativity. Work-based learning must not be tied to adaptations of existing strategy. It requires the development of intuition combined with a mental image of a future state.

The skills, competence and knowledge of the strategic human resource development practitioner

The skills, competence and knowledge of the Strategic Human Resource Development practitioner will depend upon the place the SHRD practitioner occupies in the organization. As facilitators, they will have received professional knowledge and training in behavioural/organizational science (including group dynamics, decision-making, and communications) and have come to specialize in the application of creative solutions to knowledge and techniques in order to develop pro-active change. By contrast, line managers are more likely to acquire these in a more piecemeal way as a result of the tasks they are required to oversee. Some organizations will seek to develop line managers by rotating them into a variety of roles so that they can gain skills and experience needed for higher-level management positions. Table 4.2 illustrates how these differences may occur although it is clear that there is a minimum level of awareness required by line managers.

CONCLUSION

Strategic Human Resource Development has emerged to advance a more enlightened, methodological, ethical and skills-focused change management that puts human resources back where they belong – at the top of the change

	Strategic HRD professional	Line manager
SKILLS		
Process consultation	*	
Diagnostic	*	
Intrapersonal	*	*
Interpersonal	*	*
Presentational	*	*
Research methods	*	
Analytical	*	*
Problem solving	*	*
KNOWLEDGE		
Organizational development	*	*
Organizational behaviour	*	
Methodological	*	
Data collection	*	
Organizational trends and developments	*	
VALUES AND ETHICS		
Humanistic	*	*
Ethical	*	*
EXPERIENCE		
Organizational	*	*
Strategic/managerial	*	*
Cross-functional	*	*

agenda. Strategic Human Resource Development is defined by three things. First, it recognizes the complexities of change management. In particular, that change does not simply result from a linear and cascaded top-down strategy. Indeed, it may be developed as much from within the organization as from the pressure of external forces. Second, it seeks to reposition the HRD perspective by rescuing it from a confused and mundane existence in the depths of training programmes. Finally, it results from a refined OD perspective which provides direction for the twenty-first century.

Strategic Human Resource Development can be distinguished by four main characteristics: a focus on the organization's business strategy; responsibility devolved to line managers; an employee-centred approach to learning embracing employees and managers alike; and an emphasis on workplace learning. Strategic Human Resource Development focuses on the development of personal skills and learning in order to achieve personal and organizational transformation.

FURTHER READING

The classic text on change is Lewin's (1952) three stages of change which reflects the essence of the traditional OD approach. Cummings and Worley (1997) is a useful and practical text on traditional Organizational Development and change and the text by Hamlin et al. (2001) provides practitioners and change agents with a reflective guide through the practice today. Reasons for failure have been described by Church et al. (1996) and Edmonstone and Havergal (1995) provide an interesting account of how critical challenges are removed from change programmes. Pettigrew's (1985) account of change at ICI has become a classic and Dawson's (1994; 2002) processual approach illustrates the difficulties of strategic planning. The origins of Human Resource Development can be found in the controversial debate between Swanson (1995; 1999) and McLean (1998). The development of knowledge-intensive firms and the implications for managing knowledge work are described in Tenkasi and Boland's (1996) text. To understand the importance of emergent strategy *vis-à-vis* and organization-wide incremental adjustment, the work of Mintzberg and Waters (1985) is useful.

5
Consultants, clients and change agents

INTRODUCTION

Since the late 1980s, there have been various attempts to address the dominance of rational, linear, planned OD approaches to change. The more recent focus on processual and emergent change is intended to draw attention to the routine issues – the attitudes, behaviours, actions and the unintended consequences of previous actions which are influenced by the history and by the internal politics of the organization – which determine the effective management of change. Furthermore, as organizations struggle to survive in a global marketplace, it is necessary to move away from viewing change as (a) a series of strategic episodes (the Strategic Management approach) and (b) a limited diagnostic relationship between the consultant and individual client. If processes informing internal dynamics have been paid particular attention in the recent change literature, as indicated in Chapter 4, then the dynamics of decision-making and employee involvement have forced change agents to appreciate the views of internal stakeholders. The most important aspect of the processual approach, however, is the recognition that change, borne of imagination and creative thinking, can

FIGURE 5.1

Historical, processual and contextual issues

HISTORICAL ISSUES
may include:

How change was managed in the past.
How management control had been exercised.
The design of the organization.
The decision-making process.
The growth of the organization.
The development of leadership.
The nature and extent of employee and management development.
The history of employee/management relationships.

PROCESSUAL ISSUES
may include:

- The extent to which change is proactive, driven by intrapreneurial actions, group learning and is devolved.
- The extent to which expertise is devolved through SHRD concentrating on the continuous development of tasks, skills and ideas.
- The ability to evaluate whether the organization's culture needs to change or whether to introduce change to fit the organization's culture.
- Continually defining organizational reality by tuning in to different ideological arguments by identifying whose interests the change serves – shareholders, citizens, customers and internal stakeholders?

CONTEXTUAL ISSUES
may include:

The politics of the organization: for example, how change has been managed; the nature of management control.
The leadership or management style: for example, participative or confrontational styles.
The extent of employee involvement: for example, the degree to which decision-making is devolved; the extent to which social relationships are built around team needs and the collective accomplishment of tasks; the ability to redesign jobs.
Mechanisms for managing change: for example, decision-making, employee and management development, creative thinking.

emerge from within the organization. I refer to this as *pro-active* change and it is the subject of Strategic Human Resource Development. It is contrasted to *reactive* change – the planned approaches – which are led by senior managers who react to changes in the external environment or are seeking out dysfunctions within existing practices, and informed often by management consultants. Pro-active change seeks to develop enterprise within the organization through human resources. It is strategic because it is informed not only by existing strategy but also informs changes to the strategy of the organization. This was illustrated by Figure 4.2.

Strategic Human Resource Development requires an understanding of organizational dynamics. Change agents must focus on the historical, processual and contextual issues that inform change (see Figure 5.1). The ability to analyse situations, mobilize commitment, and establish mechanisms for change requires the expertise of the change agent. Seen this way, change now becomes a learning process because it seeks to facilitate individual learning, group or team learning and organizational learning.

The learning objectives for this chapter are:

1   *The nature of management consultancy* which suggests that management consultants package their products to overcome the perceived intangibility of the consultancy service. By re-defining it as a product they are also able to build in a situation of client dependency.
2   *Strategic Human Resource Development and the role of the change agent* which is contrasted with management consultancy. It is argued that Strategic Human Resource Development, like OD consultancy, has no such pretensions to be neutral and recognizes the inevitability of a values-driven position. By contrast to management consultancy, Strategic Human Resource Development seeks to develop competencies within the organization rather than to package the expert's product.
3   *Using diagnostic techniques* which looks at process consultation and argues that being a consultant or change agent involves employing diagnostic techniques. Process consultation requires the change agent to engage employees in joint diagnosis by asking questions in order to identify the appropriate type of intervention. In addition, the consultant has to decide on the depth of the intervention.
4   *Turning data into knowledge* which argues for the need to search for appropriate data by applying a theoretical frame of reference. This is discussed in relation to four metaphors: the machine, organism, drama and discourse.

THE NATURE OF CONSULTANCY

Management consultancy: building a product base by creating dependency

In Chapter 4 it was argued that some aspects of organizational development had been sanitized and made safe from critical challenges by the role of the consultant. This meant that the mechanics of change are often manipulated by unskilled change agents who adopt the safety of the recipe book by applying problem-solving tools and techniques (Edmonstone and Havergal, 1995) and fail to pay sufficient attention to the processes of change. The result has often meant that internal and external consultants become either problem-page agony aunts while managers become ratchet tighteners. By 2002 the willingness of the employees to commit to change appears to have decreased in many organizations. Reasons often cited for this have been a 'change weariness syndrome' as employees are exposed to 'multiple transitions' resulting from Business Process Reengineering, TQM, downsizing, changes in strategy and other transitions (Marks, 1997: 268).

Turbulent environments have forced external management consultants to offer their services as a product. This, in turn, increases the dependency of managers on an external consultant. The ability to construct and sell 'expert' packages to organizations invariably creates a state of dependency with management consultants showing the way through the guide book. The tendency in recent years to become increasingly dependent on expertise sold as if it was a product is explained by Burgundy:

> In particular I am concerned that the relationship between managers and consultants has changed. As managers have been forced to face an increasingly turbulent and capricious business environment, they have come to rely, more and more, on the advice and guidance of management consultants. For example, we have seen managers turning to consultants for advice on issues such as total quality management (TQM), 'reengineering' and empowerment, to name but a few. Yet with management increasingly reliant on consultants for advice, innovation and support, the traditional relationship between power broker and messenger seems to have flipped so that nowadays it seems that the consultants are the key power brokers in the relationship with the result that the messengers now shoot the managers. (1996: 28)

In recent years, for example, McKinsey sold its BPR consultancy product as 'core process redesign'. The Boston Consulting Group sold its product of 'time-based management' (TBM). Ernst & Young sold their product of BPR method using IT called 'Navigator'. Andersen Consulting sold two parallel and integrated processes – one focusing on the organizational and human side of the change, the other on the technical or information systems development side (see Werr et al., 1997). The study of consulting approaches by Werr et al. suggests that management consultants package their products to overcome the perceived intangibility of the consultancy service. But, by redefining it as a product they are also able to build in a situation of dependency:

> The methods are thus part of a more general institutionalization of competence, which has the double function of facilitating the introduction and socialization of newly recruited consultants and of increasing the organisational (in contrast to the individual consultant's) component in the 'product' sold to the client, thus binding the consultant to the company. (Werr et al., 1997: 303)

Critics of the management consultancy literature argue that it tends to be '*fragmented* and *discursive* at best' (Lundberg, 1997) and *atheoretical* (Gallessich, 1985). Product dependency is created largely because consultants are often 'wrapped in a mystery' (Lundberg, 1997). Lundberg's proposal for a general model of consultancy suggests that it should meet a number of criteria, such as:

1   Not relying on esoteric or created constructs; where possible, it would utilize existing ideas and convey them using familiar language.
2   Ideologically neutral, and not managerially, scientifically, humanistically or critically biased.
3   Encompassing all the major schools of thought in management and being potentially compatible with all of the dominant frames/ perspectives on organizations.
4   Applicable to alternative ontological positions about the nature of reality.
5   Promoting future-oriented explanations, that is, it should be predictive and hence teleological in form, over past-only explanations, eschewing *post-hoc*, causative-explicative forms.
6   Explicit about its theoretic purpose, consciously trading off among the purposes of precision, simplicity and generality.

Although this is a useful list of recommendations, problems emerge with points 2 and 3. For example, it is unlikely that all the authors cited (for example, Bolman and Deal, 1991; Morgan and Smircich, 1980; and Weick, 1979) would agree with the possibility of neutrality since this is influenced by the methodology adopted and by the assumptions of the consultant. Furthermore, the attempt to encompass all schools of thought is unrealistic since this assumes they are complementary rather than competing forms of interpretation based on incommensurate paradigms of knowledge.

In this way, it is argued that 'management gurus offer certainty and a potential route through the complexities of modern management life' (Clark, 1995: 120). This is done by unfreezing existing attitudes, values and beliefs with one of two forms of persuasion: either the promise of the economic benefit, hoping that, as a result, performance will improve, or persuasion by the empirical foundations of the ideas being promulgated, refreezing to reinforce and permanently to fix the change (Clark, 1995: 124).

Management consultancy, therefore, has three major problems associated with it:

1   Failure to diagnose critical problems.
2   The need to sell a product fails to focus on building the competencies and thinking required for pro-active change from within the organization.
3   Over-dependency on outside expertise tends to maintain top-down management controls and maintain functional dependency.

STRATEGIC HUMAN RESOURCES DEVELOPMENT AND THE ROLE OF THE CHANGE AGENT

While management consultancy often claims to be neutral, Strategic Human Resource Development, like OD consultancy, has no such pretensions and recognizes the inevitability of a values-driven position. In contrast to management consultancy, Strategic Human Resource Development seeks to develop competencies within the organization rather than package the expert's product and create dependency.

The study of competencies has developed from three main routes: human resources literature; the business strategy literature, and the OD literature. The human resources literature argues that the jobs of individuals are highly influenced by a set of competencies that determines the skills and knowledge required for successful job performance (Spencer and Spencer, 1993). This argument suggests that organizations should focus on identifying individuals with appropriate competencies and locating them at appropriate levels in the organization. The strategy literature has been influenced by the work of Prahalad and Hamel (1990) who argue that corporations can identify a relatively small number of competencies that provide competitive advantage in the marketplace. It is, however, to the OD literature that we need to turn for the development of change agent competencies.

The role of the change agent

In their discussion of generic skills, Cummings and Huse (1989) argued that OD practitioners should possess three types of skill in order to deal with complexity and ambiguity. These are: (a) intrapersonal skills which are related to conceptual and analytical ability; (b) interpersonal skills, to create and maintain effective relationships by dealing with members' perceptions; and (c) consultation skills, which include organizational diagnosis, and the ability to design and execute interventions.

For Carnall, managing change is comparable to conducting an orchestra. The role of the change agent requires similar skills to that of the conductor in order to 'energise and motivate, build cohesion, create a sense of pace and timing, and provide a skilled performance while sustaining the performance of others' (1995: 159). To be successful at this activity requires four core competencies which demand that the change agent is able (a) to make decisions; (b) to build coalitions; (c) to achieve action; and (d) to maintain the momentum and effort required for the change initiative. Each core competency contains elements that identify specific skills to be achieved by the change agent. Similarly, Buchanan and Boddy (1992) identify a 'model of expertise' containing five clusters of attributes that appear to complement those identified by Carnall. These refer to abilities to define goals, to manage role relationships, to communicate effectively and to negotiate with key players and, finally, to 'manage up' by being skilled in the art of organizational politics.

Like Carnall, Buchanan and Boddy suggest that the acquisition of knowledge and skills is contingent on the characteristics of the organization. Thus, 'the expertise of the change agent is contextual' (Buchanan and Boddy, 1992: 115) and requires the change agent to learn how to choose which competencies are appropriate for a given situation. The choices are clearly mediated by organizational culture, leadership style and the extent of commitment throughout the organization. But the change agent has to manage three variables simultaneously: the *content* of change itself, the *context* (history, market situation, etc.) and the *process* (interpersonal factors) of change. From an interactional perspective, it follows that the main skill is the ability to establish legitimacy for change 'while conforming to accepted custom and practice in the culture of the organization' (ibid.: 70).

The recommendations offered by Carnall, and Buchanan and Boddy for developing competencies have focused on strategic leadership. Strategic Human Resource Development drives this argument for the development of internal change agent competences further down the organization because it was previously illustrated how the focus on pro-active change (the processual factors that drives change internally) is potentially more important than reactive change (the traditional planned change approach, which focused on either restoring equilibrium or reacting to the changes in the marketplace). Strategic Human Resource Development argues that in situations of pro-active incremental change, one of the key factors in the success of the change programme is the devolution of responsibilities further down the managerial line.

Examples of the various types of Strategic Human Resource Development interventions were illustrated in Table 1.1 on pp. 26 and 27. These consisted of five types of change intervention:

1   *acceptant* change which dealt with subjective attitudes;
2   *catalytic* change which was responsible for transforming the situation in some way by the change agent acting as catalyst;
3   *confrontation* which is requested by various parties;
4   *prescriptive* change which is forced on people;
5   *principles, models and theories* which inform the various OD/Strategic Human Resource Development interventions.

Each of these intervention strategies require a *modus operandi* which involved managing the relationship between the client and consultant through process consultation and employing diagnostic and expert practices that result from the application of behavioural skills and knowledge.

Managing the relationship between the client and consultant through process consultation

Both Carnall and Buchanan and Body focus on the internal change agent. By contrast, external consultants are used for a variety of reasons but predominantly as catalysts of change. Since this book is concerned with internal change agents, then it is necessary to elaborate how the relationship between the client and consultant is established through process consultation. In this respect, Schein (1997) provided principles for managing the relationship between the client and consultant. These seek to establish a partnership between the client(s) and the consultant in which ownership of the problem and the solution always lies with the client. However, care must be taken with the way in which the change agent engages with the client system:

> Any helping or change process always has a target or a client. In most discussions of consultation we refer to 'clients' as if they were always clearly identifiable, but in reality the question of who actually is the client can be ambiguous and problematical. One can find oneself not knowing for whom one is working, or working with several clients whose goals are in conflict with each other. One can identify 'targets' of change – others whose problems we can see clearly but who do not see their own problems and would resist being seen as 'clients'. One can be working with an individual, with a small or large group, or with a slice of a total organisation in a large meeting. One can be working with the same individual but in different roles, at one time counselling her as an individual manager, and at another time helping her design a large-scale intervention to bring two of her divisions into a collaborative relationship with each other. (Schein, 1997b: 202)

Problems of client over-dependence may occur if the consultant is defined unwittingly by the client as the 'expert' rather than as the catalyst in search of joint diagnosis, problem identification and solving. The client's expectations have to be managed away from dependency by engaging the activities and knowledge of other stakeholders in the organization. To clarify this Schein attempts to identify various clients:

1   Contact clients (those individual(s) who first contact the consultant with a request, question or issue).
2   Intermediate clients (the individuals or groups who or which get involved in various interviews, meetings, and other activities as the project evolves).
3   Primary clients (the individual(s) who ultimately 'own' the problem or issue being worked on; they are typically also the ones who pay the consulting bills or whose budget covers the consultation project).
4   Unwitting clients (or those who will be affected by the interventions but who are not aware of it yet).
5   Indirect clients (members of the organization who are aware that they will be affected by the interventions but who are unknown to the consultant).
6   Ultimate clients (such as 'the community, the total organisation, an occupational group, or any other group that the consultant cares about and whose welfare must be considered in any intervention that the consultant makes').

Once the client system is established, the *modus operandi* is process consultation. This is defined as a helping relationship that seeks to diagnose the clinical needs of the client through which the pathological needs of the client system are operationalized:

> When I first formulated the concept of process consultation and contrasted it with being an 'expert' or a 'doctor' in a helping relationship, I was trying

to argue that a model which I am now calling a 'clinical' model starts instead with the needs of the client, is client driven and involves the researcher in the client's issues rather than involving the client in the researcher's issues. The word clinical is deliberately introduced here in order to highlight that some perceived pathology is usually involved and that the helper takes on the obligations that are associated with being in the helping professions, i.e. the interests and the welfare of the client must be protected at all times, and all of the helper's actions, whether diagnostic or not, are de facto interventions and must be evaluated as interventions before they are undertaken. This clinical model is often also lumped into 'action research', but is fundamentally different in that the initiative remains at all times with the client. (Schein, 1995: 15)

It is imperative that the change agent recognizes that each stage of organizational diagnosis may also involve an unwitting intervention carrying unintended consequences:

If they [the workforce] acquiesce they simply reinforce the very pathology that may need to be addressed, or worse they may damage themselves by revealing data to a superior who may take advantage of it. On the other hand, if they refuse or participate only in a token fashion, they may either distort the data or create a revolt that the CEO may not have anticipated and may not know how to deal with. In both cases what is wrong is that the consultant did not operate from a clinical model which would have forced him or her to consider what the clinical consequences would be of gathering data in a certain fashion.

It is my contention that a clinical process must a priori consider all of these possibilities and must involve the initial client in an up-front process of jointly figuring out each next step. The consultant must raise the question of what would be the consequence of interviewing the subordinates or doing the survey, of how the data would be fed back and what kinds of confidentiality would be guaranteed. Of greatest importance at this stage is also to share with the contact client the possible outcomes, especially the possibility that the data will reveal a problem in the relationship of the client to the people who will be interviewed or surveyed. In other words, what if a lot of negative data comes out about the boss who is launching the project? Is he or she ready for it? How will they handle the feedback? (ibid.: 15)

USING DIAGNOSTIC TECHNIQUES

Process consultation adopts an agenda which assumes that being a consultant involves employing diagnostic and expert practices that result from the application of skills and knowledge. This is similar to a doctor/patient relationship (Schein, 1987; 1988; 1997; Cummings and Huse, 1989). Process consultation requires the change agent to 'engage organisation members in diagnosis' by asking the 'right questions' in relation to the level of intervention (organizational, group and individual) and by collecting and analysing information through a variety of methodological techniques, including the use of statistics, survey techniques and force-field analysis (Cummings and Huse, 1989: 64-105). Therefore, process consultation requires the change agent to involve the organization's members at a diagnostic stage in order to identify the appropriate type of intervention.

Depth of involvement

Careful diagnosis is performed when the change agent considers which one of the five Strategic Human Resource Development intervention strategies to pursue. Each will be guided by the level of intervention as well as by the motives for engagement. The latter are, however, determined by consultation. There is one other important consideration and that is the depth of the involvement in the intervention. Following Harrison (1996), the depth of intervention is central to the mode of consultation within the organization. Depth refers to the extent to which change agents are required to influence the attitudes, values and behaviours of organizational members. Strategies may range on a continuum from instrumental (surface level) to deep (emotionally charged). Thus, the deeper the intervention, the greater the extent to which core areas of the personality or self are the focus of the change attempt.

At the diagnostic stage, thought has to be given to the type of intervention required. As Harrison notes:

> If, on the one hand, the consultant seeks information about relatively public and observable aspects of behavior and relationship and if he tries to influence directly only these relatively surface characteristics and processes, we would then categorize his intervention strategy as being closer to the surface. If, on the other hand, the consultant seeks information about very deep and private perceptions, attitudes, or feelings and if he intervenes in a way which directly affects these processes, then we would classify his intervention strategy as one of considerable depth. (1996: 16)

The consultant has to decide the extent to which he or she wishes to intervene. For example, if it is considered necessary to deal simply with organizational roles, procedures and operational processes, then the depth of the intervention, and hence the diagnosis, is surface level. This is what Harrison refers to as a process of rational analysis in which the tasks to be performed are determined and specified and then 'sliced up into role definitions for persons and groups in the organization' (1996: 16). This level is essentially non-controversial and should not cause problems of interpersonal conflict:

> Persons are assumed to be moderately interchangeable, and in order to make this approach work it is necessary to design the organisation so that the capacities, needs, and values of the individual which are relevant to role performance are relatively public and observable, and are possessed by a fairly large proportion of the population from which organisation members are drawn. (ibid.: 16)

If, on the other hand, it is considered that the problem is more fundamentally behavioural in origin (for example, motivation, team relationships, customer-oriented behaviours, leadership issues, stress-related work roles, traumatized individuals, etc.), then the intervention is required to deal with emotional/behavioural issues and requires appropriate (socio-psychological) expertise.

Deeper strategies are more likely to be at the individual and group/team level. These may be evaluative, such as those that attempt to evaluate individual performance in order to improve it. This is carried out today by personal trainers or sports psychologists with the voluntary permission of the client. This is typical of the industrial psychologist's work in selection, placement, appraisal, in the counselling of employees and in the technical performance of difficult tasks such as flying an aeroplane or driving a car since the task is to modify behaviours, habits and, sometimes, attitudes. There may be other circumstances where coercion of certain clients occurs because a learned authority acts in the public interest. Such situations may arise with clients who have mental disorders. But the protection of the client must always be paramount. The change agent will always be guided by a code of ethics and, on some occasions, is guided by statute.

Harrison (1996) makes it clear that a consultant's role should be consciously constructed around a focus either on instrumentality (work behaviour) or on a deeper level by dealing with interpersonal and intra-personal relationships. At the interpersonal level, the focus is on:

> feelings, attitudes, and perceptions which organisation members have about others. At this level we are concerned with the quality of human relationships within the organisation, with warmth and coldness of members to one another, and with the experiences of acceptance and rejection, love and hate, trust and suspicion among groups and individuals. At this level the consultant probes for normally hidden feelings, attitudes, and perceptions. He works to create relationships of openness about feelings and to help members to develop mutual understanding of one another as persons. (ibid.: 17)

The deepest level of intervention – intrapersonal analysis – requires the consultant to use 'a variety of methods to reveal the individual's deeper attitudes, values, and conflicts regarding his own functioning, identity, and existence' (ibid.: 4). Intrapersonal analysis may deal with 'fantasy' and may be 'symbolic', involving techniques which began in the 1960s, such as T-group sessions and risk-taking laboratory approaches as well as the Tavistock model. More recent examples include the ability to use metaphors to reconstruct aspects of organizational life. Storytelling and enabling clients to represent organizational life through the construction of genre images have also been used to successfully transform clients' thinking.

The level at which the consultant operates carries implications for the client. At the surface end, the methods of intervention are easily communicated and made public and the client–consultant relationship may involve learning and understanding something of the change agent's skills. At the deeper levels (the interpersonal and intrapersonal process analyses), skills of intervention and change involve special learning and sensitivity and are usually beyond the ability of the organization since the consultant must uncover 'information which is ordinarily private and hidden' (ibid.: 20).

Action research and process consultancy are usually taken to involve the client system in both the gathering and analysis of the data in relation to the identified problem. Action research has parallels with clinical work (see the section on psychodynamics below) because the client requires research assisted by the change agent/consultant. For example:

> When Lewin first formulated action research it was clearly a case of the researchers wanting to figure out how to be more successful in implementing some changes that the researcher desired. He found that by involving the targeted population in the research process, they became more amenable and committed to the desired change. But the initial drive came from the change agent, and it was the change agent's goals that were driving the process. In this model, action research involves the client system as the beneficiary. But the client did not initiate the process and it was not the client's needs that drove the process. It was the researcher's choice to involve the client. (Schein, 1995: 14)

The socio-technical systems/psychodynamic perspective

The socio-technical systems/psychodynamic perspective has developed from the work of diverse social scientists who took on various consulting roles in organizations. While this approach to consultancy is related to the processual issues raised by process consultancy, it takes a particular direction with its focus on psychodynamics. Thus, the consultant and client system 'are partners in the process of organisational analysis and design, and there is progressively wider involvement of the client system in designing and managing the successive phases of the change itself' (Miller, 1997: 187). While the beginning of a client–consultant relationship is likely to be concerned with rational objectives in relation to the management of change, moving on logically to discuss the task of planning the stages of implementation, consultants and clients often find that the route, no matter how well planned, is littered with obstacles. These are the processual issues often referred to by the critics of planned change approaches. The major difference to other forms of management consultancy is that while many will talk about 'eliminating' resistance to change, from this perspective resistance is a natural human process. Therefore, resistance needs to be understood and worked with in order to develop ongoing learning experiences within organizations.

The systems/psychodynamic approach emerged from the work of social scientists at the Tavistock Institute in the 1950s and 1960s concerned with sociological and psychological aspects of organizations. Effectively, it combines systems theory with psychoanalysis. Thus, whereas the former is focused on holistic social and technical systems, the latter attempts to illuminate unconscious processes found in the individual's biography and in the interaction of groups.

Systems theory was informed principally by the work of functionalist sociologists influenced by the organismic approach to social life who began to see organizations as social systems with interconnected parts. Psychologists like Lewin (1946; 1947) drew attention to the 'Gestalt properties of human systems' and to the tendency of systems to move towards a 'quasi-stationary equilibrium' (Lewin, 1950; Miller, 1997: 188). As the founder of action research, Lewin informed the later work of the Tavistock Institute.

The development of human relations theory, and the later socio-technical system, emerged as a reaction to the dominance of the machine metaphor through the work of Trist and Bamforth (1951). Combined with the psychoanalytic work of Klein (1946; 1952; 1959), Jaques (1951; 1955; 1995) and Bion (1961), work relationships were increasingly investigated for their social processes and their psychic projections and defences.

The consultancy role reflects this socio-psychological concern through a humanistic perspective. Although not every practitioner embraced the medical analogy of illness and treatment, some practitioners 'saw organisational consultancy as a macro-version of psychoanalysis' (Miller, 1997: 191). The role of the psychodynamic consultant is defined by Miller when he points out that the consultant–client relationship is an attempt to gain a deep appreciation of the change relationship:

> The decision to act (or not) rests with the client; both jointly review the outcomes and, if appropriate, move to a next phase. It is an action research approach. There are two more specific influences. First, the transference is central to the analytic method. That is to say, the analyst becomes a screen onto which the patient projects underlying and perhaps unconscious feelings towards key figures in the patient's earlier life. In the analyst this evokes counter-transference: the analyst either has the experience of becoming the fantasised character in the patient's internal drama (a process of projective identification) or the projections resonate with some parallel dynamic in the analyst's own inner world. Correspondingly, the feelings evoked in the organizational consultant about the role one is being put into and the way one is being used provide data about underlying processes in the client system. The other influence is the recognition that, as with the analyst, it is an important function to provide for the client system a 'holding environment' (Winnicott, 1965) by serving as a safe container who can accept and survive the anxieties and sometimes hostile projections coming from the client system. (Miller, 1997: 191)

TURNING DATA INTO KNOWLEDGE

Attempting to understand organizational life is not simply an act of imposing oneself upon the organization and recording all the data we can lay our hands on, since we will be left with a mass of unconnected details of varying complexity and with incoherent connections. The process of data collection can overwhelm individuals to the extent that the data may not be written up satisfactorily. Skilful analysis has little to do with the accumulation of facts and more to do with the relationships between them. It also has less to do with 'facts' – the telephone directory approach which simply collects information – and more to do with interpretation and insight.

Turner's paper on connoisseurship is an inspiration for anyone engaged in organizational diagnosis. Its main contribution is the identification of two related issues. These are, first, the need to find clarity in complexity and, second, the need to deal with ambiguity. Both are related and require the analyst to possess specific skills:

> How, then, would I approach the study of an organisation? In the crudest outline, I would need to establish first my broad purpose in carrying out the study. I would need an interest in a particular type of organisation, and in particular types of activities which might go on within such milieu. I would not normally have a very cut-and-dried set of questions prepared, or a set of strong preconceptions about what I might find. I would want to negotiate entry in a way which would enable me to 'botanize', to observe and begin to sort out and name the social flora and fauna to be found in the setting concerned, so that, in the process, sharper research questions could develop. I would need to gain access to an appropriate organisation, or, in some instances, to appropriate documents, negotiating with power holders and 'gatekeepers' as necessary. (Turner, 1988: 109)

The change agent is likely to begin with a problem-oriented approach since the intervention itself would require an act of entry, scouting, data collection. But this, in itself, is not enough since we might be tempted to engage in uncoordinated activities such as recording interviews, making notes, creating a chronological record of activities, making observations, plans, speculating and hypothesizing and all the other activities required of a Strategic Human Resource Development change agent. Before any such activity, the change agent requires a perspective. A perspective enables the coherent recording and analysis of data by making certain types of information relevant and practical for the purpose of the intervention. This is because information is replaced by knowledge. This is what Turner (1988) refers to as the art of *knowing*. The art of 'knowing' takes us beyond pure description by engaging in 'intellectual passion'. Turner's reference to the work of Polanyi succinctly makes the connection between knowledge and connoisseurship:

> passionate participation in the act of knowing . . . manifested in the appreciation of probability and order in the exact sciences and . . . even more extensively in the way the descriptive sciences rely on skills and connoisseurship. At all these points the act of knowing includes an appraisal and this personal coefficient, which shapes all factual knowledge, bridges in doing so the disjunction between subjectivity and objectivity. (Polanyi, 1958, p. 16)

To become a connoisseur requires the skill of 'social knowing' in addition to 'analytic comprehension'. Thus, 'rather than merely absorbing knowledge, the connoisseur pours his or her attention into the "subsidiary awareness of particulars", passionately participating in the act of knowing and at the same time appraising the quality of that which is known' (Turner, 1988: 115).

Taking a perspective requires both knowledge of 'conceptual leverage' (Schatzman and Strauss, 1973: 118) and the ability to apply it. This ability is what Ravetz calls 'craft knowledge' (Ravetz, 1971; Turner, 1988: 116) or tacit understanding which is passed on from members of the same (behavioural) scientific community. This is similar to Kuhn's notion of paradigm in which members of a scientific community come to defend or refute scientific evidence. In this way we can contrast OD consultancy with other forms of 'expert' consultancy because of the underlying (behavioural) perspective adopted. Yet participants within this perspective can recognize a variety of approaches taken to the investigation of organizational problems. In this sense we can locate historical OD traditions of organizational theory in the form of open systems, organizational culture, systems thinking, and quality management, as well as intervention strategies and techniques such as team development, self-directed learning, training approaches to personal growth and empowerment, T-groups, and force field analysis organizational learning.

At the beginning of this section it was stated that complexity has to be reduced yet not over-simplified. This needs to be qualified, however. At too high a level of complexity, analysis is overwhelmed while at too low a level of complexity, the theorizing is sterile (Turner, 1988). The consultant will be faced with many complexities, ambiguities and overlapping perceptions yet it is necessary to tell a story that identifies the categories of events, issues and problems through causal links that specify their intensity and significance. Thus, the consultant or change agent must select and prioritize data to determine their significance through propositional statements. These statements will contain some degree of causality in which case the 'links must be made with care, tying them in a defensible manner to the data collected' (ibid.: 120).

Morgan's celebrated *Images of Organisation* (1986) is a book about the way metaphor enables a 'reading of organisation'. It belongs to a tradition that has its roots in the work of various writers on language and social thought. It is particularly the writers on metaphor that interest him. These include Vico in the eighteenth century and Nietzsche in the nineteenth century. More recently, the work of twentieth-century philosophers such as Cassirer (1946), Wittgenstein (1958), and social theorists such as Black (1962), Burke (1962), Pepper (1942) and writers on linguistics, hermeneutics, and psychoanalysis such as Eco (1976), Jakobson and Halle (1962) and Lacan (1966) are central to this debate. Although there are a number of others in this tradition such as Ortony (1979) and Sacks (1979), it is the impact of analysis through metaphor to be found in the work of Lakoff and Johnson (1980) that has clearly influenced Morgan's own thinking.

To those critics who have argued that scientific discourse should eliminate the use of figurative language Morgan cites writers such as Koestler (1969), Miller (1978) and Kuhn (1970) who discuss the role of metaphor in the creative imagination of scientists. His own work has previously explored the metaphorical basis of organization theory (Morgan, 1980; 1983). In the debates about the place of metaphor in scientific discourse there is a danger of cheering one side of the debate rather than the other. While we need to be cautious about adopting the 'supermarket' of metaphors approach, it is nevertheless apparent that the use of metaphor as a vehicle for transforming meaning and thus creating a new way of thinking is evident (even in the use of the word 'supermarket' in this sentence). It is therefore necessary to identify the limitations of metaphor before we can proceed to recommend their virtues.

First, there is the debate between positivistic and constructivist modes of enquiry. The predominant style of reporting knowledge to an audience of learned academics can be described as objective realism. This style assumes a positivistic or universally objective attitude to organizational data, implying that 'facts' speak for themselves through a 'rational' process of statistical indices and measurable variables. The 'natural' language for this style is to be found in mathematics which is considered to be unambiguous and universally valid. Although this in itself is debatable, the major problem emerges when research findings are analysed surreptitiously through a positivistic perspective and transformed into a quantifiable scientific discourse that assumes that words are uncontentious, neutral and free from multiple connotations. Research reports which depend on statistical correlations claim to be truthful representations of reality precisely because they are seen to be 'consensible' (Ziman, 1991) and logically self-consistent. The reality, however, is usually different because academic discourse, however neutral its intention, is presented in concepts with descriptive power: full of hyperbole, metaphor, simile and figures of speech which mark out the territory of natural language and distinguish it from scientific-mathematical language. Therefore, while natural language is therefore 'imperfectly consensible', its vocabulary is qualitatively richer than algebra (Ziman, 1991: 14) and yet, in positivistic accounts, is assumed to be neutral. The following example illustrates this mixture of (unexplored) metaphors, tropes and value judgements despite the authors' attempt to convince the reader of the factual nature of their statements with the use of statistical indices:

> The competitiveness just mentioned was a specific target of concern. Beyond the decreased *'battling' among managers*, several other *desirable trends* were found that indicated a *less confrontational* and *competitive organisational climate* . . . managers reported a significant decline (X pre = 3.62 vs x post = 3.17; p < 0.05) in their perception that their superiors fostered a competitive climate within the work unit. Consequently they were less likely to compete with other managers in terms of work quantity (X pre = 3.64 vs x post = 3.25; p < 0.05). (Sommer and Merritt, 1994: 58)

This 'universally objective' attitude requires authored control over the selection and presentation of data. Although informed implicitly by the researcher's values and assumptions, it is presented as a mirror of reality observable to all. The theories and assumptions which guide a particular author's objective attitude, in reality, order the data. Studies in organizational behaviour and development are no exception despite their concern for interpretative issues. As Burrell has argued: 'Counting metaphor as a replaceable rhetorical device presumes that we must always be able, sooner or later, to hit upon a proper and unambiguous description' (1973: 258). While this was, of course, the original objective of Wittgenstein's *Tractatus*, his later writings in the *Philosophical Investigations* illustrate the function of language as a continuously changing series of language games which invite the observer to participate in order to fully understand their import.

Such discourse is inherently reductionist, believing in the possibility of a non-figurative language (Tsoukas, 1993) and assumes that a science 'laced with metaphors' makes its own programme of falsifiability impossible (Pinder and Bourgeois, 1982: 644). The search for truth, the desire to eliminate bias, the assumption that facts have an existence independent from that of the observer, and the application of research techniques of proof and verification end up as fictions which go unrecognized by the researcher who fails to appreciate the artful construction of relevant data into meaningful stories that explore, explain and enable a discussion of organizational activities within the organization. This is more in keeping with the aims of action research through which the 'facts' are interrogated and presented from multiple perspectives.

The limitation of Morgan's 'mixed metaphors' results from the confusion with which he associates metaphors with entirely different functions. This is what Tsoukas (1993) refers to as a distinction between *explanatory* metaphors (domination, flux and transformation, psychic prison) and *interventionist* metaphors (machines, organismic, culture, holographic, political). Morgan, therefore, confuses the reader by implying that all metaphors carry equal weight. This is clearly not the case since their functions are very different. The first type explain something about contemporary organizations whereas the second type enable managers to intervene in the reconstruction of their organizations. Tsoukas illustrates this point clearly:

> Consider, for instance, Morgan's case study at the end of his book *Images of Organisations,* in which lie attempts to show how the insights of eight different metaphors can be used in diagnosing, critically evaluating and solving concrete organisational problems. There are two weaknesses in his approach. First, despite his earlier remarks about the equality (or rather equifinality), in terms of practical utility, of diverse metaphors, Morgan himself favours one particular type of discourse (and the accompanying machine, organismic and holographic metaphors) when he talks about effective management, improving current organisational practices, and enhancing the ability of organisations to solve problems through their emphasis on cultural socialization and decentralized control . . . Similarly, in a later book derived from empirical research, Morgan urges managers to 'become more proactive and skilled in dealing with the managerial turbulence that lies ahead' . . . and acknowledges that organisations face the dual problem of 'how to do the right thing and do it well' . . .
>
> In other words, instrumental discourse of a managerialist type is used *de facto* when attempting to comprehend and influence organisational

phenomena. To talk, however, about the 'effectiveness' of current organisations necessarily entails concessions towards a particular discourse, thus implicitly prioritizing metaphors according to the rules of such a discourse. In short, Morgan finds himself in the contradictory position of theoretically proclaiming the usefulness of all metaphors (and their associated mode of discourse), while practically privileging some of them at the expense of others.

   Second, the use of metaphors is ordered *de facto* according to the degree to which they allow human intervention in concrete organisational situations. In the beginning was the environment, and Morgan's analysis of the case study starts with the organismic metaphor to be followed by the prescriptions derived from the holographic and culture metaphors. It becomes obvious that the other metaphors have a residual status, and are thus of marginal utility, due to lack of adequate information. (1993: 32)

There are other relevant issues to consider. First, the nature of the discourse is intended to enable managers to learn how to 'read' or analyse their organizations and it is clear that only the interventionist metaphors have utility in their application to organizations. Thus, 'intervention is future-oriented and implies action within a short-term time frame, while explanation is retrospective and may or may not lead to action towards a specific problem.' (ibid.: 33). Second, because certain metaphors are algorithmic (e.g., machine, organism) in that their purpose is prescriptive and, interestingly, relate to structure, others (e.g., culture, political systems, psychic prison) are heuristic in that their purpose is to indicate (preferred) behaviour (ibid.: 33).

   Since the purpose of this chapter is to engage in debate about organizational development and the art of connoisseurship, the discussion is restricted to the nature of intervention and to suggest, therefore, how certain types of metaphors can be used productively from a Strategic Human Resource Development perspective. This is clearly only one type of discourse (interventionist) and while it should be informed by others (critical, interpretive, positivistic etc.), it is necessary to separate it from them as a discrete activity. In this way it should be clear that a form of intervention will adopt a voice that clearly identifies the type of discourse taking place.

   The central issue is the need to separate analytic insight and the creation of knowledge from intervention strategies in organizations. While the first offers the possibility of insight, the latter is inevitably political because it involves some form of mediation and control in the transformation from one state to another. From a constructivist perspective, a discourse of Strategic Human Resource Development requires an ability to speak with the subjects of investigation and provide an intelligible interpretation of social order. For participants, stories about organizational life are structured so as to provide the listener with a commitment to a valued position. From this perspective the Strategic Human Resource Development change agent/consultant is required to read the organization like a text using the conceptual levers of organizational behaviour as a grammar to provide a discourse relevant to the client. This is a skilled accomplishment akin to the acquisition of craft

TABLE 5.1
Root metaphors as
analytical tools

Root metaphor	Mode of analysis	Type of analogy
Machine	Behaviourist: observation of response to stimuli; Scientific Management	Man as machine Organization as machine
Organism	Functionalist: observation of norms; Health of system and search for dysfunctions	Organization as organic system; Culture as control
Drama	Symbolic interactionism/constructivist: observation of symbolic communication	Dramaturgic analogy; culture as negotiated order
Discourse	Talk, speech acts, discourse: observation of language in context	Language games; Meaning as innovation; Discourse as power relationships

knowledge discussed earlier. Without it the change agent will blunder into vague generalizations lacking sensitivity and meaningful significance.

In order to avoid the endless relativity of metaphor and tropes we need to locate the root metaphors of organizational theory (machine, organism, drama and discourse). These give rise to others but are themselves defined as root metaphors of organization analysis because they provide more than the array of images (or supermarket if you wish to be critical) that Morgan recommends, since they also depend upon a particular form of analysis (as illustrated in Table 5.1).

This particular type of metaphorical analysis is more useful because the image it conveys is not only analogical but located in a known analytic perspective that has generated unique theoretical insights. It gives metaphor a status similar to that of 'conjecture', as described by Popper, and enables the researcher to view knowledge as a process of rigorous criticism, hypotheses testing, and the formulation of better theories (McCourt, 1997: 517). It is sufficient to note that each root metaphor requires different research methods and techniques of investigation.

If we define the purpose of the intervention then we can begin to see how they can be used more productively. This is described in Table 5.2.

Root metaphors and their practical use as intervention strategies

The machine metaphor   The machine metaphor can be viewed in two ways, as indicated in Table 5.1. The first emerged from Behaviouristic Psychology and created a view of man as machine. The second resulted from the application of scientific management and from Taylor's ideas in particular.

Behaviouristic psychology was informed largely by the ideas of Skinner who argued that it was necessary to provide a 'functional' or causal explanation of behaviour patterns. For Skinner it was necessary to view man

Root metaphor	Role of the change agent
Machine	**Purpose of intervention: to guide and develop employees task skills** 1 To control training to predefined schedules in which consideration has to be given to the design of the system in respect of mechanistic – there can be no room for deviation from protocols, such as Health and Safety training, air traffic control etc. – or fluid features such as knowledge and experience of staff, the structure and shape of the communications networks; the nature of compliance. 2 To control systems (organization as machine) such as quality control, administration, lines of accountability, etc. Today, the exercise of control will be a democratic function of team processes. Consideration of behavioural controls will be of paramount importance in clarifying the objectives, in planning, organizing and directing the various aspects of the change process. 3 To achieve personal control and mastery by changing habits, behaviours or attitudes.
Organism	**Purpose of intervention: to transform systems needs** 1 To manage the health of the system and identify dysfunctions through an open systems framework of inputs, outputs and internal processes. 2 To continually examine the 'needs' of the system by managing the organization's culture. 3 To anticipate the consequences of change.
Drama	**Purpose of intervention: to transform perceptions and manage the service performance** 1 To identify the front and backstage performances and to critically examine the need for precise scripts in the performance of an operation (as in the case of emergency services) or innovative performances in order to deal with unique situations or events. 2 To negotiate the culture of the organization and to manage change by involving the different interests of various stakeholders. 3 To identify the effectiveness of teamwork in relation to the performance required for service encounters.
Discourse	**Purpose of intervention: to analyse opportunities for organizational learning** 1 To improve the effectiveness of organizational relationships through the analysis of talk related to continual improvement (e.g., the analysis of Speech Acts in relation to teamwork). 2 To manage change through action research to identify cognitive dysfunctions. 3 To apply a normative-reeducative method to convert the tacit causes of ineffectiveness into explicit formulations.

TABLE 5.2
Root metaphors and their practical use as intervention strategies

as analogous to a machine and thereby avoid the investigation of inner mental states. For example he argues that:

> The Practice of looking inside an organism for an explanation of behaviour has tended to obscure the variables which are immediately available for scientific analysis. These variables lie outside the organism, in its immediate environment and in its environmental history. They have a Physical status to which the usual techniques of science are adapted, and they make it possible to explain behaviour as other subjects are explained in science. (Skinner, 1953: 31)

Change results from the selective reinforcement of one element in behaviour and can be explained without any reference to mental processes. Although Skinner's experiments were conducted on animals, he saw little distinction between the human and other animal organisms since the same causal chain consisting of three links applied to both. These were: (a) an operation performed on the organism from without; (b) an inner condition; and (c) a behaviour. The behaviourist, therefore, argued that it was unnecessary to examine the middle link since action can be explained without reference to this internal mental state.

While this empirical model can be practically demonstrated, as far as humans are concerned, it is limited to training or behaviour modification programmes that require conditioned reflexes in order to deal with routine situations. Obvious examples include training programmes involving health and safety systems, which are predetermined by the trainer, and air traffic control and flight simulators, which require the control of stimulus and response. An example of behaviour modification may include the introduction and reinforcement of new stimuli in the case of addictive behaviours or the modification of habits to improve performance in the case of sports training. Similarly, fears and phobias may be overcome in this way.

In the case of Scientific Management, Taylor focused on the task in the attempt to establish a true science of work. As a management consultant at the Bethlehem Steel Corporation he demonstrated his ideas. As a starting point the task had to be analysed and when documented and understood, a series of prescribed rules were established. Taylor's work led to the so-called scientific selection and training strategies we see in organizations today. His work on the measurement of task sequences, while heavily criticized for its failure to understand the needs of the social system required to implement tasks, has, nevertheless, led to the control of many contemporary workplaces through techniques of surveillance. Such techniques include quality control and the use of sophisticated electronic technology. However, it should be stressed that there is nothing wrong with quality control or electronic techniques *per se*. It is the motives of senior decision-makers and the use to which they are put that causes the problem. While one of the major problems of the Classical school was its attempt to construct a universal solution to the management of organization, it is possible to argue that jobs, by contrast, can be functionally analysed to find the best way of doing them.

The practical role for this type of intervention today is really limited to identifying where controls are required or where they are deficient because they result in too many accidents (as in rail systems or air disasters). This is essentially an issue of reliability as Weick (1994) has pointed out:

> As organisations and their technologies have become more complex, they have also become susceptible to accidents that result from unforeseen consequences of misunderstood interventions. Recent examples include Bhopal, the Challenger, and Three Mile Island. What is interesting about these examples is that they involve issues of reliability, not the conventional organisational issues of efficiency. Organisations in which reliability is a more pressing issue than efficiency often have unique problems in learning and understanding, which, if unresolved, affect their performance adversely. (1994: 147)

Although Weick does not limit discussion to this particular form of analysis, it is clear that error-free performance is the requirement of expert systems. Therefore it can be argued that a better match between system complexity and human complexity can occur basically in one of two ways: 'either the system becomes less complex or the human more complex' (ibid.: 147).

Finally, the machine metaphor is useful as a Strategic Human Resource Development intervention in order to construct training schedules in relation to controlled systems (administration, sales marketing, production, etc.) that require quality assurance and lines of accountability. The role of the change agent is to analyse and redesign the way in which tasks can be managed and controlled more effectively. Change agents are responsible for the development of employees' task skills and training in relation to the control of all work processes. Central to this role is the need to identify the extent of mechanistic control. This distinction was first made by Burns and Stalker (1961) in their discussion of mechanistic and organic systems. For example, a mechanistic system will be required for specific reasons such as air traffic controller, health and safety, food standards, or quality control designed to achieve standardized services or products in a uniform manner. On the other hand, some systems will require a high degree of fluidity. This is the case with systems that must deal with regularly changing conditions such as knowledge systems or networks of people who are instrumental in developing ideas or exploring their imagination in a collaborative way. In reality, all organizations will contain a mixture of mechanistic and fluid systems although, in some, there will be a higher preponderance of one type over another. The key questions are: *what needs to be controlled?* And, *for what reasons?* In relation to fluidity, decisions will therefore need to be made about (a) the application of knowledge and experience of staff – whether staff must be tied to a strict script, as in the case of an air traffic controller, or not; (b) the structure and shape of the communications networks; and (c) the nature of compliance. That is, whether it is based on rigid adherence to rules (as in safety systems) or whether it requires motivation and commitment from the team to achieve the task. In saying this, however, change agents need to be mindful of the controversial nature of control. Since the prime objective is improvements in organizational performance, there is a danger that change agents or managers will resort to a classical approach. Therefore, consideration of behavioural controls will be of paramount importance in clarifying the objectives, in planning, organizing and directing the various aspects of the change process. Thus, today, the exercise of control will be a democratic function of team processes and no longer the prescriptive command of tasks without regard for the behavioural prerequisites of the organization's culture. Front-line employees have to be convinced to articulate their know-how (tacit knowledge) in order that it can be programmed (Huy, 2001: 606).

The organismic metaphor   The original Functionalist perspective on organizations was provided by the sociologist Talcott Parsons who viewed organizations as if they were small-scale societies. This form of organizational analysis was based on his social systems theory which suggested that although organizations have interdependent component parts, the organization as a whole will have basic survival needs similar to any biological organism. The whole is therefore viewed as greater than the sum of all the individual parts. When organizations interact with one another and with the environment in general, they adapt their structure and goals to changes in the environment. However, an organization that cannot adapt is unlikely to survive. As with the wider Functionalist or organismic perspective in sociological theory, organizations can be seen as analogous to organisms because they have *inputs* which are then converted to *outputs*. Just as people have inputs (such as food, water, information, ideas, symbols) which are transformed or converted to satisfy various needs, organizations similarly will have needs. When an organization's needs are fully met, it can be regarded as healthy. Central to the accomplishment of the organization's needs are decisions about the indicators that specify a healthy state. In the past, these were performance indicators relating to finance and deviations from conformance. More recently these have come to include the wider notion of performance management derived, on the one hand, from Human Resource Management and on the other, from Total Quality Management. We might regard performance indicators as critical success factors in pursuit of the mission. Deviations from this state of health, however, will lead to dysfunction. Diagnosis will therefore require an examination of critical processes beginning with inputs and ending with outputs.

The open systems framework of input–conversion–output can be applied to organizations. The four key elements (task, technology, people and structure) to be managed are the interdependent parts. When changes in one element emerge (for example, changes in the people element involving skill, knowledge, personality traits, motivations, group dynamics, political interactions etc.), they will cause subsequent changes elsewhere in the system. If this is not managed carefully, then it will have consequences for the way the other elements perform (e.g., tasks may become vague, technology – tools, machines, techniques - may become outdated and structural relationships may become increasingly inappropriate to meet the needs of the customer.

The health of the system depends upon the maintenance of these inter-changes. Although it may be difficult, it is possible to trace the causes of dysfunctions which, when discovered, may be considered to represent the manifestation of deeper (latent) behavioural traits. More recently this has become one of the central tenets of quality management which seeks to identify and remove problems by influencing culture.

Finally, the metaphor is useful: (a) to manage the health of the system and identify any dysfunctions through an open systems framework; and (b) to continually examine the 'needs' of the system by managing the organiza-tion's culture in the interests of the customer. The role of the change agent is to analyse and redesign work processes that result from the tasks. The primary role here is to consider the extent to which changes in the external and internal environments need to be identified for their implications to the management of the organization. Change agents will therefore be concerned with the consequences of causality. For example, changes in markets or legislation will determine the thinking of employees in making internal adjustments to strategy or culture. Since it is impossible to control all con-sequences of change, then dysfunctions will inevitably result. The 'needs' of the system will change and it is therefore important that change interventions are introduced in a timely manner.

The metaphor of drama　　In Chapter 3 it was argued that an inter-pretive (phenomenological) approach viewed cultural integration as problem-atic since agreement is a temporary and continuously negotiated arena of volatile social interactions. The metaphor of drama, as part of this tradition, contrasts with the positivistic metaphors of machine and organism discussed above.

Influenced by symbolic interactionism, the drama metaphor is influenced by the work of the sociologist Erving Goffman (1964), whose metaphor of *dramaturgical performance* provides a terminology for the social analysis of public performances. The idea of life as drama rests on five key concepts which are used to analyse public performances. These are *persona, perform-ance, staging, teamwork* and *roles*. Briefly, persona refers to the fact that people play multiple roles each day and each of the roles requires the adop-tion of a particular persona. As a result, we select our behaviour in order to create the impression we would like others to see. A persona is also projected with the use of a mask such as make-up, hairstyle, glasses and clothes. The second concept, performance, suggests that we put on a performance to create a desired impression in front of others. The third concept, staging, refers to the manipulation of the setting. Settings can be described as front or back stage arenas. In front stage arenas people use props to convey impressions to the audience. It is the front stage where the careful crafting of the performance is organized. Front stage refers to office, reception areas, living rooms, shops or ceremonial occasions. The fourth concept, teams, refers to the way that people work at teamwork in order to present a united front whether or not that is the case in reality. Finally, roles are performed for the benefit of others. By adopting this vocabulary it is possible to analyse the way people in organizations perform. This is particularly obvious in a service encounter where the ability to convey a convincing performance is crucial.

The drama metaphor begins with the phenomenological critique of functional analysis. This is illustrated by Bolman and Deal (1994) who argue that such interventions usually assume a linear cause and effect sequence between activities and outcomes or between problems and their solutions. In this way too much credibility is given to rational decision-making criteria through the usual assumptions such as 'Leaders make things happen', 'Administrators administer', 'Structures co-ordinate activity' and 'Planning shapes the future'. As they point out, 'Such statements seem so obvious that they are rarely questioned', yet 'these "obvious" connections often fail in the everyday world' (Bolman and Deal, 1994: 93). A good example is provided by the 'Front' and 'Backstage' performances that in reality shaped the drama of the Polaris Missile System:

> The development in the United States of the Polaris Missile System was heralded as an example of government activity at its best. One of its distinctive characteristics was the introduction of modern management techniques such as PERT charts and Program Planning and Budgeting System (PPBS) into the public sector. Those techniques were reflected in several structural forms, such as specialist roles, technical divisions, management meetings, and a Special Projects Office. Since Polaris turned out to be a highly successful project, it was easy to conclude that the modern management techniques were a major causal factor of this success. The admiral in charge of the project received a plaque recognizing his contribution in bringing modern management techniques to the US Navy. A visiting team of British experts recommended PERT to the British Admiralty.
>
> However, a later study of the Polaris project suggested a different interpretation of what really happened. The activities of the specialists were in fact only loosely coupled to other aspects of the project. The technical division produced plans and charts that were largely ignored. The management meetings served two primary purposes: they were arenas that the admiral used to publicly chide poor performers, and they were revival meetings that reinforced the religious fervor around the Polaris project. The Special Projects Office served as a briefing area in which members of Congress and other visiting dignitaries were informed about the progress of Polaris through an impressive series of diagrams and charts that had little to do with the actual status of the project. The team from the British navy apparently surmised this on their visit and therefore recommended a similar approach . . . . (Bolman and Deal 1994: 93–94)

According to Bolman and Deal, symbolic management suggests that: (a) the interpretive meanings in organizations are more important than the superficial appearances; (b) organizations are more accurately characterized by ambiguity and uncertainty than by the usual rational problem solving and decision-making processes; and (c) organizational members attempt to reduce ambiguity through symbols in order to gain a sense of direction and purpose. The notion of performance is central to this and as such percolates through to most organizational activities, from persuading organizational members that change is unavoidable, to exaggerating the characteristics of a service in front of the customer. In this respect Goffman links impression management with the performance offered to the audience:

> When the individual has no belief in his own act and no ultimate concern with the beliefs of his audience, we may call him cynical, reserving the term 'sincere' for individuals who believe in the impression fostered by their own performance. It should be understood that the cynic, with all his professional disinvolvement, may obtain unprofessional pleasures from his masquerade, experiencing a kind of gleeful spiritual aggression from the fact that he can toy at will with something his audience must take seriously. (1966: 98)

The analysis of performance is useful to Strategic Human Resource Development because, as Casey argues, 'Post industrial corporations are now attempting to design their own organizational culture more explicitly and more carefully than industrial culture was ever planned' (1996: 319). Leaving the fabrication of post-industrial experience to one side, it has become clear that organizations are increasingly turning to scripted performances to manage the service features of an organization. However, since getting close to the customer is an unavoidable feature of service encounters, some form of dramaturgical performance will invariably take place. For example, the service encounter is a process that usually requires the service provider to either persuade the customer or to negotiate a desired outcome from the performance. Because customers have the opportunity to observe the minutiae of service provision (which carries significant interpersonal consequences including: non-verbal behaviour, linguistic competence, and logical consistency between the development of ideas and definitions), a poor service encounter may damage a customer relationship because s/he sees through the act (Grieves and Mathews, 1997).

Performances require the service provider to display three types of competence:

1 *Articulation* is the ability of the service producer to articulate clearly the nature of the service offered and the ability to display listening skills appropriate to the type of encounter. This usually means being sensitized to the typical requests of the service encounter as well as displaying the ability to deal adequately with *atypical* requests that may occur sporadically.
2 *Linguistic competence*, which refers to the ability to display conversational ability, through knowledge appropriate to the context. This competence also presupposes a sensitivity to linguistic rules through which conversations are structured (Garfinkel, 1967; Schegloff, 1972).
3 *Logical consistency* refers to the speaker's ability to express a consistent message enabling the customer to clearly understand the definitions provided.

The service encounter presents an opportunity to engage in experiential learning of this type in order to deal with the intangibility of the service encounter. A good example of this is the type of scripted performance required by the emergency services. Another is the activity of the change agent or consultant.

Finally, the dramaturgic analogy enables interventions which (a) critically examine the need for precise scripts in the performance of an operation (as in the case of emergency services or healthcare) or innovative performances in order to deal with unique situations or events and (b) continually negotiate the culture of the organization and to manage change by involving the different interests of various stakeholders. Table 5.3 is intended as a heuristic device for thinking about performances we encounter each day. Simply fill in your responses to a performance your have encountered recently. The role of the change agent is to engage employees in a dialogue about the effectiveness of the performance. In doing this the team will consider the use of props, the nature of the scripted performance and the effectiveness of teamwork.

Discourse as metaphor   It was noted in Chapter 3 how discourse is a tool for analysing and explaining culture. The analysis of discourse should be considered a critical element in enabling people to change their attitudes and behaviours and in their gaining ownership of the change. Rather than seeing discourse as something that occurs in the change process, it is useful to also see change resulting from discourse.

As noted in Chapter 3, discourse reveals certain things about speakers. For example:

- The complexity of discourse is expressed in various ways. Ideas can be expressed literally or figuratively. Language can express open and conscious intentions or it can reveal involuntary expressions that indicate hidden ideas or feelings. Analysis of discourse can also reveal rational thoughts or emotional constructs.
- Metaphors communicate elliptical expressions of legitimate issues by symbolically expressing cognitive or emotional constructs. We can therefore use metaphors to change or influence something (as in a management development activity) or we can analyse metaphors as elliptical expressions about situations in which people find themselves and about which they may not be consciously aware.

Furthermore, Marshak argues:

> With these premises serving as a reminder to constantly pay attention to the symbolic aspects of communications, a paradoxical principle informs the diagnostic process: explore literal messages symbolically, and symbolic messages literally. This principle requires the diagnostic process to remain open to the potential multiple meanings that may be conveyed by a seemingly single communication. (1996: 156)

For example, to explore the symbolic – 'This office is like a prison' – literally can be heard as a symbolic way of expressing the range of feelings and

TABLE 5.3 The drama metaphor. Simply fill in your responses to a performance you have encountered recently.

Features of the drama	Well crafted. An inspiration to us all.	A competent performance with minor inconsistencies.	Unconvincing performance. S/he does not appear to give everything to it.	Laughable. I will not go there again.
What drama is being performed?				
How effective is the drama? Provide description for your answers	Highly aesthetic: refers to specific codes of . . . Highly psychological: refers to Highly emotional: refers to	Aesthetic: refers to Psychological: refers to Emotional: refers to	Aesthetic: refers to Psychological: refers to Emotional: refers to	Aesthetic: refers to Psychological: refers to Emotional: refers to
What scripts are used?	Well articulated Highly convincing Highly emotional	Factual Convincing Emotional	Not factual Unconvincing Unemotional	Not factual Unconvincing Unemotional
What props are used?				
What impressions are being managed?				

thoughts about the workplace (ibid.: 156). Conversely, the literal statement 'you can't tell the truth around here because too many people would get hurt' symbolically suggests that people in this organization experience truth as a weapon (ibid.: 157).

The discussion of discourse in Chapter 3 referred to Austin's (1962) description of performative utterances to illustrate that any speech act produces a changed reality and does not simply provide a report. This was extended by Searle (1976) who classified speech acts into five categories: *assertives, directives, commissives, expressives* and *declarations*. This is useful since these categories constitute the five different ways a change agent can take action in communication. They are performative, in that each type of speech act seeks to establish, negotiate or contest a version of reality.

An example of the analysis of Speech Acts in relation to change is provided by Ford and Ford (1995) who argue that although participants will engage in a variety of change-related conversations, 'there are four different types of conversation that correspond to four different types of interaction in the intentional change process' (ibid.: 546). The four types of conversation referred to are:

1   Conversations that seek to *initiate* something which use assertions, directives, commissives and declarations.
2   Conversations that seek *understanding* and are characterized by (counter-) assertions and expressives which seek to comprehend the cause and effect relationships and attempt to specify the conditions of satisfaction for the change.
3   *Performance* conversations are conversations as action which focus on 'doing' through directives (requests) and commissives (promises) designed to achieve a desired result;
4   Conversations seeking *closure* which involve ending something through expressives and declarations designed to complete the cycle. (ibid. my emphasis)

Listening to discourses about change, we can identify different dimensions of talk in relation to the use of power. For example, if a change conversation is initiated with a directive, then one might reasonably infer an unequal power relationship exists between the speakers. This may also be the case where conversations about change fail to seek understanding because counter-assertives or expressives are curtailed. One might simply ask the question: 'What is s/he doing with this discourse?' Alternatively, company documents, written statements and other verbal exchanges may be the focus for an interrogation of the political dimensions of talk. It is possible to envisage that in more enlightened organizations change may be managed through such critical debates used as a stimulus for change and resulting in a resolution by identifying opportunities for innovation and organizational learning.

A change agent can use this constructively by using techniques that involve *framing, advocating, illustrating* and *inquiring* (see Fisher et al.

2001). This is illustrated in the case study 'Reframing the business idea' in Chapter 6. The nature of this type of intervention is informed by collaborative learning. This is described as a teaching intervention because: '[it] refers to an analytical and guided learning approach in which change targets participate in their own reeducation through the active involvement of change agents' (Huy, 2001: 607). The change agent will require an ability to analyse the shifts and tensions in organizational culture and to act as teachers in order to bring employees' deep beliefs to the surface. Cognitive dysfunction may be the root cause of problems or taken-for-granted assumptions may have unintended consequences (ibid.: 607). The following account provides some useful examples of this 'normative-reeducative' (Chin and Benne, 1994) method:

> For instance, Argyris's (1993) theory of action method probes and reveals the incongruence between espoused theories and theories in use. Schein's (1992) culture diagnosis method seeks to elicit the tacit, shared assumptions of the organization's culture. With his system dynamics method, Senge (1990) tries to map the organization's structure as complex dynamic systems in order to uncover vicious causal loops and decision makers' erroneous mental causal attributions. These scholars believe in sound, cognitive diagnoses of root causes as a prelude to change in behaviors. They use a normative-reeducative method (Chin & Benne, 1994) and believe that outsider intervention is necessary to convert the tacit causes of ineffectiveness into explicit formulations, since employees are cognitively limited and trapped by their own hidden assumptions. Organizations are viewed as psychic prisons (Morgan, 1986) that can be liberated by outside action researchers. Once cognitively liberated, employees are assumed to be able to learn freely, and this enhances the organzation's ability to innovate and adapt to uncertain environments.
>
> To expose relationship difficulties in the client systems, teachers try uncovering past beliefs and reconstituting them in the present through retrospective sensemaking (Weick, 1979). These deep beliefs link space and time together within individuals' consciousness to reject a sense of stability and coherence. Challenging these beliefs is tantamount to upsetting a person's inner time, and this causes personal distress. *Inner time* refers to qualitative time experienced at the subjective level of individual. (Huy, 2001: 607)

CONCLUSION

Traditional texts describing the actions of the OD consultant invariably begin with a problem-oriented approach to an organizational situation. The chapter sought to establish Strategic Human Resource Development as proactive change from the inside. This type of change requires the change agent to develop and be responsive to imagination and creative thinking. This is not change led by senior managers reacting to changes in the external environment or to dysfunctions within existing practice. Pro-active change means developing enterprise through human resources. It is strategic because it develops the strategy of the organization.

To become a change agent requires an awareness of how to achieve knowledge of 'conceptual leverage' and the ability to apply it. To do this, the chapter considered the weaknesses of management consultancy and suggested that Strategic Human Resource Development is based on process skills that seek to develop strategy within the organization. The various types of Strategic Human Resource Development interventions require an ability to manage the relationship between the client and consultant through process consultation as well as the ability to use diagnostic skills. Sensitivity to clients' needs was considered in relation to the depth of the intervention as well as to socio-technical and psychodynamic perspectives. This 'craft knowledge' is based on four metaphors – machine, organism, drama and discourse – from which the mode of analysis is linked to the purpose of the intervention.

FURTHER READING

While the text by Lundberg (1997) provides a useful model of consultancy, consideration should be given to the competencies of the OD consultant illustrated by Cummings and Worley (1997). A very comprehensive coverage of the role of the change agent is given by Hamlin et al. (2001). Because change agents should be aware of the implications of intervention, attention should be directed to the concerns of Harrison (1996) which should be read in conjunction with Blake and Mouton's (1972) classic work illustrated in Chapter 1. A very useful text on organizational diagnosis and assessment is provided by Harrison and Shirom (2001).

Strategic human resource development interventions

I am scared that nothing is real.
That's called existential angst, or dread, and is, as a rule only a stage on the way to new consciousness.
(Jostein Gaarder, 'Sophie's World')

INTRODUCTION

In Chapter 5 it was suggested that to become a change agent required an awareness of how to achieve knowledge of 'conceptual leverage' and the ability to apply it. This chapter extends these ideas with practical examples that demonstrate the application of knowledge and skills to be acquired by the Strategic Human Resource Development practitioner or change agent.

The chapter begins with an example of the need to manage the relationship between the client and consultant through process consultation. In particular, it demonstrates the dangers of client over-dependence and reliance on the definition provided by the contracting party. The art of conceptual leverage means managing the client's expectations when soundings have been taken from the wider client system. Following this is an example of the personal changes involved in becoming an internal change agent. The chapter then moves on to provide examples of change narratives that illustrate how each of the metaphors – machine, organism, drama and discourse/learning – have been applied in practice. It is important to note that in taking these concepts further with some practical examples, their relationship depends upon the culture of the organization. In this sense culture is viewed not as a component of the organization but as the totality of all actions, beliefs and values. This is illustrated in Figure 6.1. Thus, how each of these models is used will be constrained by or will seek to change the culture. Central to this is the relationship with power, politics and decision-making, motivation, leadership, role conflict and stress. Finally, strategic learning is discussed as a flexible solution to the demands of contemporary organizations.

The learning objectives for this chapter are:

1   *The role of the change agent* through five examples which demonstrate (a) the need to manage the relationship between the client and consultant through process consultation and the danger of client over-dependence on the definition provided by the contracting party; (b) the problems associated with becoming an internal change agent; (c) exploring the organismic analogy by managing the systems inputs, the conversion processes and the outputs; (d) exploring the production of meaning though the drama analogy in the case study, 'The graveyard of ambition'.

2   *Strategic learning* as a flexible solution to the demands of contemporary organizations. Change today requires the change agent to be aware of key learning processes. Strategic learning requires managers and employees to look inward and to critically reflect on their own defensive reasoning as well as on strategies to develop individual and organizational learning.

Learning is critical to survival and the change agent will need to know how and why to apply each of the analytical frameworks identified in the previous chapter. It is in this sense that the examples provided here reflect only a small portion of the possibilities for management development. Many more and very different examples can be found to apply to each paradigm. Each, however, represents a more flexible alternative to the early twentieth-century command-and-control, bureaucratic machine model.

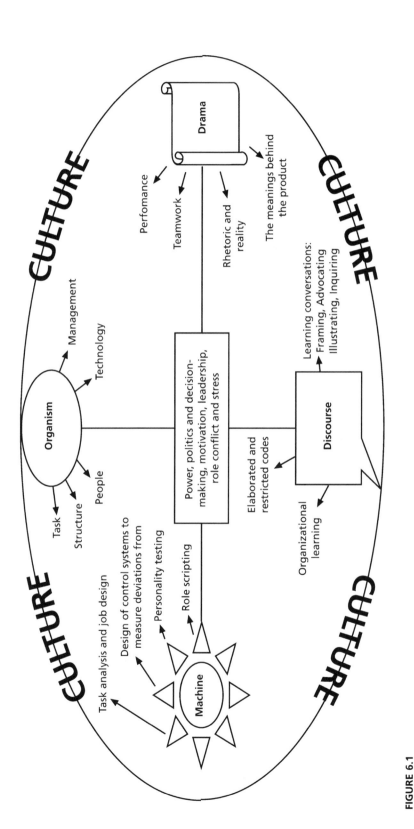

FIGURE 6.1
Strategic Human Resource Development interventions

CONTRACTING WITH THE CLIENT

The following case study indicates the difficulty of assuming that the client's definition of the situation is accurate at the outset of an investigation. In this case, it is seen that while the client appears to have a clear strategy, in reality it is based on a partial awareness of how the goals might be achieved. In addition, the road to achieving the strategy defined by the client ignored operational issues that need to be addressed. Thus, his attempt to devise and plan what he considered to be a straightforward change led to a series of 'emergent' difficulties that needed to be addressed. These were discovered by the consultants only when they collected data from the wider client system. This example refers to external consultants but the method demonstrates how, once conducted, and with the right training, the organization's teams can continue to develop their skills and abilities. Encouraging the development of independent learning rather than over dependence of the external consultant became a major achievement. However, the case also reminds us that there are times when an external consultant is essential.

Case study 1: process consultation at the George Hotel

Background   Set in 15 acres of wooded parkland on the outskirts of Castlebridge, the George Hotel is an accessible luxury hotel. The location of the hotel means that it is adequately serviced by road, rail and air. The hotel building is a seventeenth-century mansion house that has recently been refurbished and awarded a four-star rating from the AA and RAC. The English Tourist Board has classified it as a 5 crown awarded hotel.

The hotel was recently bought by new owners. The hotel has a range of facilities suitable for a variety of customers. Facilities include the following:

- 120 bedrooms;
- conference and banqueting facilities;
- two public bars;
- a leisure club;
- 18-hole golf course.

The hotel has traditionally accommodated a mixture of celebrities, business travellers and holidaymakers. The restaurant is able to take up to 120 people and it provides a full à la-carte menu. The leisure club offers a number of health and fitness facilities including an indoor heated swimming pool, sauna, solarium and gymnasium. Croquet, golf and tennis can also be played in the hotel grounds. There are four main conference rooms and eight syndicate rooms which are well equipped with projectors, video recorders and flip charts. Functions such as weddings and dinner dances also take place in the hotel. There are two bars, both of which are open to the public as well as to hotel residents.

The problem as seen by the client   The client was the new general manager of the hotel, Andrew Collins. When he first met with the consultants he stated that their purpose was to identify ways: 'to increase profitability in the area of food and beverage by 10 per cent'. Andrew was of the opinion that in order to increase profitability it was necessary to attract a new client base of a lower socio-economic status. Traditionally, the hotel has focused on the B1 social class group. It was able to do so in the past because it had a niche market and there were no other luxury hotels in the immediate area. However, other luxury hotels have recently been built and competition has increased significantly.

Andrew's brief to the consultants was constrained by the fact that the budget allocated to him by the Board of Directors for improving the hotel and offering a higher quality of service was limited. This meant that the hotel could not compete at the quality end of the market.

Other incidental issues for improving the quality of service to customers included teamwork and communication. This is because 'different parts of the hotel do not always co-ordinate their activities as effectively as they should', he stated. Because 'the different functions of the hotel have different managers and different staff', resulting 'in their failure to identify with the customer's needs as seen holistically by the hotel'. As an example of ineffective teamwork he cited a breakdown in communication in which the restaurant ran out of paper napkins because the conference staff, having already used the linen napkins, proceeded to use the reserve supply of paper napkins without informing the restaurant and without ordering more from the supplier. Another aspect of Andrew's strategy was his desire to attract local people who lived near the restaurant as their obvious first choice. Therefore, Andrew's main strategy was to do the following:

1   Target customers from a lower socio-economic group.
2   Attract local people to use the restaurant which would also be run as a separate business.
3   Develop teamwork throughout the hotel in order to identify with the needs of the business and in so doing address the customer's needs.

His first strategy was therefore to develop the thinking of the managers.

The consultants' strategy   Further discussions with Andrew Collins revealed the existence of a number of customer satisfaction measures. These were designed to identify the perceived level of service provided within the hotel. The consultants decided to use this existing information in order to obtain a snapshot of customer perception. This information was collected from (a) a mystery customer programme; and (b) a questionnaire collected from bedrooms, the restaurant, conference and leisure facilities.

In addition, the consultants originally considered undertaking a financial appraisal of the last five years. A study of recording stock control and wastage would have identified inefficient ways of working, or recording practices and suggested possibilities for improvement. This would have provided the financial background information necessary to address the problem defined by the client.

The consultants recognized that points 1 and 2 in Andrew's strategy were directly related to possible ways of increasing profitability but point 3 was only indirectly related to the problem definition but its effectiveness would, nevertheless, determine the success of the strategy. As a result, they considered that point 3 – to develop teamwork – might be the logical place to start with a training programme designed to 'increase profitability'. Consequently, the consultants decided to begin the process of inquiry by consulting with the wider client system by means of interviews and questionnaires.

Preliminary findings of the wider client system Of the seven department managers interviewed, four had not been invited to participate in the development of the new strategic plan for the hotel. The three heads who had been involved in this long-term planning were the newest members of the management team. Only the four older 'time served' department managers could quote the mission statement (which was: 'Our mission is to exceed your expectations') but considered it to be 'relatively meaningless' and 'banal'.

Two of the department heads stated that there was a 'blame culture' and that no one accepted responsibility when things went wrong. They said that it was not uncommon to hear people say 'this has nothing to do with me'. Another head of department stated, 'two subcultures are beginning to develop in the hotel, one of which was based on the past and the other based on a future'. This clearly reflected the four heads who represented the old team and the three heads who were part of the new team. One of the new heads said that a 'culture of inflexibility' had developed and that staff needed a 'good shake-up'. By contrast, the four older department heads stated that low morale was one of the major obstacles to change and that the hotel had 'no buzz' about it. The four older heads agreed that the low morale was caused mainly by exceedingly low wages at about, or just above, the minimum wage. But, because of the increased competition they felt that there was little chance of increasing wages. Hence an intractable problem had developed. As one of them, paraphrasing Hertzberg, stated, 'It [money] may not be a motivator but it is the most important hygiene factor in this industry – it determines who you get, how long they stay and why they move on to other things.' He went on, 'the amount of training given to new staff is determined by how long you can keep them and this is now a high turnover hotel in a high turnover industry'. Another problem was the hours staff were expected to work. On some occasions staff were called in to work but never knew in advance if they would work a full shift or whether they would be sent home early as a result of slack business. On other occasions, when business was brisk, they were often kept hours longer than their normal finishing time. This uncertainty about knowing the hours they were to work was a major source of dissatisfaction.

In addition, the mystery customer programme indicated that standards across departments varied. This appeared to be particularly the case in the bars and restaurants. Service in the bar was said to be slow and expensive. The beer was criticized for being badly kept and customers were often kept waiting due to the limited number of staff on duty at any one time. Training was generally done on the job and in front of the customer and often carried out at high speed causing the new member of staff some anxiety in meeting the demands of both the customer and her more experienced colleague.

Interviews with staff also revealed that quality standards throughout the hotel were not written down. Instead, they were passed on by word of mouth. A snapshot of perceptions across departments suggested that quality standards varied according to which head of department they were working for.

Therefore, the preliminary investigation of managers and their staff seemed to suggest contradictions and underlying dynamics that might not only impede any effective changes to the improvement strategy but might, if they could be addressed, provide a more effective strategy in the long run. In the attempt to avoid bias these were summarized as 'working facts'. For example:

- Four of the department managers felt they were not part of the management team.
- Three of the newer managers felt that the management team worked well together.
- Employees, generally, obtained very low wages.
- Employees, generally, were uncertain about the number of hours they would work on any one shift.
- Quality standards across the hotel varied and were not written down.
- Training was ineffective, did not satisfy staff, and detracted from the quality of service perceived by the customer.

The need to refocus the problem The original problem statement identified by the new general manager, Andrew Collins, was 'to increase the profitability in the area of food and beverage by 10 per cent'. This can be regarded as a surface intervention as defined by Harrison (1996). The consultants began by investigating the various systems at the George Hotel, including the financial control system and the quality system, and wanted to know more about service expectations which would inform them about how various services were being delivered. However, the interviews of the managers and staff suggested that there were deeper issues to address which would impact on any solution recommended. This required an examination of interpersonal relationships and the extent to which employees considered themselves to be 'valued resources' involved in the process of service delivery (this is even more important in service encounters where staff are in front line contact with customers and where the products are intangible). The interviews with managers and staff therefore revealed dysfunctions that were likely to inhibit a change strategy that focused simply on a 10 per cent increase in profitability linked to food and beverage.

In addition to the discovery of dysfunctions that would clearly detract from effective team-work, a series of *critical incidents* were identified. In August 2001 the restaurant manager left unexpectedly. As a solution, the managing director, Andrew Collins, decided to give responsibility for running the restaurant to the staff and at the same time increased their wages by £1 per hour. However, this caused major discontent to the remaining staff in the hotel who had previously been told they had to regard themselves as a team.

As a result, the consultants decided it was necessary to re-examine the original problem statement. They began with a task-related issue which developed into what appeared to be a more deep-seated socio-emotional concern with the effectiveness of the organization and the relationships within it. It was therefore agreed that the original aims and objectives had changed. As a result, the consultants approached Andrew Collins to discuss their concerns with the original remit and present a revision to it. They concluded that they needed to reappraise the situation and change the focus of the consultancy.

Their primary concern was the healthy development of the organization and they argued that, in order for the objectives to be embraced (which included the original goal of increasing productivity by 10 per cent), senior management needed to develop and share the new vision of the organization with all staff. In order to do this, it was necessary to share concerns and develop a vision with all managers in order to ensure they developed the idea collectively rather than as two distinct groups. This was to be followed by communicating the vision, asking employees to identify opportunities, including productivity bonuses and pay increases to all staff, training and personal development resulting from the effort and commitment they were prepared to invest in the development of their own organization.

Postscript   The top team set about the task of investigating its external environment and considered the position of the hotel over the next five years. They agreed to change the organization structure to a flatter style. An examination of the industry's external environment found that other factors needed to be considered. The general manager's 'value for money' focus was informed by data from the industry (which reported trends throughout the UK suggesting a growth in both the 'value for money' and 'luxury' markets of the hotel industry) that suggested the hotel needed to attract more tourists rather than rely on their history of attracting celebrities. Furthermore, a value chain analysis illustrated the interconnectedness of the organization's strategy and its operational processes. This called into question a complete re-examination of its human resource strategy and the processes by which it managed its staff.

A new mystery customer survey set criteria against which the hotel's performance could be measured. There has since been a steady improvement in standards within the hotel. In addition, an annual employee survey has been introduced. This has revealed, in particular, the need to manage change in a more integrated way by involving all staff in the process. Deficiencies in communications have been identified and small teams of staff have been given the task of solving communication problems. Quality standards have also been identified for all areas – once again by staff working in teams – and regular training has been introduced in order to maintain the standards and, where possible, improve the quality of service offered to customers.

By the end of the first year, February 2002, profitability was informed more by efficiencies and by focusing on raising quality standards. Wastage on perishables, such as food and drink, was reduced. The number of returning customers increased by 5 per cent. Variations in standards were eliminated. The payment of part-time staff increased to well beyond the minimum wage. Profitability increased by 23 per cent which represented 13 per cent more than originally expected by Andrew Collins.

BECOMING AN INTERNAL CONSULTANT

In Chapter 5 we noted that process consultation requires the change agent to engage organization members in diagnosis and to collect and analyse data through a variety of methodological techniques, including the use of statistics, survey techniques and force field analysis. Central to this is the ability to 'find your feet' by developing new skills and new knowledge by involving the organization's members at various stages of the intervention. The following case study 'Becoming an internal change agent in the National Health Service' illustrates this.

Case study 2: discovering the role of internal change agent in the National Health Service

I was appointed as a project manager on secondment to review the theatre processes in an NHS hospital and their link to all specialities. The advantages and disadvantages of being an internal change agent became apparent very soon. Having managed theatres was obviously beneficial when reviewing theatre processes. Relationships were already established with most of the staff, and I was aware of the informal structures. I was respected by staff, especially clinicians, who were the major stakeholders. However, being an internal change agent rather than an external one can also be disadvantageous. Although I no longer officially work for the division of anaesthesia/ theatres, I feel I am still seen to be working for theatres, thus staff from other departments may feel I am biased towards theatre objectives only.

To ensure the different boundaries are managed, I have had to ensure that I effectively communicate with and involve all the relevant stakeholders, informing them initially of my role and objectives, sharing the theatre problems with them, and also discovering their problems. By demonstrating motivation and enthusiasm at all times, selling ideas to gain support by presenting information clearly, and ensuring information is accurate, progress was made. I have used these skills, along with persevering to sell ideas and gain support from those opposing any change, continuously. However, this has been time-consuming but critical to managing change. I have also had to deploy political tactics, such as building internal relationships and alliances. I developed my persuasion skills further in order to influence key stakeholders, especially clinicians. Empathy became essential when managing cross-cultural issues. I discovered how important it was to be sensitive to the needs of people in other departments and to explore any prejudicial judgements I may have made in the past with responsibility for one area only.

One particular theatre process that required reviewing was the theatre list planning process. This was influenced by the external political agenda in relation to waiting times and waiting lists. During my first few months in the post, I obtained a good deal of data from the Theatreman system regarding theatre utilization. I conducted interviews with the surgeons to identify what their own system was for planning lists. Having documented and obtained information regarding the production of lists, I then produced an impact analysis chart to highlight the problems associated with the lack of a standardized system for effectively managing the theatre lists against the time available. The major reasons could then be identified using Pareto analysis. In a six-month period 157 operations had been cancelled. Furthermore, this revealed other impacts such as a high level of anxiety from patients and incidents of complaints. Problems included: no bed available, lack of theatre time, the patient cancelled at short notice, late starts and delays, poor planning, etc. This was presented to stakeholders – surgeons, anaesthetists, divisional staff, theatre and ward staff. I involved many of the ward and theatre staff in the collection of the data to establish a degree of ownership and validity. The graphs and statistics highlighted the problems.

After six months in the post I persuaded two surgeons, who were chiefs of service, to trial a new list planning procedure by using their average operating times as a means of avoiding both over- and under-utilization of theatre sessions. During a theatre briefing, I informed staff of the trial we were to run and highlighted that this was a major breakthrough for them, because it gave them an opportunity to take control of the over-running of lists. This had always been a major complaint from the theatre staff. However, to 'sell' the trial to surgeons, their own late starts had to be addressed and in order for it to work, the theatre managers had to ensure lists commenced on time. The theatre staff, along with ward staff, identified three performance standards to work towards (theatre list will commence on time; patients will be in the anaesthetic room 5 minutes prior to list start time; all areas of patient documentation will be completed as accurately as possible). These were placed on the theatre notice walls.

My role as an internal change agent already feels more positive and collaborative and open relationships have emerged. Working together to meet the standards, rather than blaming each other when things go wrong, is now much more apparent.

MAINTAINING EQUILIBRIUM – MANAGING THE SYSTEMS FITS

An organization that cannot adapt is unlikely to survive. When organizations are seen as analogous to organisms, the focus must be on the vitality of the *inputs*, the *conversion processes* and the *outputs*. An organization's needs are not met when examples of effectiveness, or declining health, begin to emerge.

At some point decisions will be made about the factors that indicate an unhealthy state. The most obvious one is financial. When the sub-systems (task, structure, people, technology, management) become uncoupled, deviations from conformance occur. This will lead to the search for dysfunctions and an examination of critical processes beginning with inputs and ending with outputs.

The open systems framework of *input–conversion–output* can be applied to organizations. When changes in one sub-system occur, they will cause subsequent changes elsewhere in the system. If this is not managed carefully then it will have consequences for the way the other elements perform.

The following example demonstrates the role of the change agent in this process. In this organization there is a need to analyse and redesign work processes.

Case study 3: improving processes by examining functional inter-relationships

Machine Products manufacture gearbox components for diesel engines. It employs approximately 300 people. The company has two sites: a head office which employs a wide range of people who are generally well educated and enthusiastic about their work, and a factory site which employs semi-skilled local men who are generally disinterested in the products of the company and who have an instrumental attitude to work, seeing the wage as the only reward.

The problem The senior management team became concerned about the performance of the factory. Objectives were suggested by the executive team and an external consultant indicated specific changes to relationships and tasks. The objectives were:

1   To review and improve formal communications within the organization.
2   To restructure the organization and to review teamwork practices.
3   To review leadership across all departments.
4   To create a quality focus across the company.

In relation to the need to create a quality focus, a change agent – John – was appointed and given responsibility for improving process control and review procedures for ISO9001 in the factory. John identified a mixture of facts and perceptions that needed to be tackled. The facts were:

1   Wastage within the factory was costing the company approximately £32K a month.
2   Observation and records confirmed differences in the work standards of different individuals.
3   Processes were not standardized and resulted in repeated problems.
4   Management made all decisions and cascaded the results down to employees.

Perceptions suggested:

1   The existence of a 'them and us' attitude between the office and the factory which appeared to influence attitudes to work.
2   Production employees appeared complacent and showed little responsibility for the quality of their work.
3   Production employees were isolated by the technology and appeared alienated from the products and from the success of the company.

The factory environment was highly mechanized and the production employees were seen as unskilled workers. Their work involved the performance of repetitive tasks on an assembly line.

The change strategy   In consultation with team leaders, John selected a team to recommend a change strategy. Ten production employees were selected at random with certain conditions:

•   Each should have worked for the company for at least six months.
•   None should have received warnings on their work records.
•   Each must be willing to help and be interested in the challenge offered.

The team had authorization to experiment and make changes to the design of the process. The planning process took two months and consisted of analysing the production output, staff rotas, levels of training.

Potential obstacles to implementation and strategies to overcome them   Before analysing the task the team identified three potential obstacles to performance. First, many managers did not want to relinquish control. To overcome this the team was enlarged to include a manager who would keep other managers informed about the activities of the team. In this way it was made clear that no changes would threaten their role. Second, production employees felt that they did their jobs and that quality control was the responsibility of the supervisors. This attitude was tackled through a series of meetings which addressed the responsibilities of everyone. A solution could only emerge when the team considered the restructuring of the job with the redesign of tasks and processes. Since this team was representative of production employees, John suggested that the redesign and implementation of a new methodology would be placed in the hands of the team. Third, discussions with production employees indicated that they did not wish to take on extra responsibility without reward. To address this the team put forward a proposal to senior management that any measured improvements in productivity would be rewarded by paying bonuses related to increased profitability.

Identifying critical problems   The team then set about identifying critical problems. To do this they constructed a cause and effect diagram which produced some useful insights into the variety of issues that contributed to the problem of wastage within the factory.

The root causes revealed that systems were defective because there was frequent variation in standards set and accepted by different operators. Decisions were made by supervisors who were too remote from the immediate task, operators received no feedback on their performance other than negative comments about defects. The structure and materials revealed that the job was rigidly defined and the quality of incoming materials from suppliers was often defective. The process or method revealed that as a result of poor systems and inadequate control of materials, work was often repeated or delayed in the attempt to make corrections. In addition, the methods of manufacture had been designed *ad hoc* over many years and needed to be reviewed and redesigned. Discussions revealed the need to understand the importance of internal customers in order to eliminate misunderstandings and improve the service. This was particularly important between the office and the factory. Finally, tasks needed to become more coherent in order that production operators could identify with the end product. This required the elimination of repetitive and monotonous work. The root causes are illustrated in Figure 6.2.

Improving system fits   Once the problems were identified, the next step for the team was to identify opportunities for improvement. They began by producing a flowchart of the current process and from this they identified improvement opportunities. This is illustrated in Table 6.1. The improvements carried costs in relation to training, personal development and time required for review meetings. These costs were agreed with senior management and measured against the costs of the overall problem. By the end of the first year the savings to the company had averaged out to £21,500 per month.

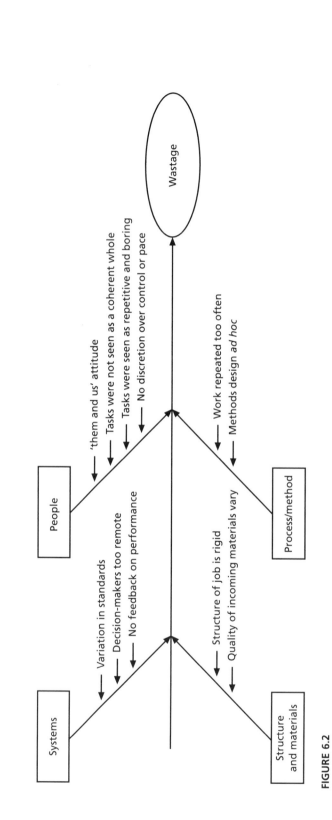

FIGURE 6.2

Cause and effect diagram identifying wastage within factory

TABLE 6.1 Opportunities for improvement

Systems	People	Structure and materials	Process/method
Identify work standards through training programme	Introduce personal development to enhance self-esteem	Move to multi-skilled teams in order to reduce repetition and boredom. Pace of work in hands of the team who set targets for improvement	Methods to be redesigned by team following monthly review
Decisions to be made at source to (1) empower staff, (2) minimize the costs of defects and (3) reduce the activities of the inspection department	Training to relate tasks to finished product. External and internal customers involved in demonstrating the function of the product	Team to inspect quality of incoming materials	Any repeat work to be subject to monthly reviews to eliminate cause
Feedback on performance will no longer be provided by supervisor but by team			Measure process improvements and feed into review
	Change reward structure with bonuses related to targets for the type of work		

THE PRODUCTION OF MEANING: UNDERSTANDING DRAMA

As the previous chapter indicated, the metaphor of drama is concerned with the production of meaning in organizations rather than a set of rational formulas for organizational success. Indeed, the elegance of this metaphor turns the very idea of rationality on its head by showing that what really matters is how people feel and what they really think as opposed to what they say in public. The following account demonstrates one of the most important change interventions. It is important precisely because it challenges the taken-for-granted assumptions of organizational life. The account demonstrates that if managers manage and planners shape the future and administrators administer, then why are the tasks within such organizations carried out so ineffectively? The case study provided – 'The graveyard of ambition' – resulted from an activity that required participants to analyse their own organization through a literary genre. They were asked to portray their organization as they really felt it to be in order to identify some of the underlying tensions and tacit frameworks that inform the judgements that people make. To do this they were required to write a story using a fictional device. They were asked to identify a novel or film they were familiar with and use the narrative to tell a story about their own organization. Various genres were offered such as: journey (usually transformational and often spiritual), political thriller (used to portray intrigue and complexity), western (typically used to portray good versus evil), science fiction (often used to create an image of the future which is often cast as a warning), a game (used to demonstrate the function of strategy, tactics and personal struggle to overcome the odds).

Essentially the drama metaphor is used to explore and improve performance, teamwork, the gap between rhetoric and reality and the meanings behind the product or service offered to the organization. Towards the end of the following extract you will notice how the writer has used this as a discussion for making changes to the organization. This, of course, is much easier to do with teams or groups of people than it is with an entire organization, since the change agent can use this technique to inform strategy.

Case study 4: the graveyard of ambition

Step one   The novel is set in 1998 in 'Dulltown' No. 103 Sanctum, otherwise known as the 'graveyard of ambition'. The No. 103 Sanctum comprises the Inner Sanctum, the Outer Sanctum and the Lower Sanctum. The Inner Sanctum represents the Corporation and is divided into eight Superpowers led by the 'Inner Sanctees'. Their position is one of power, privilege, and secrecy. They huddle frequently together in the Corporate Room. They reside in the 'Corridors of Power'.

The language frequently used is 'recognition', 'corporate', 'authority', 'discipline', 'procedures', 'protocols', 'rules', 'secrecy', 'regulations', 'conditions', and not least of all *'do as I say not as I do'* (I will not say this directly, but you must infer it implicitly).

These words are expected to be cultivated and internalized by the 'Outer Sanctum'. They are charged with the job of 'educating' the Lower Sanctum or the masses at the bottom of the pyramid. This must be done in such a way that the Lower Sanctum are unaware of the continual stream of brainwashing – but of course they are!

The Outer Sanctum comprise a hundred Sanctees who have long forgotten how to exude a true 'sanctimonious' air – a corporate value. Instead they are a core of Sanctees who work 9–5 every day in an unquestioning, apathetic way and who protect the Inner Sanctum from the true feelings of the masses. This is also in their own interest.

The Lower Sanctum, representing some 2,000, get on with their work. They know, or have learned to their cost, that they must be *'seen and not heard'*. They speak pure 'Sanctspeake' a mumbled, jittery, hesitant, hurried speech exchanged in coffee lounges and in quiet corners. They take orders from the 'Outer Sanctum', many of whom are known as 'Suits'. They rarely see the Inner Sanctum but their presence is felt nevertheless. They know that to cross the 'suits' could result in dismissal, 'movement', 'scapegoating' or suicide. Their tactics for survival are to maintain a low profile, to appear busy and to use the right 'buzz-led' phrases exalting the agreed 'sanctimonious' speak.

The Sanctum is not without its enemies – consisting of the 'Lower Sanctum United', a group set up to meet the criteria laid down by the Upper and Over Sanctum but detested secretly by the Inner Sanctum. Lucy Cannon, known as the 'poisonous dwarf', and Arthur Trotsky lead the Lower Sanctum United. Juliet Scapegoat is the 'heroine', an Outer Sanctum Sanctee of the upper middle variety, and Winsome-Loosem is of the same order.

The visit   Mr Thrashem from the Upper and Over Sanctum is due to visit Dulltown No. 103 Sanctum.

His purpose is to be *'seen and heard'*. The press, photographers and TV will be there in significant numbers.

Mr Thrashem is *important* to the Inner Sanctum who are all scurrying around. When they bump into each other, a sort of high-pitched voice emanates 'recognition', 'must be corporate' and everyone looks even more busy!

Mr Thrashem is opening a sub-unit in Dulltown and Sanctee No. 2 will be there with his minions. Minions 1 and 2 are particularly ferocious and everyone, even their peers, always speak 'sanctimonious' in their presence. It's a sort of unwritten rule. To get Sanctee No. 2 on your back is 'career limiting'.

Juliet Scapegoat and Winsome-Loosem are friends and behind the scenes have organized a programme for the masses which they call 'Return to the Real World'. Ten people from the Lower Sanctum have successfully completed this. These were organized in conjunction with Lucy Cannon.

Lucy Cannon has 'big ideas!' Cannon et al. have links with the Upper Sanctum United. Without a care in the world Cannon et al. go direct for talks to the Upper Sanctum United. They have links to Mr Thrashem et al. direct! Without reference to Dulltown and the Inner Sanctum, Mr Thrashem is to present the 'Return to the Real World' sanctees (Lower Sanctum) with their Certificates! Lucy Cannon liaises with Miss Scapegoat who is to finalize the arrangements with the Inner Sanctum! Cannon et al. make themselves scarce. The Corporate balloon at its hottest hits the proverbial fan!

Miss Scapegoat and Winsome-Loosem find themselves at the centre of attention and with nowhere to hide. Winsome-Loosem, who is used to political infighting and who thrives on conflict, finds a way out! Miss Scapegoat awaits her fate.

Lucy Cannon finds herself questioned by Upper Sanctee No. 3 with Minion Control. This has the appearance of informality but you should 'never judge the book by its cover' and all the Upper Sanctum are poised and eager for feedback. 'Feedback' being a form of language largely used by the Upper Sanctum for their exclusive use.

The Upper Sanctum huddle even more closely over meetings such as the Upper Sanctum Meeting and Upper Sanctum subgroup. They devise a cunning plan using the rational approach to decision-making – New Rule One!

> *Rule 1 is called 'Co-ordination of Upper and Over Sanctum and Crown United visits'.*
> *Rule 2 All visits must be co-ordinated by No. 1 Upper Sanctee.*
> *Rule 3 This applies to everyone* (particularly the Outer and Lower Sanctum but formally this is not emphasized. It may upset the delicate 'ba-ba-balance' of power and spoil splendid relations with Upper and Over Representatives).

A new order will be circulated by Minion Control as a matter of priority.

Lucy Cannon et al. also meet and, true to their counter-culture unit, devise further interventions.

Step two
- The plot is based on rigid hierarchical structure with tight controls emanating primarily from the top of the organization.
- It has by necessity many rules and regulations which provide a large organization with a consistent framework.
- The Taylorist approach, however, is also overlaid by a strong political dimension. It is a government body and is in the public domain.
- In addition, professional bodies and trade unions are prevalent as semi-counter cultures which modify the extremes of regulation.

This story gives a picture of a visit by a Senior Parliamentarian and a strong trade unionist influence.

Changes to be made

1   The Inner Sanctum should identify its values and the symbolism of its actions. It should involve entrenched, apathetic middle managers in some of the decision-making to break down the barriers between them.
2   Middle managers should be valued for their contributions and should be encouraged to have ownership.
3   Jargon words should be unpacked so that there is shared understanding of their implicit and explicit meanings.
4   Senior Managers should 'walk the talk', to be visible, available and approachable.
5   Lucy Cannon represents the strong counter-culture which is in direct proportion to the dark side of the culture. This should be recognized and acted upon positively. Lucy is a powerful informal, political leader. Her links to the Parliamentarian should have been anticipated by the Inner Sanctum. As soon as dialogue was detected, Cannon et al. should have been involved more formally to minimize any misrepresentation of the organization.
6   Miss Scapegoat should have insisted that Lucy Cannon take responsibility for her actions and report directly to the Senior Team. Not to do so was a misjudgement on her part.
7   Winsome-Loosem does not exist although elements of his character represent 'Minion Control'.

Summary   The culture of the organization is very much 'do as I say' and 'don't question too much'. There needs to be more openness and risk taking. Senior managers need to identify with staff, presenting the values of the organization. These need to be a 'lived-out' experience especially by senior and middle managers. The organization will remain political but involvement of the trade unions may limit the sabotaging effects on the organization.

All names and descriptions are of course entirely coincidental.

STRATEGIC LEARNING

What conclusion can we come to regarding Strategic Human Resource Development in organizations today? In times of turbulence Ashby's *law of requisite variety* provides a potential direction. This principle states that for a system to preserve its integrity and survive, its rate of learning must at least match the rate of change in its environment (Ashby, 1956).

The first two models for Strategic Human Resource Development interventions identified in the previous chapter – the *machine* and the *organism* reflect four basic values: (a) to maintain unilateral control; (b) to maximize 'winning' and minimize 'losing'; (c) to suppress negative feelings; and (d) to be as 'rational' (defining clear objectives and evaluating their behaviour in terms of whether or not they have achieved them) as possible. The problem is that these values are created to avoid embarrassment, threat or feeling vulnerable or incompetent. As such, this is regarded as defensive reasoning since it 'encourages individuals to keep private the premises, inferences, and conclusions that shape their behavior and to avoid testing them in a truly independent, objective fashion' (Argyris, 1997: 206).

In discussing an example of defensive reasoning Argyris cites managers who continually attribute the problem elsewhere rather than recognize their own contribution to it:

> Because the attributions that go into defensive reasoning are never really tested, it is a closed loop, remarkably impervious to conflicting points of view. The inevitable response to the observation that somebody is reasoning defensively is yet more defensive reasoning. With the case team, for example, whenever anyone pointed out the professionals' defensive behavior to them, their initial reaction was to look for the cause in somebody else – clients who were so sensitive that they would have been alienated if the consultants had criticized them or a manager so weak that he couldn't have taken it had the consultants raised their concerns with him. In other words, the case team members once again denied their own responsibility by externalizing the problem and putting it on someone else . . . Needless to say, such a master program inevitably short-circuits learning. And for a number of reasons unique to their psychology, well-educated professionals are especially susceptible to this. (ibid.: 207)

If these are inevitable human behaviours, then how can organizations break out of this vicious circle? Argyris' first point is motivational. That is, 'despite the strength of defensive reasoning, people genuinely strive to produce what they intend' because they 'value acting competently' and because their 'self-esteem is intimately tied up with behaving consistently and performing effectively' (ibid.: 207). His second point is about method. That is, individuals 'can be taught how to recognize the reasoning they use when they design and implement their actions' and they can begin by identifying the 'inconsistencies between their espoused and actual theories of action' (ibid.: 207). Inevitably, as with all human learning, there is no quick fix or recipe for change. There is, however, a growing awareness among practitioners that organizational learning and change are intertwined and need to begin with reflective awareness. As Argyris argues, the first step is for managers at the top to critically examine and change their own theories-in-use.

Organizational learning provides a flexible solution to the demands of contemporary organizations. The point here is that change requires awareness of key learning processes. Organizational learning represents the organizational responses to turbulence by creating solutions to the daily routine of unforeseen events that create everyday problems. In this respect Shrivastava (1983) has suggested that there are three kinds of learning for the organization to deal with: (a) 'adaptive learning' which identifies critical processes in the external environment, thereby bringing about emergent changes from new knowledge about the environment; (b) learning to influence the organization's theories-in-use (Shrivastava calls this 'assumption sharing' and changing) as defined originally by Argyris and Schön (1978); and (c) learning that develops a wider 'knowledge base'.

Argyris has argued for more than a decade that most companies have difficulty addressing the learning dilemma. That is, most are not even aware that it exists or if they have some interest, they often 'misunderstand what learning is and how to bring it about' (Argyris, 1997: 201). A major problem is that learning is defined too narrowly as mere problem-solving, 'so they focus on identifying and correcting errors in the external environment' (ibid.: 201). Although he regards solving problems as an important activity, it is not essentially strategic learning. Strategic learning therefore requires managers and employees to look inward, to reflect critically on their own behaviour and identify the ways 'they often inadvertently contribute to the organization's problems'. In particular, they must learn how the very way they go about defining and solving problems can be a source of problems in its own right (ibid.: 201). Argyris call this problem 'defensive reasoning and the doom loop' by which he refers to the essential contradiction between what people say (action) and what they do (behaviour). This is evident in the case of: 'The graveyard of ambition'.

LEARNING AND CHANGE

As Lorange has argued, 'In an entirely stable world, learning would be largely a luxury which one would not necessarily have to pursue systematically, and certainly not one on which to spend organizational resources extensively' but with the risk of becoming obsolete and no longer being relevant to one's customers there are strong pressures to learn (1996: 5). Therefore, at both the individual and organizational levels, learning has to be inspired by change (ibid.: 5). That is to say, critical factors impacting either at the individual or the organizational level need to be identified, managed and reflected upon as a process. Consequently, because organizational environments are changing rapidly 'one might perhaps say that change, as a phenomenon, represents the very rationale for the necessity to learn' (ibid.: 5). The turbulence experienced in recent years has been depicted by a series of change-related metaphors such as Charles Handy's, 'the age of unreason' (1990), Vaill's description of 'permanent white water' (1989), Morgan's 'riding the waves of change' (1988), and Stacey's 'managing the unknowable' (1992). However, because of the need to operate in turbulent environments, contemporary organizations will have to consider newer and more imaginative ways of developing employees and changing their organizations. Personal development and management development will require a greater focus on types of learning.

Individual learning

Individual learning has been identified through a number of models such as Kolb's cycle of (a) concrete experience; (b) reflection; (c) abstract conceptualization; and (d) active experimentation. Argyris (1989; 1991; 1993), on the other hand, has been more concerned to develop a theory of learning through a recognition of an individual's espoused theories, theories-in-use and defensive justifications. Another direction was taken by Senge (1990) to identify 'mental models' based on underlying beliefs, habits and values through which people define reality. Thus by challenging these, individuals can either modify or transform their ideas.

Organizational learning

Argyris and Schön (1978) suggested the term 'organizational learning' refer to an organization's adaptability to a changing environment. Learning in organizations can be said to require the development of both systems and processes in order that changes in the external (and internal) environments filter through to attitudes, procedures and practices in a way that facilitates constant review of operating norms at a variety of levels throughout the organization. Organizational growth appears to be a determinant of organizational learning and as Appelbaum and Reichart point out, 'In the early stages of an organization's existence, organizational learning is often synonymous with individual learning because the organization consists of a small group of people and has minimal structure. As an organization grows, a distinction between individual and organizational learning evolves' (1997: 228).

Organizational learning is not the same as individual learning since the sum of the parts do not equal the collaborative effort of the team. This follows Senge's comment that a team of committed managers with individual IQs above 120 can have a collective IQ of 63 as a result of their learning disability (Senge, 1990: 9). Current literature suggests that there is no definitive agreed definition of a learning organization since it is not possible to identify an organizational blueprint. Marsick and Watkins, for example, argue that 'the learning organization is not a prescription, but rather a template for the examination of current practices' (1994: 354).

For March and Olsen (1976), organizational learning begins with individual learning. Their account views organizational learning in behaviouristic terms as a 'stimulus-response system' in which individuals' beliefs inform organizational decision-making. They identified four learning conditions which inhibited learning:

1   *Role-constrained learning* which occurred when the constraints of the role limited the development of knowledge (typical of bureaucratic situations in which rules and regulations prevented individuals from integrating their learning with others).
2   *Superstitious learning* which is based on untested belief and inference rather than fact (this represents a failure to establish causal relationships

between facts and leads either to partial misinterpretation, or to the development of an entire mythology).

3 *Audience learning* which results from the separation of learning from doing.

4 *Ambiguous learning* which results from an inconsistency between external reality (established or potential fact) and individuals' beliefs. (see Bedeian, 1984)

The learning organization

The concept of the learning organization is summed up by Senge's phrase 'metanoia', or a shift in mindset. This is 'the basic meaning of a "learning organization" – an organization that is continually expanding its capacity to create its future' (Senge, 1990: 13). In order to give the concept greater tangibility, Garvin (1993) argued that the learning organization should be 'meaningful, manageable and measurable'. Others, however, have argued that the concept of learning organization should be viewed as a metaphor rather than a distinct type of structure, (Drew and Smith, 1995; Pedler et al., 1991). Drew and Smith suggest that a useful way of thinking about the metaphor is as a 'social system' whose members have learned conscious communal processes: (a) for continually generating, retaining and leveraging individual and collective learning to improve performance of the organizational system in ways important to all stakeholders; and (b) by monitoring and improving performance (Drew and Smith, 1995). Their approach attempts to relate permanent change to learning by suggesting a model consisting of three elements: 'focus', 'will' and 'capability'. Focus refers to a clear sense of direction and vision. It is 'rooted in the shared mental maps of the top teams' and in the 'shared vision throughout the organization'. It is useful to distinguish between a necessary 'high degree of focus' which 'requires a well-developed knowledge of the business and an extraordinary understanding of critical players, relationships, events and timings affecting the future' and 'excessive focus' which can be dangerous if it leads to rigidity (Drew and Smith, 1995: 5).

The second aspect 'will' is similar to Hamel and Prahalad's (1989) concept of 'strength of strategic intent' which refers to an inclination to set 'stretch' targets and face up to challenges. Will creates a 'winners' culture because it is 'influenced by strength and styles of leadership throughout the organization, not just at the top by generating self-confidence and a desire to succeed' but it requires 'emotional commitment and high energy levels' which may result from internal tensions 'evoked by dissatisfaction with the status quo' leading to a desire to 'unfreeze' (Drew and Smith, 1995: 5).

The third element is 'capability' which, although influenced by stakeholder interests and preferences which themselves may exert critical constraints, refers to: (a) specific learned competences that are related to the organization's current situation; and (b) the ability and freedom to take action. Capability may be limited by the dynamics of the context such as power and ownership.

The point here is that change requires awareness of key learning processes which include:

1   benchmarking (which is described as a process of learning from other firms in the same or related industries);
2   action learning through teamwork and through executive development programmes resulting in learning-by-doing;
3   an organizational climate 'which tolerates failures associated with greater learning and experimentation' and displays openness and trust through teamwork;
4   a commitment to support continuous learning;
5   creative planning techniques, 'such as scenarios, visualization and interactive planning . . . which can stimulate strategic thinking and faster learning' (Drew and Smith, 1995: 6).

CONCLUSION

This chapter has attempted to illustrate the role of the change agent in Strategic Human Resource Development through a series of case studies. These examples reflect the subtlety of the role required by internal change agents. Examples of managing change through each of the four models (machine, organism, drama, discourse) carry their own set of boundary rules related to defining the task, maintaining equilibrium, managing the drama and negotiating the discourse. As Figure 6.1 indicates, the culture of the organization is critical to how each of these models will be used by change agents. Thus, power, politics and decision-making, motivation, leadership, role conflict and stress will all be related to how well the different types of intervention are managed. It has also become apparent that the management of change has not only become an activity for managers, it requires a co-ordinating role for the Strategic Human Resource Development change agent (or internal consultant). It has also become apparent that change today deals with processual issues and requires awareness of organizational learning. The learning organization is effectively the flexible solution to the problem of change because it seeks to promote continuous learning and develop the potential of all employees. In addition, it seeks to integrate the individual's learning with that of the organization.

FURTHER READING

Useful texts on learning are Argyris (1997), and Easterby-Smith et al. (1999). Two useful text on change agent practice are Gilley et al. (2001a) and Gilley et al. (2001b).

Conclusion 7

Business gurus and consultants have merely interpreted the world, the point is to change it. This book is written for managers as change agents who wish to understand the frameworks and practical applications for a new Strategic Human Resource Development. The word 'strategy' in SHRD incorporates the underpinning knowledge of three domains – Organizational Development, Human Resource Development and Strategic Management. To that end, this book attempts to provide a better understanding of the concepts and ideas that influence contemporary SHRD practice. The starting point is the need to understand the limitations of the top-down formulas of change management.

The ability to analyse and diagnose change depends upon a complex mix of knowledge, skill and experience. The balance between these three elements is critical. Knowledge applied without skill and experience leads to complacency. Skill without knowledge and experience leads to frustration when things fail to work out as expected. Experience without knowledge or skill leads to a myopic sense of sublime detachment and self-importance. There are two implications for organizations. First, is the requirement that organizations create management development programmes to facilitate the acquisition of change skills. Second, is the need for change agents to develop sensitivity to the dynamics of process in order to deliver meaningful services and products to customers or clients.

The knowledge and sensitivity encouraged by this book seek to enhance the abilities of managers as observers, communicators, and assimilators of knowledge. Strategic Human Resource Development should therefore be regarded as a form of craft knowledge that enables managers to develop an authoritative understanding of change processes. The ability to facilitate pro-active change is, above all else, the distinguishing characteristic of the SHRD change agent.

SHRD craft knowledge requires the change agent to become competent at processing information. This craft knowledge requires acute powers of perception and an ability to recognize critical issues and problems confronting organizations. For example, Chapter 1 introduced Blake and Mouton's

(1972) concern to understand the motives and ethics behind different intervention strategies. Furthermore, in Chapter 5, it was argued that an effective change agent required an ability to identify a course of action through root metaphors intended to guide the focus of the intervention. In Chapter 6 we discover what it is to become a change agent and how each of the root metaphors inform the change agent role as mentor, critical thinker, strategist, interpreter, communicator and, above all, as co-worker.

The skills of the change agent will be shaped by experience, on the one hand, and by conceptual schemes on the other. Finding the right balance between each is rather like equating rules with hedges, as Thomas Hobbes did in the seventeenth century when he suggested that hedges exist not to constrain people but to guide them in their way so they will not get lost in the wilderness. When the rules become moribund, however, they need to be challenged by new ideas and imaginative symbolic constructs. An example of this was 'The graveyard of ambition' case study illustrated in Chapter 6. The ability to understand the social dynamics of change, however, requires awareness of organizational culture as a concept that is dynamic and fluid, except, of course, in certain circumstances where conformity to a well-defined norm is itself a virtue.

The processes by which we build pictures of the world from subjective experience or from objective maps require an ability to visualize a pattern that is not always immediately obvious to others. The change agent operates with experimental instruments often transforming the subjective thinking of others. A word of caution is recommended when using the word subjective. To call organizational knowledge subjective is to argue that it is knowledge performed by a knowing subject who is informed by historical and contextual circumstances but seeks ways to transform them.

It is not enough to simply have technical expertise in, for example, accountancy, retail marketing, or electronic design. The reflective practitioner needs to think about change as a long and complex series of processes.

It would be useful to conclude with a few words on the nature of change. In one sense, change can be regarded as flux. That is, as a regular but constantly changing pattern of ideas and actions performed by people in organizations. However, for practical purposes it is useful to think about change as comprised of human actions that transform the status quo.

There is a sense in which we can also regard change as either reactive or pro-active. Reactive change carries its own set of dynamics which we can define as radical in the sense that they seek to totally transform an organization. This can happen with mergers or take-overs or when a new chief executive attempts to re-invent an entire organization. Chapter 2, for example, illustrated six strategies that became central to the development of organizational efficiency in the twentieth century and were regarded as precursors to our understanding of the management of change in the twenty-first century. For the purpose of this book, however, we have focused on incremental change which is much more positive and less confrontational, and is driven by internal actions performed on an organization through volition and methodical enquiry.

Pro-active change is concerned with the act of transforming products or services by focusing on the key processes. It proceeds as a succession of events that modify or replace previous patterns of activity in temporal sequences. That is, as a series of short-term, medium-term and long-term transformations that are marked by calendar time. Finally, it was also noted in Chapter 4 that Strategic Human Resource Development practitioners need to understand three things. First, they need to understand the complexity of change management. Second, that being a change agent is a role of facilitation and not a training role. Third, that they are required to promote a more enlightened, ethical and skills-focused change management that puts human resources back where they belong – at the top of the change agenda. Ultimately, the skills of the change agent will depend on the ability to apply the craft knowledge in order to gain the 'conceptual leverage' illustrated by Chapter 6. Such people do manage to go beyond interpretation and transform the world for the better.

Bibliography

Ackers, H.P., Marchington, M., Goodman, J. and Wilkinson, A. (1992) *New Developments in Employee Involvement*. Research Series 2. Sheffield: Employment Department.

Albrecht, K. (1983) *Organization Development: A Total Systems Approach to Positive Change in any Business Organization*. New Jersey: Prentice-Hall.

Alimo-Metcalfe, B. (1997) 'Machiavelli, Mother Theresa and the concept of empowerment', *Management Development Review*, 10 (4/5): 4–18.

Alpander, G.G. and Carroll, R.L. (1995) 'Culture, strategy and teamwork: the keys to organizational change', *Journal of Management Development*, 14 (8): 4–18.

Alvesson, M. (1993) 'The play of metaphors', in J. Hassard and M. Parker (eds) *Postmodernism and Organizations*. London: Sage. pp. 114–31.

Alvesson, M. and Deetz, S. (2000) *Doing Critical Management Research*. London: Sage.

Alvesson, M. and Willmott, H. (eds) (1992) *Critical Management Studies*. London: Sage.

Anderson, A.H. (1992) *Successful Training Practice: A Manager's Guide to Personal Development*. Oxford: Blackwell.

Andrews, P.H. and Herschel, R.T. (1996) *Organizational Communication: Empowerment in a Technological Society*. Boston: Houghton Mifflin.

Appelbaum, S.H. and Reichart, W. (1997) 'How to measure an organization's learning ability: a learning orientation: part I', *Journal of Workplace Learning*, 9 (7): 225–39.

Argyle, M., Furnham, A. and Graham, J. (1981) *Social Situations*. Cambridge: Cambridge University Press.

Argyris, C. (1957) *Personality and Organization*. New York: Harper and Row.

Argyris, C. (1962) *Interpersonal Competence and Organizational Effectiveness*. Homewood, IL: Irwin.

Argyris, C. (1989) 'Strategy implementation: an experience in learning', *Organizational Dynamics*, 18 (2): 5–15.

Argyris, C. (1990) *Overcoming Organizational Defenses: Facilitating Organizational Learning.* Boston: Allyn and Bacon/Simon and Schuster.

Argyris, C. (1991/1997) 'Teaching smart people to learn', *Harvard Business Review,* May/June: 99–109.

Argyris, C. (1993) 'Education for leading-learning', *Organizational Dynamics,* 21 (3): 5–17.

Argyris, C. and Schön, D. (1974) *Theory in Practice: Increasing Professional Effectiveness.* San Francisco: Jossey-Bass.

Argyris, C. and Schön, D. (1978) *Organizational Learning: A Theory of Action Perspective.* New York: Addison-Wesley.

Ashby, W.R. (1956) *An Introduction to Cybernetics.* London: Methuen and Co.

Austin, J.L. (1962) *How to Do Things with Words.* Oxford: Oxford University Press.

Bales, R.F. (1970) *Personality and Interpersonal Behaviour.* London: Holt, Rinehart and Winston.

Bales, R.F. (1950) 'A set of categories for the analysis of small group interaction', *American Sociological Review,* 15 (25): 7–63.

Band, D.C. and Tustin, C.M. (1995) 'Strategic downsizing', *Management Decision,* 33 (8): 36–45.

Barley, S.R., Meyer, G.W. and Gash, D.C. (1988) 'Cultures of culture: academics, practitioners and the pragmatics of normative control', *Administrative Science Quarterly,* 33 (1): 24–60.

Barnard, C. (1938) *The Functions of the Executive.* Cambridge, MA: Harvard University Press.

Barry, D. (1997) 'Telling changes: from narrative family therapy to organizational change and development', *Journal of Organizational Change Management,* 10 (1): 30–4.

Barter, R.F. (1994) 'In search of excellence in libraries: the management writings of Tom Peters and their implications for library and information services', *Library Management,* 15 (8): 4–15.

Bate, P. (1995) *Strategies for Cultural Change.* Oxford: Butterworth-Heinemann.

Bateson, G. (1972) *Steps to an Ecology of Mind.* New York: Ballantine.

Bavelas, A. (1948) 'A mathematical model for group structures', *Applied Anthropology,* 7: 19–30.

Bavelas, A. (1951) 'Communication patterns in task-oriented groups', in H.N. Lasswell and D. Lerner (eds), *The Policy Sciences.* Stanford, CA: Stanford University Press.

Beardwell, I. and Holden, L. (1994) *Human Resource Management: A Contemporary Perspective.* London: Pitman.

Beck, A.S. and Jones, T. (1988) 'From training manager to human resource development manager – not a rose by any other name!', *Industrial and Commercial Training,* May–June: 7–12.

Beckhard, R. (1969) *Organisation Development: Strategies and Models.* Reading, MA: Addison-Wesley.

Bedeian, A.G. (1984) *Organizations: Theory and Analysis*. New York: Dryden Press.

Beech, N. (1996) 'Organisational change interventions: a new set of beliefs?', in C. Oswick and D. Grant (eds), *Organisation Development, Metaphorical Explorations*. London: Pitman. pp. 175–89.

Beekun, R.L. (1989) 'Assessing the effectiveness of sociotechnical interventions: Antidote or fad?', *Human Relations*, 47 (10): 877–97.

Beer, M. and Walton, A.E. (1987) 'Organisation change and development', *Annual Review of Psychology*, 38: 339–67.

Beetham, D. (1985) *Max Weber and the Theory of Modern Politics*. 2nd edn. London: Allen and Unwin.

Belbin, R.M. (1981) *Management Teams: Why They Succeed or Fail*. Oxford: Butterworth-Heinemann.

Belbin, R.M. (1993) *Team Roles at Work*. Oxford: Butterworth-Heinemann.

Bell, D. (1988) *The End of Ideology: On the Exhaustion of Political Ideas in the Fifties*. Cambridge: Harvard University Press.

Benne, K.D. and Sheats, P. (1948) 'Functional roles of group members', *Journal of Social Issues*, 4: 41–9.

Bennis, W.G. and Slater, P.E. (1968) 'The temporary society', in W.G. Bennis and P.E. Slater (eds), *The Temporary Society*. New York: Harper and Row.

Bennis, W. (1969) *Organization Development: Its Nature, Origins and Prospects*. Reading, MA: Addison-Wesley.

Berger, H.S. and Luckmann, T. (1967) *The Social Construction of Reality*. New York: Anchor.

Bessant, J. (1990) *Managing Advanced Manufacturing Technology: The Challenge of the Fifth Wave*. Oxford: Basil Blackwell.

Bevan, J. (1987) 'What is co-makership?', *International Journal of Quality and Reliability Management*, 4 (3): 7–21.

Beyer, J.M. and Trice, H.M. (1988) 'The communication of power relations in organisations through cultural rites', in M.D. Jones, M.D. Moore and R.C. Sayder (eds), *Inside Organisations: Understanding the Human Dimension*. Newbury Park, CA: Sage, pp. 141–57.

Biggart, N.W. (1989) *Charismatic Capitalism: Direct Selling Organizations in America*. Chicago: University of Chicago Press.

Bion, W.R. (1961) *Experiences in Groups and Other Papers*. London: Tavistock Publications.

Black, M. (1962) *Models and Metaphors*. Ithaca, NY: Cornell University Press.

Blake, R.B. and Mouton, J.S. (1972) *Strategies of Consultation*. Austin, TX: Scientific Methods.

Blau, P.M. (1965) *Bureaucracy in Modern Society*. New York: Random House.

Blauner, R. (1966) *Alienation and Freedom*. Chicago: University of Chicago Press.

Bleecker, S.E. (1994) 'The virtual organization', *The Futurist*, 28 (2): 9–12.

Bloch, M. (1975) *Political Language and Oratory in Traditional Society*. New York: Academic Press.

Blumberg, P. (1968) *Industrial Democracy: The Sociology of Participation*. London: Constable.

Boisot, M. (1995) 'Preparing for turbulence', in B. Garratt (ed.), *Developing Strategic Thought*. Maidenhead: McGraw–Hill. pp. 29–45.

Boje, D.M. (1994) 'Organizational storytelling: the struggles of pre-modern, modern and postmodern organizational learning discourses', *Management Learning*, 25 (3): 46–57.

Boje, D.M. (1995) 'Stories of the storytelling organization: a postmodern analysis of Disney as "Tamara-land"', *Academy of Management Journal*, 38 (4): 997–1035.

Boje, D.M. and Winsor, R.D. (1993) 'The resurrection of Taylorism: total quality management's hidden agenda', *Journal of Organizational Change Management*, 6 (4): 57–70.

Boje, D.M., Fedor, D.B. and Rowland, K.M. (1982) 'Myth making: a qualitative step in OD interventions', *Journal of Applied Behavioral Science*, 18 (1): 17–28.

Boland, R.J. and Tenkasi, R.V. (1995) 'Perspective making and perspective taking in communities of knowing', *Organization Science*, 4 (6): 350–72.

Bolman, L.G. and Deal, T.E. (1991) *Reframing Organizations: Artistry, Choice and Leadership*. San Francisco, CA: Jossey-Bass.

Bolman, L.G. and Deal, T.E. (1994) 'The organization as theatre', in H. Tsoukas (ed.), *New Thinking in Organizational Behaviour*. Oxford: Butterworth-Heinmann.

Bounds, G., Yorks, L., Adams, M. and Ranney, G. (1996) *Beyond Total Quality Management: Toward the Emerging Paradigm*. New York: McGraw Hill.

Bourgeois, W.V. and Pinder, C.C. (1983) 'Contrasting philosophical perspectives in administrative science: a reply to Morgan', *Administrative Science Quarterly*, 28 (4): 608–13.

Bowen, D.E. and Lawler, E.E. (1992) 'The empowerment of service workers: why, how and when?', *Sloan Management Review*, Spring, 33 (3): 31–9.

Bowles, M.L. (1989) 'Myth, meaning, and work organization', *Organization Studies*, 10 (3): 405–21.

Bowles, M.L. and Coates, G. (1993) 'Image and substance: the management of performance as rhetoric or reality?', *Personnel Review*, 22 (2): 3–21.

Bowonder, B. and Miyake, T. (1993) 'Japanese innovation in advanced technologies, an analysis of functional integration', *International Journal of Technology Management*, 8 (1/2): 135–56.

Boyce, M.E. (1996) 'Organizational story and storytelling: a critical review', *Journal of Organizational Change Management*, 9 (5): 5–26.

Braverman, H. (1974) *Labor and Monopoly Capitalism: The Degradation of Work in the Twentieth Century*. Monthly Review Press.

Broadbent, J., Laughlin, R. and Read, S. (1991) 'Recent financial and administrative changes in the NHS: a critical theory analysis', *Critical Perspectives on Accounting*, 2: 1–29.

Brown, A. (1995) *Organisational Culture*. London: Pitman.

Brown, P. and Fraser, C. (1979) 'Speech as a marker of situation', in U. Scherer and H. Giles (eds), *Social Markers in Speech*. Cambridge: Cambridge University Press. pp. 49–57.

Brown, R.K. (1992) *Understanding Industrial Organizations: Theoretical Perspectives in Industrial Sociology*. London: Routledge.

Buchanan, D. and Boddy, D. (1992) *The Expertise of the Change Agent: Public Performance and Backstage Activity*. Hemel Hempstead: Prentice-Hall.

Burgundy, J. de (1996) 'Shoot the messenger! Crazy management fads and faddish management "crazies"', *Empowerment in Organizations*, 4 (4): 28–35.

Burke, K. (1945) *A Grammar of Motives*. New York: Prentice-Hall.

Burke, K. (1950) *A Rhetoric of Motives*. New York: Prentice-Hall.

Burke, K. (1968) 'Dramatism', in *International Encyclopedia of the Social Sciences*, vol. VII, New York: Macmillan, pp. 445–52.

Burke, K.A. (1962) *Grammar of Motives and a Rhetoric of Motives*. Cleveland, OH: Meridian.

Burke, W. (1986) 'Leadership as empowering others', in S. Srivastra (ed.), *Executive Power*. San Francisco: Jossey-Bass, pp. 51–77.

Burke, W. (1992) *Organization Development: A Process of Learning and Change*. Reading, MA: Addison-Wesley.

Burnes, B. (1996a) 'No such thing as a "one best way" to manage organizational change', *Management Decision*, 34 (10): 11–18.

Burnes, B. (1996b) *Managing Change*. 2nd edn. London: Pitman.

Burnes, B. (1997) 'Organizational choice and organizational change', *Management Decision*, 35 (10): 753–9.

Burns, T. and Stalker, G.M. (1961) *The Management of Innovation*. London: Tavistock.

Burrell, D. (1973) *Analogy and Philosophical Language*. New Haven, CT: Yale University Press.

Burrell, G. (1988) 'Modernism, postmodernism, and organizational analysis 2: the contribution of Michel Foucalt', *Organization Studies*, 9 (2): 221–35.

Burrell, G. and Morgan, G. (1979) *Sociological Paradigms and Organisational Analysis*. London: Heinemann.

Calas, M.B. and Smircich, L. (1992) 'Re-writing gender into organizational theorizing: directions from feminist perspectives', in M. Reed and M. Hughes (eds), *Rethinking Organization: New Directions in Organization Theory and Analysis*. Newbury Park, CA: Sage, pp. 227–53.

Cameron, K.S., Freeman, S.J. and Mishra, A.K. (1991) 'Best practices in white-collar downsizing: managing contradictions', *Academy of Management Executive*, 5 (3): 57–73.

Campbell, T. and Cairns, H. (1994) 'From buzz words to behaviours: developing and measuring the learning organization', *Industrial and Commercial Training*, 26 (7): 10–15.

Canney Davison, S. (1994) 'Creating a high performance international team', *Journal of Management Development*, 13 (2): 81–90.

Carnall, C. (1995) *Managing Change in Organizations*. Hemel-Hempstead: Prentice-Hall.

Casey, C. (1996) 'Corporate transformations, designer culture, designer employees and "post-occupational" solidarity', *Organization*, 3 (3): 317–39.

Cassirer, E. (1946) *Language and Myth*. New York: Dover Publications.

CBI (1989) *Managing the Skills Gap*. London: Confederation of British Industry.

Chelsom, J.V. (1997) 'Total quality through empowered training', *Training for Quality*, 5 (4): 139–45.

Cheng, C. (1994) 'Diversity as community and communions: a Taoist alternative to modernity', *Journal of Organisational Change Management*, 7 (6).

Child, J. (1972) 'Organizational structure, environment and performance: the role of strategic choice', *Sociology*, 6: 1–22.

Chin, R. and Benne, K.D. (1994) 'General strategies for effecting changes in human systems', in W.L. French, C.H. Bell and R.A. Zawachi (eds), *Organisation Development and Transformation: Managing Effective Change (4th ed.)*. Boston: Irwin. pp. 22–45.

Chomsky, N. (1959) 'Review of Skinner's verbal behaviour', *Language*, 35 (1): 26–58.

Church, A.H., Burke, W.W. and van Eynde, D.F. (1994) 'Values, motives, and interventions of organization development practitioners', *Group and Organization Management*, 19 (1): 1–50.

Church, A.H. and McMahan G.C. (1996) 'The practice of organization and human resource development in the USA's fastest growing firms', *Leadership and Organization Development Journal*, 17 (2): 37–45.

Church, A.H., Siegal, W., Javitch, M., Burke, W. and Waclawski J. (1996) 'Managing organizational change: what you don't know might hurt you', *Career Development International*, 1 (2): 25–30.

Clark, T. (1995) *Managing Consultants*. Milton Keynes: Open University Press.

Clark, T. and Salaman, G. (1996) 'Telling tales: management consultancy as the art of story telling', in D. Grant and C. Oswick (eds), *Metaphor and Organizations*. London: Sage. pp. 137–61.

Clegg, R.S. (1990) *Modern Organizations: Organization Studies in a Postmoderm World*. London: Sage.

Clegg, S. (1981) 'Organization and control', *Administrative Science Quarterly*, 26: 532–45.

Clegg, S. (1994) 'Weber and Foucault: social theory for the study of organizations', *Organization*, 1 (1): 149–178.

Clemson, B., Keating, C. and Robinson, T. (1997) 'Development of high performance organisational learning units', *The Learning Organization*, 4 (5): 228–34.

Cleveland, H. (1990) 'The age of spreading knowledge', *The Futurist*, March–April: 35–9.

Clutterbuck, D. and Crainer, S. (1990) *Makers of Management: Men and Women Who Changed the Business World*. London: MacMillan, pp. 218–224.

Collins, D. (1995) 'Rooting for empowerment?' *Empowerment in Organizations*, 3 (2): 25–33.

Collins, D. (1997) 'Two cheers for empowerment: some critical reflections', *Leadership and Organization Development Journal*, 18 (1): 23–8.

Conger, J.A. (1986) *Empowering Leadership*, working paper. Montreal: McGill University.

Cooper, C.L. and Mangham, I.L. (1971) (eds). *T-Groups: A Survey of Research*. Chichester: Wiley.

Cooper, C.L. and Williams, S. (1994) *Creating Healthy Work Organizations*. Chichester: John Wiley and Sons.

Cordery, J.L., Mueller, W.S. and Smith, L.M. (1991) 'Attitudinal and behavioral effects of autonomous group working: a longitudinal field study', *Academy of Management Journal*, 34 (2): 464–76.

Cotton, B. (1995) *The Cyberspace Lexicon*. London: Kogan Page.

Cummings, T.G. and Griggs, W.H. (1976) 'Worker reactions to autonomous work groups: conditions for functioning, differential effects, and individual differences', *Organization and Administrative Sciences*, 1996/77, 7 (4): 87–100.

Cummings, T.G. and Huse, E.F. (1989) *Organisational Development and Change*. St. Paul, MN: West.

Cummings, T.G., Molloy, E.S. and Glen, R. (1977) 'A methodological critique of fifty-eight selected work experiments', *Human Relations*, 30: 675–708.

Cummings, T.G. and Worley, C.G. (1997) *Organisational Development and Change*. Ohio: South Western College Publishing.

Cunningham, I. (1994) *The Wisdom of Strategic Learning*. Maidenhead: McGraw-Hill.

Currie, G. and Kerrin, M. (1996) 'English football as a metaphor for organizational change', in C. Oswick and D. Grant (eds), *Organization Development: Metaphorical Explorations*. London: Pitman.

Daloz, L.A. (1986) *Effective Mentoring and Teaching*. San Francisco: Jossey-Bass.

Davenport, T.H. (1993) *Process Innovation: Re-engineering Work through Information Technology*. Boston: Harvard Business School Press.

Davenport, T.H. and Short, J.E. (1990) 'The new industrial engineering: information technology and business process redesign', *Sloan Management Review*, 31 (4): 11–27.

Davidson, K.M. (1991) 'Why acquisitions may not be the best route to innovation', *Journal of Business Strategy*, 12 (3): 50–2.

Dawson, P. (1994) *Total Quality Management: A Processual Approach*. London: Paul Chapman.

Dawson, P. (2002) *Managing Change*. London: Sage.

Dawson, P. and Palmer, G. (1995) *Quality Management*. Melbourne: Longman.

Deadrick, D.L., McAfee, R.B. and Champagne, P.J. (1996) 'Preventing workplace harassment: an organisational change perspective', *Journal of Organisational Change Management*, 9 (2): 66–75.

Deakins, E. and Makgill, H.H. (1997) 'What killed BPR? Some evidence from the literature', *Business Process Management Journal*, 3 (1): 81–107.

Deal, T.E. and Kennedy, A.A. (1988) *Corporate Cultures: The Rites and Rituals of Corporate Life*. Harmondsworth: Penguin.

Dean, J.W. and Evans, J.R. (1994) *Total Quality: Management, Organisation and Strategy*. St Paul, MN: West.

Dehler, G.E. and Welsh, M.A. (1994) 'Spirituality and organizational transformation: implications for the new management paradigm', *Journal of Managerial Psychology*, 9 (6): 17–26.

Derrida, J. (1967) *Writing and Difference*. Chicago, IL: University of Chicago Press.

Despres, C. and Hiltrop, J.M. (1995) 'Human resource management in the knowledge age: current practice and perspectives on the future', *Employee Relations*, 17 (1): 9–23.

DiPadova, L.M. (1996) 'Towards a Weberian management theory: lessons from Lowell Bennion's neglected masterwork', *Journal of Management History*, 2 (1): 59–74.

Dixon, N. (1994) *The Organisational Learning Cycle*. Maidenhead: McGraw-Hill.

Doherty, N., Bank, J. and Vinnicombe, S. (1996) 'Managing survivors: the experience of survivors in British Telecom and the British financial services sector', *Journal of Managerial Psychology*, 11 (7): 51–60.

Donnellon, A. (1996) *Team Talk: The Power of Language in Team Dynamics*. Cambridge, MA: Harvard Business School Press.

Dougherty, D. (1992) 'Interpretive barriers to successful product innovation in large firms', *Organization Science*, 3: 179–202.

Drew, S. and Coulson-Thomas, C. (1996) 'Transformation through teamwork: the path to the new organization?', *Management Decision*, 34 (1): 7–17.

Drew, S.A.W. (1994) 'Downsizing to improve strategic position', *Management Decision*, 32 (1): 4–11.

Drew, S.A.W. and Smith, P.A.C. (1995) 'The learning organization: "change proofing" and strategy', *The Learning Organization*, 2 (1): 4–14.

Drucker, P. (1988) 'The coming of the new organization', *Harvard Business Review*, (January–February): 45–53.

Drucker, P. (1993) *Post-Capitalist Society*. London: Butterworth-Heinemann.

Dunn, S. (1990) 'Root metaphors in the old and new industrial relations', *British Journal of Industrial Relations*, 28 (1): 1–31.

Dunphy, D. and Stace, D. (1988) 'Transformational and coercive strategies for planned organisational change', *Organisation Studies*, 9 (3): 317–34.

Dunphy, D. and Stace, D. (1990) *Under New Management*. Sydney, NSW: McGraw-Hill.

Durkheim, E. (1938) [1895] *Rules of Sociological Method*. Chicago: University of Chicago Press.

Dyck, B. (1994) 'Build in sustainable development and they will come: a vegetable field of freams', *Journal of Organizational Change Management*, 7 (4): 47–63.

Easterby-Smith, M., Burgoyne, J. and Araujo, L. (1999) *Organizational Learning and the Learning Organization*. London: Sage.

Eco, U. (1965) 'Towards a semiotic enquiry into the TV message' in *Working Papers in Cultural Studies*. Birmingham: University of Birmingham, No. 3 1972.

Eco, U. (1976) *Theory of Semiotics*. Bloomington: Indiana University Press.

Edmonstone, J. (1995) 'Managing change: an emerging new consensus', *Health Manpower Management*, 21 (1): 16–19.

Edmonstone, J. and Havergal, M. (1995) 'The death (and rebirth?) of organization development', *Health Manpower Management*, 21 (1): 23–33.

Ekman, P. and Friesen, W.V. (1969) 'Non-verbal leakage and clues to deception', *Psychiatry*, 31 (1): 88–106.

Ekman, P. and Friesen, W.V. (1974) 'Detecting deception from the body or face', *Journal of Personality and Social Psychology*, 29 (3): 288–298.

Elliott, D. and Smith, D. (1992) 'Safety in numbers?: sports stadia disasters in the UK', paper presented at the conference, 'Crisis management in the 1990s', Home Office Emergency Planning College, 15–17 September.

Emery, F.E. and Trist, E.L. (1969) 'The causal texture of organizational environments', in F.E. Emery (ed.) *Systems Thinking*. Harmondsworth: Penguin, pp. 241–57.

Etzioni, A. (1964) *Modern Organizations*. Englewood Cliffs, NJ: Prentice-Hall.

Etzioni, A. (1975) *A Comparative Analysis of Complex Organizations*. New York: The Free Press.

Farace, R.V. Monge, P.R. and Russell, H.M. (1977) *Communicating and Organizing*. Reading MA: Addison-Wesley.

Fayol, H. (1949) *General and Industrial Administration*. London: Pitman.

Felts, A.A. and Jos, P.H. (1996) 'The contemporary challenge to the administrative state: a Weberian analysis', *Journal of Management History*, 2 (1): 21–36.

Ferguson, K. (1984) *The Feminist Case against Bureaucracy*. Philadelphia, PA: Temple University Press.

Fisher, D. Rooks, D. and Torbert, B. (2001) *Personal and Organizational Transformations.* Boston: Edge/Work Press.

Fisher, D. and Torbert, W. (1995) *Personal and Organizational Transformations.* Maidenhead: McGraw-Hill.

Fisk, R.P. and Grove, S.J. (1996) 'Applications of impression management and the drama metaphor in marketing', *European Journal of Marketing*, 30 (9): 6–12.

Fitzgerald, T.H.(1988) 'Can change in culture really be managed?', *Organisational Dynamics*, 17 (2): 5–15.

Fletcher, C. (1996) 'The 250lb man in an alley: police storytelling', *Journal of Organizational Change Management*, 9 (5): 36–42.

Ford, J.D. and Ford, L.W. (1995) 'The role of conversations in producing intentional change in organizations', *Academy of Management Review*, 20 (3): 541–570.

Foucault, M. (1972) *The Archaeology of Knowledge.* London: Routledge.

Foucault, M. (1984) *The History of Sexuality: An Introduction.* Harmondsworth: Penguin.

Francis, S. (1997) 'A time for reflection: learning about organizational learning', *The Learning Organization*, 4 (4): 168–79.

Freire, P. (1985) *The Politics of Education: Culture, Power, and Liberation*, trans. by D. Macedo. Westport, CT: Bergin and Garvey.

French, W.L. and Bell, C.H. (1995) *Organization Development–Behavioral Science Interventions for Organization Improvement*, 5th edn. New York: Prentice-Hall.

Fromm, E. (1963) *The Sane Society.* London: Routledge and Kegan Paul.

Frosdick, S. (1995) '"Safety cultures" in British stadia and sporting venues: understanding cross-organisational collaboration for managing public safety in British sports grounds', *Disaster Prevention and Management*, 4 (4): 13–21.

Gaarder, J. (1995) *Sophie's World.* London: Phoenix.

Gagliardi, P. (1986) 'The creation and change of organisational cultures: a conceptual framework', *Organization Studies*, 7 (2): 117–34.

Gallessich, J. (1985) 'Toward a meta-theory of consultation', *Counseling Psychologist*, 13 (3): 336–54.

Gantt, H.L. (1974[1921]) *Industrial Leadership.* Easton, MD: Hive.

Garavan, T.N. (1995) 'Stakeholders and strategic human resource development', *Journal of European Industrial Training*, 19 (10): 11–16.

Garavan, T.N. (1997) 'Training, development, education and learning: different or the same?', *Journal of European Industrial Training*, 21 (2): 39–50.

Garavan, T.N., Costine, P. and Heraty, N. (1995) 'The emergence of strategic human resource development', *Journal of European Industrial Training*, 19 (10): 4–10.

Garfinkel, H. (1967) *Studies in Ethnomethodology.* London: Prentice-Hall.

Garfinkel, H. (1974) 'The origins of the term "ethnomethodology"', in R. Turner (ed.), *Ethnomethodology.* Harmondsworth: Penguin. pp. 15–18.

Garratt, B. (1987) *The Learning Organization*. London: Collins.

Garratt, B. (1994) *Developing Strategic Thought*. Maidenhead: McGraw-Hill.

Garvin, D.A. (1993) 'Building a learning organization', *Harvard Business Review*, 71 (4): 78–91.

Geertz, C. (1975a) 'Thick description, towards an interpretive theory of culture', in C. Geertz, *The Interpretation of Cultures*. London: Hutchinson.

Geertz, C. (1975b) 'Notes on the Balinese cockfight', in C. Geertz, *The Interpretation of Cultures*. London: Hutchinson. pp. 421–53.

Ghobadian, A. and Speller, S. (1994) 'Gurus of quality: a framework for comparison', Total Quality Management, 5 (3): 53–69.

Gilbreth, F.B. (1911) *Motion Study*. New York: Van Nostrand.

Giles, H. and Hewstone, M. (1982) 'Cognitive structures, speech and social situations: two integrative models', *Language Sciences*, 4, 187–219.

Giles, H., Scherer, K. and Taylor, C. (1979) 'Speech markers in social interaction', in U. Scherer and H. Giles (eds), *Social Markers in Speech*. Cambridge: Cambridge University Press. pp. 108–114.

Gilley, J.W. Dean, P. and Bierema, L. (2001b) *Philosophy and Practice of Organizational Learning, Performance and Change*. Cambridge, MA: Perseus.

Gilley, J.W. and Eggland, S.A. (1989) *Principles of Human Resource Development*. Reading, MA: Addison-Wesley.

Gilley, J.W., Quatro S.A., Hoekstra, E., Whittle, D.D. and Maycunich, A. (2001). *The Manager as Change Agent: A Practical Guide to Developing High Performance People and Organizations*. Cambridge, MA: Perseus.

Giroux, H.A. (1992) *Border Crossings: Cultural Workers and the Politics of Education*. New York: Routledge.

Giroux, H.A. (1993) *Living Dangerously: Multiculturalism and the Politics of Difference*. New York: Peter Lang.

Goffman, E. (1966) *The Presentation of Self in Everyday Life*. Harmondsworth: Penguin.

Goodman, P.S., Devadas, S. and Hughson, T.L. (1988) 'Groups and productivity: analyzing the effectiveness of self-managing teams', in J.P. Campbell, R.J. Campbell and Associates (eds), *Productivity in Organizations*. San Francisco: Jossey-Bass and Associates, pp. 295–325.

Gramsci, A. (1971) *Selections from the Prison Notebooks*. New York: International Publishers.

Grant, D. (1996) 'Metaphors, human resource management and control', in C. Oswick and D. Grant (eds), *Organisation Development: Metaphorical Explorations*. London: Pitman.

Granville, D. (1996) 'Developing logistics potential through people', *Logistics Information Management*, 9 (1): 39–44.

Green, C. (1996) 'Globalization, borderless worlds, and the Tower of Babel: metaphors gone awry', *Journal of Organizational Change Management*, 8 (4): 55–68.

Greiner, L.E. (1980) 'OD values and the bottom line', in W.W. Burke and L.D. Goodstein, (eds), *Trends and Issues in Organization Development: Current Theory and Practice*. San Diego, CA: University Associates Inc, pp. 319–32.

Grice, S. and Humphries M. (1997) 'Critical management studies in postmodernity: oxymorons in outer space?', *Journal of Organizational Change Management*, 10 (5): 412–25.

Grieves, J. (1996) 'Stories and fictions as representations of organizational experience', in C. Combes, D. Grant, T. Keenoy and C. Oswick (eds), *Organisational Discourse: Talk, Text and Tropes*. London: KMCP.

Grieves, J. and Matthews, B.P. (1997) 'Healthcare and the learning service', *The Learning Organization*, 4 (3): 88–98.

Guimaraes, T. and Bond, W. (1996) 'Empirically assessing the impact of BPR on manufacturing firms', *International Journal of Operations and Production Management*, 16 (8): 5–28.

Gumperz, J.J. (1971) 'The speech community, language in social groups', in A.S. Dil (ed.), *Essays by John J. Gumperz*. Stanford, CA: Stanford University Press. pp. 98–102.

Gumperz, J.J. and Hymes, D. (eds) (1964) 'The ethnography of communication', *American Anthropologist*, 66 (6): part 2.

Hackman, J.R. and Oldham, G.R. (1975) 'Development of the job diagnostic survey', *Journal of Applied Psychology*, 60: 159–70.

Halliday, M.A.K. (1970) 'Language structure and language function', in J. Lyons (ed.), *New Horizons in Linguistics*. Harmondsworth: Penguin. pp. 34–47.

Hamel, G. and Prahalad, C.K. (1989) 'Strategic intent', *Harvard Business Review*, 67 (3): 63–74.

Hammer, M. (1990) 'Reengineering works: don't automate, obliterate', *Harvard Business Review*, 68 (4) 104–12.

Hammer, M. and Champy, J. (1993) *Reengineering the Corporation*. New York: Harper Business.

Hamlin, R.G., Keep, J. and Ash, K. (2001), *Organisational Change and Development: A Reflective Guide for Managers, Trainers and Developers*. London: Financial Times Prentice Hall.

Handy, C. (1985) *Understanding Organizations*. Harmondsworth: Penguin.

Handy, C. (1990) *The Age of Unreason*. Boston: Harvard Business School Press.

Harrigan, K.R. and Dalmia, K. (1991) 'Knowledge workers: the last bastion of competitive advantage', *Planning Review*, November/December: 5–48.

Harrison, M.I. and Shirom, A. (2001) *Organisational Diagnosis and Assessment: Bridging Theory and Practice*. London: Sage.

Harrison, R. (1963) 'Defenses and the need to know', *Human Relations Training News*, 6 (4) 1–3.

Harrison, R. (1966) 'Cognitive change and participation in a sensitivity training laboratory', *Journal of Consulting Psychology*, 30 (6): 517–520.

Harrison, R. (1970) 'Choosing the depth of organizational intervention', *Journal of Applied Behavioral Science*, 6 (2): 189–202.

Harrison, R. (1972) 'Developing autonomy, initiative, and risk taking through a laboratory design', *European Training*, 2: 100–16.

Harrison, R. (1992) *Employee Development*. London: Institute of Personal Management.

Harrison, R. (1996) *The Collected Papers of Roger Harrison*. Maidenhead: McGraw-Hill.

Heery, E. (1996) 'Academics 0, Consultants 4', *British Universities Industrial Relations Association Newsletter*, No. 14, April, p. 8.

Hertzberg, R. (1966) *Work and the Nature of Man*. Cleveland, OH: World.

Hickman, C.R. and Silva, M.A. (1987) *The Future 500: Creating Tomorrow's Organizations Today*. London: Unwin Hyman.

Hilb, M. (1995) 'The challenge of management development in western Europe in the 1990s', *International Journal of Human Resource Management*, 3 (3): 575–84.

Hodge, R. and Kress, G. (1993) *Language as Ideology*. London: Routledge.

Höpfl, H. (1994a) 'Empowerment and the management prerogative', *Empowerment in Organizations*, 2 (3): 39–44.

Höpfl, H. (1994b) 'Organisational transformation and the commitment to safety', *Disaster Prevention and Management*, 3 (3): 49–58.

Höpfl, H. and Maddrell, J. (1996) 'Can you resist a dream? Evangelical metaphors and the appropriation of emotion', in D. Grant and C. Oswick (eds), *Metaphors and Organizations*. London: Sage. pp. 200–12.

Hubbert, A.R., Sehorn, A.G. and Brown S.W. (1995) 'Service expectations: the consumer versus the provider', *International Journal of Service Industry Management*, 6 (1): 6–21.

Huczynski, A.A. (1993) *Management Gurus: What Makes Them and How to Become One*. London: Routledge.

Huy, Q.N. (2001) 'Time temporal capability, and planned change', *The Academy of Management Review*, 26 (4): 601–23.

Inns, D. (1996) 'Organisation development as a journey', in C. Oswick and D. Grant (eds), *Organisation Development, Metaphorical Explorations*. London: Pitman.

Isabella, L.A. (1989) 'Downsizing: survivors' assessments', *Business Horizons*, May–June: 35–41.

Isabella, L.A. (1990) 'Evolving interpretations as a change unfolds: how managers construe key organisational events', *Academy of Management Journal*, 33 (1): 7–41.

Jakobson, R. and Halle, M. (1962) *Fundamentals of Language*. The Hague: Mouton.

Jankowicz, A.D. (1994) 'Etymology as cultural encoding: the stories hidden in the words which we use'. Paper given at the 2nd European Conference of the European Personal Construct Association, St Andreasberg, Harz, Germany, 19–23 April.

Jaques, E. (1951) *The Changing Culture of a Factory*. London: Tavistock Publications.

Jaques, E. (1955) 'Social systems as a defence against persecutory and depressive anxiety', in M. Klein, P. Heimann and R.E. Money-Kyrl (eds), *New Directions in Psychoanalysis*. London: Tavistock Publications, pp. 478–98.

Jaques, E. (1995a) 'Why the psychoanalytical approach to understanding organizations is dysfunctional', *Human Relations*, 48: 343–9.

Jaques, E. (1995b) 'Reply to Dr Gilles Amado', *Human Relations*, 48: 359–65.

Jeffcutt, P. (1994) 'From interpretation to representation in organizational analysis: postmodernism, ethnography and organizational symbolism', *Organization Studies*, 15 (2): 241–74.

Joby, J. (1996) 'A dramaturgical view of the health care service encounter: cultural value-based impression management guidelines for medical professional behaviour', *European Journal of Marketing*, 30 (9): 60–74.

Johnson, G. (1992) 'Managing strategic change: strategy, culture and action', in D. Faulkner and G. Johnson (eds), *The Challenge of Strategic Management*. London: Kogan Page, pp. 202–19.

Johnson, G. and Scholes, K. (1988) *Exploring Corporate Strategy*. 2nd edn. London: Prentice-Hall.

Kanter, R.M. (1983) *The Change Masters: Innovation and Entrepreneurship in the American Corporation*. New York: Simon & Schuster.

Kanter, R.M. (1989) *When Giants Learn to Dance*. New York: Simon and Schuster.

Kapstein, J. and Hoerr, J. (1989) 'Volvo's radical new plant: the death of the assembly line?', *Business Week*, 28 August: 92–3.

Katz, D. and Kahn, R. (1978) *The Social Psychology of Organizations*. New York: John Wiley.

Keenoy, T. (1990) 'Human resource management: rhetoric, reality and contradiction', *International Journal of Human Resource Management*, 1 (3): 363–84.

Keenoy, T. (1991) 'The roots of metaphor in the old and the new industrial relations', *British Journal of Industrial Relations*, 29: 313–27.

Keizer, J.A. and Post, G.J.J. (1996) 'The metaphoric gap as a catalyst of change', in C. Oswick and D. Grant (eds), *Organisation Development, Metaphorical Explorations*. London: Pitman.

Kilmann, R.H. (1982) 'Getting control of the corporate culture', *Managing*, 3: 11–17.

Klein, M. (1946) 'Notes on some schizoid mechanisms', in M. Klein, P. Heimann, S. Isaacs and J. Riviere (eds), *Developments in Psychoanalysis*. London: Hogarth Press, pp. 292–320.

Klein, M. (1952) 'Some theoretical conclusions regarding the emotional life of the infant', in M. Klein, P. Heimann, S. Isaacs and J. Riviere (eds) *Developments in Psychoanalysis*. London: Hogarth Press, pp. 198–237.

Klein, M. (1959) 'Our adult world and its roots in infancy', *Human Relations*, 12: 291–303.

Kobasa, S.C., Maddi, S.R. and Carrington, S. (1981), 'Personality and constitution as mediators in the stress-illness relationship', *Journal of Health and Social Behavior*, 22: 368–78.

Koestler, A. (1969) *The Act of Creation*. London: Hutchinson.

Kolb, D. and Frohman, A. (1970) 'An organisational development approach to consulting', *Sloan Management Review*, 12: 51–65.

Kolb, D.A., Rubin, I.M. and McIntyre, J.M. (1971) *Organizational Psychology: An Experiential Approach*. Englewood Cliffs, NJ: Prentice-Hall.

Koonce, R. (1991) 'The "People Side" of Organizations Change', *Credit Magazine*, 17 (6), November–December: 22–5.

Kotler, P. (1991) 'From mass marketing to mass customization', *Planning Review*, September–October: 11–47.

Kramar, R. (1992) 'Strategic human resource management: are the promises fulfilled?', *Asia Pacific Journal of Human Resources*, 30 (1): 1–15.

Kuhn, T.S. (1970) *The Structure of Scientific Revolutions*. Chicago: University of Chicago Press.

Lacan, J. (1966) *Ecrits*. Paris: Seuil.

Lakoff, C. and Johnson, M. (1980) *Metaphors We Live By*. Chicago: University of Chicago Press.

Lakoff, G. and Johnson, M. (1981) 'Conceptual metaphor in everyday language', in M. Johnson (ed.), *Philosophical Perspectives on Metaphor*. Minneapolis: Universitry of Minnesota Press.

Lash, S. and Urry, J. (1987) *The End of Organised Capitalism*. London: Polity Press.

Lawler, E.E. (1986) *High Involvement Management: Participative Strategies for Improving Organisational Performance*. San Francisco: Jossey-Bass.

Lawrence, E.R. and Lorsch, J.W. (1967) 'Differentiation and integration in complex organizations', *Administrative Science Quarterly*, 12: 1–47.

Leavitt, H.J. (1951) 'Some effects of certain communication patterns on group performance', *Journal of Abnormal and Social Psychology*, 46: 38–50.

Leavitt, H.J. (1978) *Managerial Psychology*. 4th edn. Chicago: University of Chicago Press.

Legge, K. (1989) 'Human resource management: a critical analysis', in J. Storey (ed.), *New Perspectives on Human Resource Management*. London: Routledge. pp. 33–59.

Leitch, C. and Harrison, R. (1996) 'Learning organizations: the measurement of company performance', *Journal of European Industrial Training*, 20 (1): 31–44.

Levy, P., Bessant, J., Sang, B. and Lamming, R. (1995) 'Developing integration through total quality supply chain management', *Integrated Manufacturing Systems*, 6 (3): 4–12.

Lewin, J.E. and Johnston, W.J. (1996) 'The effects of organizational restructuring on industrial buying behavior: 1990 and beyond', *Journal of Business and Industrial Marketing*, 11 (6): 93–111.

Lewin, K. (1946) 'Action research and minority problems', *Journal of Social Issues*, 2: 34–46.

Lewin, K. (1947) 'Frontiers in group dynamics: concept, method and reality in social sciences; social equilibria and social change', *Human Relations*, 1: 5–41.

Lewin, K. (1952) *Field Theory in Social Science*. London: Tavistock.

Lewin, K. (1958) 'Group decision and social change', in E.E. Maccoby, T.M. Newcombe and E.L. Hartley (eds), *Readings in Social Psychology*. New York: Holt, Rinehart and Winston. pp. 197–211.

Likert, R. (1961) *The Human Organization*. New York: McGraw-Hill.

Lim, B. (1995) 'Examining the organizational culture and organizational performance link: a critical review of the methodologies and findings of recent researchers into the presumed link between culture and perfomance', *Leadership and Organizational Development Journal*, 16 (5): 16–21.

Lippitt, R., Watson, J. and Westley, B. (1958) *The Dynamics of Planned Change*. New York: Harcourt, Brace and World.

Lloyd, B. (1995) 'Waterman's views of excellence', *Management Development Review*, 8 (4): 36–40.

Lorange, P. (1996) 'A business school as a learning organisation', *The Learning Organization*, 3 (5): 5–13.

Lundberg, C.C. (1985) 'On the feasibility of cultural intervention', in P.J. Frost, L.F. Moore, M.R. Louis, C.C. Lundberg and J. Martin (eds), *Organisational Culture*. Newbury Park, CA: Sage, pp. 169–85.

Lundberg, C.C. (1997) 'Towards a general model of consultancy', *Journal of Organizational Change Management*, 10 (3): 193–201.

Mair, M. (1989) 'Kelly, Bannister and a storytelling psychology', *International Journal of Personal Construct Psychology*, 2 (1): 1–14.

Malone, M. and Davidow, W. (1992) 'Virtual corporation', *Forbes*, 7 December: 102.

Mann, S. (1997), 'Emotional labour in organizations', *Leadership and Organization Development Journal*, 18: 14–12.

Manz, C.C. and Sims, H.P. (1987) 'Leading workers to lead themselves: the external leadership of self-managing work teams', *Administrative Science Quarterly*, 32: 106–28.

March, J.G. and Olsen, J.P. (1976) *Ambiguity and Choice in Organization*. Bergen: Universitetsforlaget.

March, J.G. and Simon, H.A. (1958) *Organizations*. Wiley: New York.

Margulies, N. and Raia, A. (1990) 'The significance of core values on the theory and practice of organization development', in F. Massarik (ed.), *Advances in Organization Development*. Vol. 1, Norwood, NJ: Ablex Publishing Co., pp. 27–41.

Marks M.L. (1997) 'Consulting in mergers and acquisitions interventions spawned by recent trends', *Journal of Organizational Change Management* 10 (3): 267–79.

Marshak, R.J. (1993) 'Lewin meets Confucius: a re-view of the OD model of change', *Journal of Applied Behavioural Science*, 29 (4): 147–65.

Marshak, R.J. (1996) 'Metaphors, metaphoric Fields and organizational change', in D. Grant and C. Oswick (eds), *Metaphor and Organizations*. London: Sage. pp. 147–65.

Marshall, C.C., Shipman, F.M. and McCall, R.J. (1995) 'Making large-scale information resources serve communities of practice', *Journal of Management Information Systems*, 11 (4), Spring: 65–86.

Marsick, V.J. and Watkins, K.E. (1994) 'The learning organisation: an integrative vision for HRD', *Human Resource Development Quarterly*, 5 (4): 353–60.

Martin, J. (1990) 'Deconstructing organizational taboos: the suppression of gender conflict in organizations', *Organization Science*, 1: 1–21.

Martin, J. (1992) *Cultures in Organizations: Three Perspectives*. New York: Oxford University Press.

Maslow, A.H. (1954) *Motivation and Personality*. New York: Harper and Row.

Maslow, A.H. (1965) *Eupsychian Management*. Homewood, IL: Richard D. Irwin.

Matteson, J.M. and Ivancevich, M.T. (1987) *Controlling Work Stress*. San Francisco: Jossey-Bass.

Mayer, J.P. (1956) *Max Weber and German Politics, Second edition*. London: Faber and Faber.

McClelland, D.C. (1975) *Power: The Inner Experience*. New York: Iryington Press.

McCourt, W. (1997) 'Discussion note: using metaphors to understand and to change organizations, a critique of Gareth Morgan's approach', *Organization Studies*, 18/3: 511–22.

McGregor, D. (1960) *The Human Side of Enterprise*. New York: McGraw-Hill.

McHugh, M. (1993) 'Stress at work: do managers really count the costs?', *Employee Relations*, 15 (1): 18–32.

McHugh, M. (1995) 'Stress and strategic change', in D. Hussey (ed.), *Rethinking Strategic Management*. Chichester: John Wiley and Sons. pp. 65–81.

McHugh, M. (1997) 'The stress factor: another item for the change management agenda?', *Journal of Organizational Change Management*, 10 (4): 345–62.

McHugh, M. and Brennan, S. (1994) 'Managing the stress of change in the public sector', *International Journal of Public Sector Management*, 7 (5): 29–41.

McKenna, S.D. (1994) 'Leveraging complexity: the middle manager's dilemma', *The Learning Organization*, 1 (2): 6–14.

McKinley, W., Sanchez, C. and Schick, A. (1995) 'Organizational downsizing: constraining, cloning, learning', *Academy of Management Executive*, 9, August: 32–44.

McLagan, P. (1989) *Models for the HRD Practice: The Practitioners Guide*. Alexandria, VA: American Society for Training and Development.

McLaughlin, M. and Thorpe, R. (1993) 'Action learning – a paradigm in emergence: the problems facing a challenge to traditional management education and development', *British Journal of Management*, 14: 19–27.

McLean, A.J., Sims, D.B.P., Mangham, I.L. and Tuffield, D. (1982) *Organization Development in Transition: Evidence of an Evolving Profession*. Chichester: Wiley.

McLean, G.N. (1998) 'HRD: a three legged stool, an octopus, or a centipede?', *Human Resource Development International*, 1 (4): 375–7.

McLoughlin, I. and Clark, J. (1994) *Technological Change at Work*. Milton Keynes: Open University Press.

McLuhan, M. (1964) *Understanding Media: The Extensions of Man*. New York: McGraw-Hill.

McLuhan, M. (1967) *The Medium is the Message*. New York: Bantam Books.

Meakin, D. (1976) *Man and Work: Literature and Culture in Industrial Society*. London: Methuen.

Meek, V.L. (1988) 'Organizational culture: origins and weaknesses', *Organization Studies*, 9 (4): 453–73.

Megginson, D., Matthews, J.J. and Banfield, P. (1993) *Human Resource Development*. London: Kogan Page.

Mennell, S. (1974) *Sociological Theory: Uses and Unities*. London: Nelson.

Merton, R.K. (1968) *Social Theory and Social Structure*. New York: The Free Press.

Metcalf, H.C. and Urwick, L. (eds) (1942) *Dynamic Administration: The Collected Papers of Mary Parker Follett*. New York: Harper and Brothers.

Meudell, K. and Gadd, K. (1994) 'Culture and climate in short life organisations: sunny spells or thunderstorms?', *International Journal of Contemporary Hospitality Management*, 6 (5): 27–32.

Miller, E. (1997) 'Effecting organizational change in large complex systems: a collaborative consultancy approach', in J.E. Newman, K. Kellner and A. Dawson-Shepherd, (eds), *Developing Organizational Consultancy*. London: Routledge.

Miller, E.J. and Rice, A.K. (1967) *Systems of Organization*. Tavistock Publications.

Miller, J.G. (1978) *Living Systems*. New York: McGraw-Hill.

Mills, A.J. (1988) 'Organization, gender, and culture', *Organization Studies*, 9 (3): 351–69.

Mills, A.J. and Murgatroyd, S.J. (1991) *Organizational Rules: A Framework for Understanding Organizational Action*. Milton Keynes: Open University Press.

Mills, A.J. and Tancred, P. (eds) (1992) *Gendering Organizational Analysis*. Newbury Park, CA: Sage.

Minson, J. (1986) 'Strategies for socialists? Foucault's conception of power', in M. Cane (ed.), *Towards a Critique of Foucault*. London: Routledge and Kegan Paul, pp. 106–48.

Mintzberg, H. and Waters, J.A. (1985) 'Of strategies, deliberate and emergent', *Sloan Management Journal*, 6: 257–72.

Mirvis, P.H. (1996) 'Historical foundations of organization learning', *Journal of Organizational Change Management*, 9 (1): 13–31.

Moreno, J.L. (1953) *Who Shall Survive*. Boston, MA: Beacon House.

Morgan, C. and Murgatroyd, S. (1994) *Total Quality Management in the Public Sector*. Milton Keynes: Open University Press.

Morgan, G. (1980) 'Paradigms, metaphors and puzzle solving in organization theory', *Administrative Science Quarterly*, 25: 605–22.

Morgan, G. (1983) 'More on metaphor: why we cannot control tropes in administrative science', *Administrative Science Quarterly*, 28: 601–607.

Morgan, G. (1986) *Images of Organization*. Newbury Park, CA: Sage.

Morgan, G. (1988) *Riding the Waves of Change: Developing Managerial Competencies for a Turbulent World*. San Francisco, CA: Jossey-Bass.

Morgan, G. (1993) *Imaginization: The Art of Creative Management*. Newbury Park, CA: Sage.

Morgan, G. and Smircich, L. (1980) 'The case for qualitative research', *Academy of Management Review*, 5 (4): 491–500.

Morley, M.J. and Garavan, T.N. (1995) 'Current themes in organizational design implications for human resource development', *Journal of European Industrial Training*, 19 (11): 3–13.

Mulholland, J. (1991) *The Language of Negotiation: A Handbook of Practical Strategies for Improving Communication*. London: Routledge.

Mumford, A. (1991) 'Individual and organization learning: the pursuit of change', *Industrial and Commercial Training*, 23 (6): 24–31.

Murphy, L.R. (1995) 'Managing job stress: an employee assistance/human resource management partnership', *Personnel Review*, 24 (1): 41–50.

Nadler, D.A. and Tushman, M.L. (1977) 'A diagnostic model for organization behaviour', in J.R. Hackman, E. Lawler and L. Porter (eds), *Perspectives on Behaviour in Organizations*. New York: McGraw-Hill. pp. 86–101.

Nadler, L. and Nadler, Z. (1989) *Developing Human Resources*. 3rd edn. London: Jossey-Bass.

Newell, S. (1995) *The Healthy Organization: Fairness, Ethics and Effective Management*. London: Routledge.

Nijhof, W.J. and de Rijk, R.N. (1997) 'Roles, competences and outputs of HRD practitioners – a comparative study in four European countries', *Journal of European Industrial Training*, 21 (6/7): 247–55.

Nwankwo, S. and Richardson, W. (1996) 'Organizational leaders as political strategists: a stakeholder management perspective', *Management Decision*, 34 (10): 43–9.

Oakland, J.S. (1989) *Total Quality Management*. Oxford: Heinemann Professional.

Organization Development Institute (1992) *The International Registry of Organization Development Professionals and Organization Handbook*. Cleveland, OH: Organization Development Institute.

Ortony, A. (1979) *Metaphor and Thought*. Cambridge: Cambridge University Press.

Ott, J.S. (1989) *The Organizational Culture Perspective*. Pacific Grove, CA: Brooks/Cole.

Ouchi, W.G. (1981) *Theory Z. How American Business Can Meet the Japanese Challenge*. Reading, MA: Addison-Wesley.

Ouchi, W.G. and Jaeger, A.M. (1978) 'Type Z organisation: stability in the midst of mobility', *Academy of Management Review*, April: 305–14.

Pacanowsky, M. (1987) 'Communication in the empowering organization', in J. Anderson, (ed.), *Communication Yearbook 11*. Beverley Hills, CA: Sage, pp. 356–79.

Page, C.H. (1965) 'Foreword' in P.M. Blau, *Bureaucracy in Modern Society*. New York: Random House.

Palmer, I. and Dunford, R. (1996) 'Reframing and organizational action: the unexplored link', *Journal of Organizational Change Management*, 9 (6): 12–25.

Parker, M. and Slaughter, J. (1988) *Choosing Sides: Unions and the Team Concept*. Boston: South End Press.

Pasmore, W., Francis, C., Haldeman, J. and Shani, A. (1982) 'Sociotechnical systems: a North American reflection on empirical studies of the seventies', *Human Relations*, 35: 1179–204.

Pateman, C. (1983) 'Some reflections on participation and democratic theory', in C. Crouch and F.A. Heller (eds), *International Yearbook of Organizational Democracy for the Study of Participation, Co-operation and Power*. Vol. 1, Organizational Democracy and Political Processes. Chichester: Wiley.

Pearce, W.B. and Cronen, V.E. (1980) *Communication, Action, and Meaning: The Creation of Social Realities*. New York: Preager.

Pedler, M., Burgoyne, J. and Boydell, T. (1991) *The Learning Company*. London: McGraw-Hill.

Pepper, S. C. (1942) *World Hypotheses*. Berkeley, CA: University of California Press.

Peters, M. and Robinson, V. (1984) 'The origins and status of action research', *The Journal of Applied Behavioural Science*, 2 (1): 9–24.

Peters, T. (1987) *Thriving on Chaos: Handbook for the Management Revolution*. New York: HarperCollins.

Peters, T. (1992) *Liberation Management: Necessary Disorganization for the Nanosecond Nineties*. New York: Ballantine.

Peters, T. and Austin, N. (1985) *A Passion for Excellence: The Leadership Difference*. New York: Random House.

Peters, T. and Waterman, R.H. (1986) *In Search of Excellence: Lessons from America's Best-Run Companies*. New York: Warner Books.

Pettigrew, A. (1985) *The Awakening Giant: Continuity and Change in ICI*. Oxford: Blackwell.

Pettigrew, A. and Whipp, R. (1993) 'Understanding the environment', in C. Mabey and B. Mayon-White (eds), *Managing Change*. 2nd edn. London: The Open University/Paul Chapman. pp. 5–19.

Pettigrew, A.M. (1979) 'On studying organizational cultures', *Administrative Science Quarterly*, 24 (December): 570–81.

Pfeffer, J. (1994) *Competitive Advantage through People*. Boston: Harvard University Press.

Pinder, C.C. and Bourgeois, W.V. (1982) 'Controlling tropes in administrative science', *Administrative Science Quarterly*, 27: 641–53.

Polanyi, M. (1958) *Personal Knowledge: Towards a Post-Critical Philosophy*. London: Routledge and Kegan Paul.

Poole, M. and Mansfield, R. (1993) 'Patterns of continuity and change in managerial attitudes and behaviour in industrial relations, 1980–1990', *British Journal of Industrial Relations*, 31: 11–34.

Porter, M. (1980) *Competitive Advantage*. New York: The Free Press.

Porter, M.E. (1990) *The Competitive Advantage of Nations*. Basingstoke: Macmillan.

Potter, C.C. (1989) 'What is culture: and can it be useful for organizational change agents?', *Leadership and Organization Development Journal*, 10 (3): 17–24.

Prahalad, C.K. and Hamel, G. (1990) 'The core competence of the corporation', *Harvard Business Review*, 68 (3): 79–93.

Purser, R.E and Pasmore, W.A. (1993) 'Designing work systems for knowledge workers', *Journal for Quality and Participation*, July–August: 78–84.

Rafaeli, A. and Sutton, R.I. (1989) 'The expression of emotion in organizational life', in L.L. Cummings and B.M. Staw (eds), *Research in Organizational Behavior*. Vol. 11. Greenwich, CT: JAI Press, pp. 1–42.

Rappaport, J. (1984) 'Studies in empowerment: introduction to the issue', *Prevention in Human Services*, 3: 1–7.

Ravetz, J.R. (1971) *Scientific Knowledge and its Social Problems*. Oxford: Clarendon Press.

Redman, T. and Allen, P. (1993) 'The use of HRM consultants: evidence from manufacturing companies in the North East of England', *Personnel Review*, 22 (2): 56–64.

Reed, D. (1995) 'Critical theory and the Catholic Church's ambivalence about capitalism', *International Journal of Social Economics*, 22 (2): 19–39.

Reed, M. (1990) 'From paradigms to images: the paradigm warrior turns postmodernist guru', *Personnel Review*, 19 (3): 35–40.

Reed, M. (1992) *The Sociology of Organizations: Themes, Perspectives and Prospects*. London: Harvester Wheatsheaf.

Reeves, C.A. and Bednar, D.A. (1994) 'Defining quality: alternatives and implications', Academy of Management Review, 19 (3): 419–45.

Regan, W. (1963) 'The Service Revolution', Journal of Marketing, 27 (3): 247–53.

Reid, M. and Barrington, H. (1994) Training Interventions. 3rd edn. London: Institute of Personnel and Development.

Revans, R. (1982) The Origins and Growth of Action Learning. Bromley: Chartwell Bratt.

Revans, R.W. (1984) The Sequence of Managerial Achievement. Bradford: MCB University Press.

Richardson, W. (1994) 'Socio-technical disasters: profile and prevalence', Disaster Prevention and Management, 3 (4): 41–69.

Roberts, K. and Corcoran-Nantes, Y. (1995) 'TQM: the new training and industrial relations', in A. Wilkinson and H. Willmott (eds), Making Quality Critical: New Perspectives on Organisational Change. London: Routledge.

Roethlisberger, F.J. and Dickson, W.J. (1966) Management and the Worker. Cambridge, MA: Harvard University Press.

Rose, E. (1994) 'The "Disorganized Paradigm": British industrial relations in the 1990s', Employee Relations, 16 (1): 27–40.

Sacks, R.E. (1979) On Metaphor. Chicago: University of Chicago Press.

Schaafsma, H. (1997) 'A networking model of change for middle managers', Leadership and Organization Development Journal, 18 (13): 41–49.

Schall, M. (1983) 'A communication rules approach to organizational culture', Administrative Science Quarterly, 28: 557–81.

Schatzman, L. and Strauss, A.L. (1973) Field Research: Strategies for a Natural Sociology. Englewood Cliffs, NJ: Prentice-Hall.

Schegloff, E. (1972) 'Notes on a conversational practice: formulating place', in D.N. Sudnow (ed.), Studies in Social Interaction. New York: Free Press: pp. 75–119.

Schegloff, E., Jefferson, G. and Sacks, H. (1977) 'The preference for self-correction in the organization of repair in conversation', Language, 33: 361–82.

Schein, E.H. (1984) 'Coming to a new awareness of organisational culture', Sloan Management Review, 25: 3–6.

Schein, E.H. (1985) Organisational Culture and Leadership. San Francisco: Jossey-Bass.

Schein, E.H. (1988) Process Consultation. Vol. 1, rev. edn. Reading, MA: Addison-Wesley.

Schein, E.H. (1987) Process Consultation. Vol. 2. Reading, MA: Addison-Wesley.

Schein, E.H. (1992) Organizational Culture and Leadership 2nd edn. San Francisco: Jossey-Bass.

Schein, E.H. (1995) 'Process consultation, action research and clinical inquiry: are they the same?', Journal of Managerial Psychology, 10 (6): 14–19.

Schein, E.H. (1997a) 'Process consultation principles in respect of clients', *Journal of Organizational Change Management*, 10 (3): 206–10.

Schein, E.H. (1997b) 'The concept of "client" from a process consultation perspective: a guide for change agents', *Journal of Organizational Change Management*, 10 (3): 202–16.

Schein, E.H. and Bennis, W.G. (1965) *Personal and Organizational Change Through Group Methods: The Laboratory Approach*. New York: Wiley.

Schor, J.B. (1993) *The Overworked American: The Unexpected Decline of Leisure*. New York: Basic Books.

Schwartz, H. and Davis, S. (1981) 'Matching corporate culture and business strategy', *Organizational Dynamics*, 10: 30–48.

Searle, J. (1976) 'A classification of illocutionary acts', *Language in Society*, 5: 1–23.

Searle, J.R. (1969) *Speech Acts: An Essay in the Philosophy of Language*. Cambridge: Cambridge University Press.

Senge, P. (1990) *The Fifth Discipline: The Art and Practice of the Learning Organization*. New York: Doubleday/Currency.

Sexton, C. (1994) 'Self-managed work teams: TQM technology at the employee level', *Journal of Organizational Change Management*, 7 (2): 42–52.

Shaw, P. (1997) 'Intervening in the shadow systems of organizations: consulting from a complexity perspective', *Journal of Organizational Change Management*, 10 (3): 235–50.

Shrivastava, P. (1983) 'A typology of organizational learning systems', *Journal of Management Studies*, 20 (1): 7–20.

Silver, J. (1987) 'The ideology of excellence: management and neo-conservatism', *Studies in Political Economy*, 24, Autumn: 105–29.

Skinner, B.F. (1953) *Science and Human Behaviour*. New York: MacMillan.

Skinner, B.F. (1957) *Verbal Behaviour*. New York: Appleton-Century-Crofts.

Skinner, B.F. (1972) *Beyond Freedom and Dignity*. New York: Knopff.

Smircich, L. (1983) 'Concepts of culture and organizational analysis', *Administrative Science Quarterly*, 28 (2): 339–58.

Smith, K.K. (1982) 'Philosophical problems in thinking about organizational change', in P.S. Goodman and Associates (eds), *Change in Organizations: New Perspectives on Theory, Research and Practice*. London: Jossey-Bass.

Sokal, A. and Bricmont, J. (1997) 'The naked postmodernists', *The Times Higher Educational Supplement*, 10 October.

Sommer, S.M. and Merritt, D.E. (1994) 'The impact of a TQM intervention on workplace attitudes in a health-care organization', *Journal of Organizational Change Management*, 7 (2) May: 53–62.

Spencer, L.M. and Spencer, S.M. (1993) *Competence at Work*. New York: Wiley.

Stacey, R.D. (1992) *Managing the Unknowable*. San Francisco: Jossey-Bass.

Starbuck, W.H. (1992) 'Learning by knowledge-intensive firms', *Journal of Management Studies*, 29 (6): 713–40.

Steadman, M., Albright, T. and Dunn, K. (1996) 'Stakeholder group interest in the new manufacturing environment', *Managerial Auditing Journal*, 11 (2): 4–9.

Stebbins, M.W. (1989) 'Downsizing with "Mafia model" consultants', *Business Forum*, Autumn 1988/Winter 1989: 45–7.

Steingard, D.S. and Fitzgibbons, D.E. (1993) 'A postmodern deconstruction of total quality management (TQM)', *Journal of Organizational Change Management*, 6 (5): 27–37.

Steingard, D.S. and Fitzgibbons, D.E. (1995) 'Challenging the juggernaut of globalisation: a manifesto for academic praxis', *Journal of Organizational Change Management*, 8 (4): 30–54.

Stewart, J. and McGoldrick, J. (1996) *Human Resource Development: Perspectives, Strategies and Practice*. London: Pitman.

Sudnow, D. (1978) *Studies in Social Interaction*. New York: Free Press.

Swanson, R.A. (1995) 'Human resource development: performance is the key', *Human Resource Development Quarterly*, 6 (2): 207–13.

Swanson, R.A. (1999) 'HRD theory, real or imagined?', *Human Resource Development International*, 2 (1): 46–53.

Swenson, D.X. (1997) 'Requisite conditions for team empowerment', *Empowerment in Organizations*, 5 (1): 16–25.

Swieringa, J. and Wierdsma, A. (1992) *Becoming a Learning Organisation: Beyond the Learning Curve*. Reading, MA: Addison-Wesley.

Tayeb, M. (1995) 'The competitive advantage of nations: the role of HRM and its sociocultural context', *International Journal of Human Resource Management*, 6 (3): 588–605.

Taylor, F.W. (1967[1911]) *The Principles of Scientific Management*. New York: WW Norton and Co.

Taylor, S. (1992) 'Managing a learning environment', *Personnel Management*, 24 (10): 54–7.

Tenkasi, R.V. and Boland, R.J. (1996) 'Exploring knowledge diversity in knowledge intensive firms: a new role for information systems', *Journal of Organizational Change Management*, 9 (1): 79–91.

The Times (1995) 'Consultants given £320 million for advice on privatization', article by N. Williamson, 18 September, p. 8.

Thomas, K. and Velthouse, B. (1990) 'Cognitive elements of empowerment: an interpretive model of intrinsic task motivation', *Academy of Management Review*, 19: 666–81.

Thomas, W.I. (1931) *The Underadjusted Girl*. Boston: Little, Brown & Co.

Thompson P. and McHugh, D. (1995) *Work Organizations: A Critical Introduction*. London: MacMillan.

Thompson, P. and O'Connell Davidson, J. (1995) 'The continuity of discontinuity: managerial rhetoric in turbulent times', *Personnel Review*, 24 (4): 17–33.

Tichy, N.M. (1983) *Managing Strategic Change: Technical, Political and Cultural Dynamics.* New York: John Wiley and Sons.

Tichy, N.M., Brimm, M.I., Charan, R. and Takeuchi, H. (1992) 'Leadership development as a lever for global transformation', in V. Pucik, N.M. Tichy and C.K. Barnett (eds) *Globalizing Management.* New York: Wiley. pp. 17–32.

Tichy, N.M. and Devanna, M.A. (1986) *The Transformational Leader.* New York: John Wiley and Sons.

Tichy, N.M., Hornstein, H. and Nisberg, J. (1976) 'Participative organization diagnosis and intervention strategies: developing emergent pragmatic theories of change', *Academy of Management Review,* April: 347–56.

Tichy, N.M. and Sherman, S. (1993) *Control Your Destiny or Someone Else Will.* New York: Doubleday/Currency.

Tierney, W.G. (1989) 'Advancing democracy: a critical interpretation of leadership', *Peabody Journal of Education,* 66 (3): 157–75.

Tierney, W.G. (1993) *Building Communities of Difference: Higher Education in the Twenty-first Century.* Westport, CT: Bergin and Garvey.

Toffler, A. (1980) *The Third Wave.* New York: Bantam Books.

Tomasko, R.M. (1992) 'Restructuring: getting it right', *Management Review,* 81 (4): 10–15.

Touraine, A. (1988) 'Modernity and cultural specificities', *International Social Science Journal,* 11 (8): 443–57.

Trist, E.L. and Bamforth, K.W. (1951) 'Some social and psychological consequences of the longwall method of coal-getting', *Human Relations,* 4: 3–38.

Tsoukas, H. (1991) 'Missing link: a transformational view of metaphors in organizational science', *Academy of Management Review,* 16 (3): 566–85.

Tsoukas, H. (1993) 'Analogical reasoning and knowledge generation in organisation theory', *Organization Studies,* 14 (3): 323–46.

Tsoukas, H. (ed.) (1994) *New Thinking in Organizational Behaviour.* Oxford: Butterworth-Heinemann.

Tsui, A.S. and Milkovich, G.T. (1987) 'Personnel department activities: constituency perspectives and preferences', *Personnel Psychology,* 40 (3): 519–37.

Turner, A.N. (1988) 'Guiding managers to improve their own performance', *Journal of Management Consulting,* 4 (4): 8–12.

Turner, B.A. (1989) 'How can we design a safe organisation?', paper presented at the 2nd International Conference on Industrial and Organisational Crisis Management, New York, November.

Turner, B.A. (1988) 'Connoisseurship in the study of organisational cultures', in A. Bryman (ed.), *Doing Research in Organisations.* London: Routledge and Kegan Paul. pp. 8–12.

Tylor, E.B. (1891) *Primitive Culture.* London: John Murray.

Vaill, P.B. (1989) *Managing as a Performing Art.* San Francisco: Jossey-Bass.

Van Maanen, J. (1991) 'The smile factory: work at Disneyland', in P.J. Frost, L.F. Moore, M. Reis-Louis, C.C. Londberg and J. Martin (eds), *Reframing Organisational Culture*. Newbury Park, CA: Sage. pp. 58–76.

Van Maanen, J. and Kunda, G. (1989) 'Real feelings: emotional expression and organizational culture', in L.L. Cummings and B.M. Staw (eds), *Research in Organizational Behavior*. Vol. 11, Greenwich, CT: JAI Press. pp. 43–103.

Waclawski, J., Church, A.H. and Burke, W.W. (1995) 'Women in organization development: a profile of the intervention styles and values of today's practitioners', *Journal of Organizational Change Management*, 8 (1): 12–22.

Walck, C.L. (1997) 'Organizations as places: a metaphor for change', *Journal of Organizational Change Management*, 9 (6): 26–40.

Walters-York, L.M. (1996) 'Metaphor in accounting discourse', *Accounting, Auditing and Accountability Journal*, 9 (5): 45–70.

Walton, R.E. (1972) 'How to counter alienation in the plant', *Harvard Business Review*, Nov/Dec.: 70–81.

Watson, S. and D'Annunzio-Green, N. (1996) 'Implementing cultural change through human resources: the elusive organisation alchemy?', *International Journal of Contemporary Hospitality Management*, 8 (2): 25–30.

Watson, T.J. (1995) 'In search of HRM: beyond the rhetoric and reality distinction or the case of the dog that didn't bark', *Personnel Review*, 24 (4): 6–16.

Weber, M. (1948) *From Max Weber: Essays in Sociology*. Translated, edited and with an introduction by H.H. Gerth and C.W. Mills. London: Routledge and Kegan Paul.

Weber, M. (1968) *Economy and Society: An Outline of Interpretative Sociology*. 3 volumes. London: Bedminster Press.

Weick, K. (1979) *The Social Psychology of Organizing*. 2nd edn. Reading, MA: Addison-Wesley.

Weick, K.E. (1994) 'Organizational culture as a source of high reliability', in H. Tsoukas (ed.), *New Thinking in Organizational Behaviour*. Oxford: Butterworth-Heinemann. pp. 147–62.

Weihrich, H., Seidenfuss, K-U. and Goebel, V. (1996) 'Managing vocational training as a joint venture – can the German approach of co-operative education serve as a model for the United States and other countries?', *European Business Review*, 96 (1): 31–40.

Weinberger, L.A. (1998) 'Commonly held theories of human resourse development', *Human Resource Development International*, 1 (1): 75–93.

Weisbord, M.R. (1976) 'Organizational diagnosis: six places to look for trouble with or without a theory', *Group and Organization Studies*, 1 (4): 430–47.

Werr, A., Stjernberg, T. and Docherty, P. (1997) 'The functions of methods of change in management consulting', *Journal of Organizational Change Management*, 10 (4): 288–307.

West, P. (1994) 'The learning organization: losing the luggage in transit?', *Journal of European Industrial Training*, 18 (11): 30–8.

Wheatley, M. (1992) *Leadership and the New Science*. San Francisco: Berrett-Koehler.

White, M. (1991) 'Deconstruction and therapy', *Dulwich Centre Newsletter*, 1: 6–46.

White, R.F. and Jacques, R. (1995) 'Operationalizing the postmodernity construct for efficient organizational change management', *Journal of Organizational Change Management*, 8 (2): 45–71.

Whyte, W.A. (1963) *The Organization Man*. Harmondsworth: Pelican.

Winnicott, D.W. (1965) *The Maturational Process and the Facilitating Environment*. New York: International Universities Press.

Wittgenstein, L. (1958) *Philosophical Investigations*. Oxford: Basil Blackwell.

Woodall J. (1996) 'Managing culture change: can it ever be ethical?', *Personnel Review*, 25 (6): 26–40.

Woodward, J. (1965) *Industrial Organization: Theory and Practice*. London: Oxford University Press.

Zeffane, R. and Mayo, G. (1994) 'Rightsizing: the strategic human resource management challenge of the 1990s', *Management Decision*, 32 (9): 5–9.

Zeithaml, V.A., Berry, L.L. and Parasuraman, A. (1988) 'Communication and control processes in the delivery of service quality', *Journal of Marketing*, 52, April: 35–48.

Zenger, J.H. (1985) 'Training for organizational excellence', *Journal of European Industrial Training*, 9 (7): 3–8.

Ziman, J. (1991) *Reliable Knowledge: An Exploration of the Grounds for Belief in Science*. Cambridge: Canto.

Index